# The Unsheltered Woman

# The Unsheltered Woman:
# Women and Housing in the 80's

### Edited by
### Eugenie Ladner Birch

Published in the United States of America
by the Center for Urban Policy Research
Building 4051 — Kilmer Campus
New Brunswick, New Jersey 08903

**Library of Congress Cataloging in Publication Data**
Main entry under title:

The Unsheltered woman.

   Bibliography: p.
   Includes index.
   1. Lodging-houses—New York Region—Addresses, essays, lectures  2. Women heads of households—New York Region—Addresses, essays, lectures.  3. Housing policy—New York Region—Addresses, essays, lectures.  4. Homelessness—New York Region—Addresses, essays, lectures.  I. Birch, Eugenie Ladner.
HD7288.6.U6U57   1985        363.5'9        84-23749
ISBN 0-88285-104-7 (pbk.)

# Contents

# About the Contributors

*Susan Cotts Watkins* is currently an assistant professor in the Department of Sociology and the Population Studies Center at the University of Pennsylvania. Her current research concerns trends in marriage, fertility, and infant mortality in Western Europe and the United States over the last century, and the interrelation between these demographic changes and changes in the family.

Her paper in this volume focuses on the demographic determinants of the differences between male and female living arrangements in the United States in the 1980s.

*Eugenie Ladner Birch*, AICP, is an associate professor of urban planning at Hunter College of CUNY. Originally drawn to the topic of the role of women in housing reform through her research and publications on nineteenth- and twentieth-century housers and planners, she is currently working with Deborah S. Gardner on a book entitled, *The Impatient Crusaders, Women and the Fight for Low-Cost Housing in Britain and America, 1860-1970*.

In her essay she provides a statistical portrait of female householders in the United States and especially in New York City, chosen for its extreme manifestations of the issues discussed.

*Evelyn S. Mann* is Director of Population Research for the New York City Department of City Planning, a position she has held since 1958. For several years, she has also been the official New York City liaison with the U.S. Bureau of the Census. Currently President of the Regional Data User Network (RDUN) and New York Census Statistical Area Key Person, she participates in numerous census planning and evaluation committees. She has testified many times on census matters before various federal, state, and city legislative committees including the House Select Committee on Population.

Her article was drawn from her testimony before the New York City Commission on Human Rights, presented in March 1983, and provides advance statistical material on gender-related concerns.

*May Engler* and *Roberta R. Spohn* are affiliated with the New York City Department for the Aging. The Department, one of the oldest and most progressive in the nation, was founded in 1967. Its mission is to provide support and data for service agencies and to act as an advocate for the elderly on local, state, and federal levels.

Engler is a senior research associate and Spohn is Deputy Commissioner. They collaborated on their article as part of an ongoing departmental monitoring of the status of the elderly in the city's rental housing. This report, and earlier ones, were instrumental in the passage and amendment of the New York City Senior Citizens Rent Increase Exemption legislation, first enacted in the early 1970s. In December 1983, 71,330 households were being assisted under this program.

*Olivia Schieffelin Nordberg* is a senior editor at McCall's *Working Mother* in New York City, where she has responsibility for careers and business. She has written extensively on various aspects of marketing and consumer behavior for *American Demographics*, a Dow Jones publication to which she was a contributing editor. Her background includes two years with the United Nations Fund for Population Activities as an evaluation officer and publishing experience with E.P. Dutton, John Wiley & Sons, and The Population Council, where she edited *Studies in Family Planning*, among other publications.

For *Savvy* magazine, she designed and analyzed the ''Savvy Survey of Executive Behavior.'' Her presentation provides an introduction to the lifestyle and values of a pioneering group of managerial women.

*Barbara Behrens Gers* has been writing and speaking about real estate for almost a decade. Formerly senior editor of *Housing* magazine, a McGraw-Hill publication for professionals in the homebuilding and light-construction industries, she edited *Cost, Rent, and Profit Computer: Rental Apartments* (1979) and was the recipient of both the Jesse H. Neal and National Association of Real Estate Editors awards for journalistic excellence in 1982. In October 1982, *Housing* was incorporated into *Builder* magazine. Since that time, Gers has written articles for *Builder* and is also a regular contributor to the real-estate section of *Newsday*. She is currently an information specialist with the Nassau County (New York) Board of Cooperative Educational Services.

Her presentation highlights some of the findings of a consumer survey which *Housing* conducted in 1981. These results offer a look at the realities of the housing market as perceived by Americans who were in the process of shopping for a new home at a time when housing prices—and interest rates—were at all-time highs.

*Susan Saegert* is an associate professor of environmental psychology at the Graduate School of the City University of New York; *Theodore Liebman* and *R. Alan Melting* are principals of Liebman, Ellis Melting. Saegert is a specialist on the effects of residential densities on mental health. Liebman was chief of architecture for the New York State Development Corporation between 1969 and 1975. Melting has acted as principal planner in charge of the urban design division of the Detroit City Plan Commission as well as project manager for urban design at Gruzen and Partners in New York City.

In their article, the authors describe the extensive planning process they developed to ascertain the market for downtown, residential family housing in Denver. They give special attention to developing a schema for incorporating the concerns of working women.

*Elizabeth Mackintosh* is a senior planner in the Queens office of the New York City Planning Department where she supervises liaisons to community boards and oversees housing and waterfront development in the borough.

In her article, based on a survey conducted under the auspices of the National Institute of Mental Health, she looks at the experiences of middle-income families with children in three highrise apartment buildings in New York City. She dispels some common misconceptions about highrise living and suggests that well-designed highrise buildings can provide healthy and satisfying housing for middle-income families desiring to live in the city.

*Gwendolyn Wright* is an associate professor in the School of Architecture and Urban Planning, Columbia University. An architectural historian specializing in the history of American housing, she has taught and lectured at colleges in the United States, France, and Canada. Widely published, she is author of *Building the Dream: A Social History of Housing in America* (Pantheon, 1983) and *Moralism and the Model Home, Domestic Architecture and Cultural Conflict in Chicago* (University of Chicago Press, 1980). Currently she is completing a monograph entitled "At Home and Abroad: French Colonial Urbanism, 1880-1913."

In her article Wright focuses on theories of domestic architecture and how they have evolved over time. She presented this material as the keynote speaker at the Symposium on Gender-Related Design Issues at the University of Washington (May, 1983).

*Dolores Hayden* is professor of urban planning at the University of California, Los Angeles. She is author of *Seven American Utopias, The Architecture of Communitarian Socialism, 1780-1975* (MIT Press, 1976); *The Grand Domestic Revolution: A History of Feminist Designs for American Homes, Neighborhoods, and Cities* (MIT Press, 1981); and *Redesigning the American Dream: The Future of Housing, Work, and Family Life* (Norton, 1984) and numerous articles in the fields of architecture, housing, and urban planning. She has traveled extensively in China, Cuba, Denmark, England, and Sweden. She is a recipient of a Rockefeller Humanities Fellowship and a Guggenheim Fellowship for research on the built environment. The National Endowment for the Arts has just recognized her two books on women and housing as exemplary design research in a national competition.

In her presentation, she outlines the contribution of several nineteenth- and twentieth-century feminists who addressed gender-related issues of housing and community design. Not only does she present the hitherto undocumented work of these women, but she also sets the stage for exploration of the potential for architectural and social innovation in the modern day. Although a more detailed account of the work of early feminists is to be found in her *Grand Domestic Revolution*, her essay is useful for its crisp analysis of many of the questions addressed by women today.

*Jacqueline Leavitt* is acting associate professor of urban planning at the University of California, Los Angeles. She has been a pioneer in the research on planning and women, creating courses at Columbia and Cornell universities, and writing extensively on the subject including "Planning and Women, Women in Planning," her Ph.D. dissertation for Columbia. In conjunction with this work, she was a founder of the Planning and Women Division of the American Planning Association. Currently, she is engaged, with environmental psychologist Susan Saegart, of The City University of New York, in a study of elderly females in New York City-owned buildings. Also a practitioner, Leavitt worked on the first advocacy planning projects in New York City and recently prepared a report on the reuse of New York State's Montauk Air Force Station for the General Services Administration.

In her presentation, Leavitt articulates the housing needs of single parents, presents a review of European and American solutions, and outlines her recent experience of creating a suburban prototype for a northern New Jersey community.

*Ronnie Feit* is a founder of the National Congress of Neighborhood Women and has served as a member of its corporate board since its founding. She practices law in Washington, D.C., and acts as a consultant to small businesses and nonprofit organizations. During the Carter administration she served on the White House staff and in the Small Business Administration where she headed the women's business program and was executive director of the President's Interagency Committee on Women's Business Enterprise. She coordinated the founding convention of the National Women's Political Caucus in 1971 and is a former member of the New York City Commission on the Status of Women.

*Jan Peterson* is co-director and founder of the National Congress of Neighborhood Women. Long a political activist, she was the liaison for women's, ethnic, and neighborhood concerns for the White House Office of Public Liaison in the Carter administration. In addition, as assistant to the director of Action's office of Policy and Planning, she developed a national women's program for the agency. In her 20-year career as a community organizer, she has developed numerous locally based organizations encompassing a wide range of activities, including advocacy of senior citizens' needs, childcare, education, housing, and the rights of abused women. In these efforts she has sought to bridge the gaps between neighborhood women and the feminist movement and between men and women in terms of community development and leadership.

In their paper the authors summarize and update the activities of the National Congress of Women in promoting housing and neighborhoods responsive to the needs of poor and low-income women.

*Michael Mostoller* is an adjunct associate professor of architecture at Columbia University and associate professor of architecture at New Jersey Institute of Technology. Engaged in private practice as well, he specializes in residential design. He has been a member of the New York Settlement Housing Fund Single-Room Occupancy Task Force which has been working since 1981 to legitimize single-room occupancy housing as a residential option for low- and moderate-income people. Among other activities, this group has developed plans for a Mini Dwelling Unit (MDU) designed to replace the traditional single-room occupancy shelter characteristic of New York City and other large cities across the nation.

In his presentation, Mostoller, whose research was funded by the New York State Council of the Arts, traces how single people have been housed since the nineteenth century, documents their plight today, and explains the features of the proposed Mini Dwelling Unit.

*Clara Fox* is executive director emeritus of the Settlement Housing Fund, a non-profit developer of low- and moderate-cost housing located in New York City. Between 1969 and 1982, as SHF Executive Director, she oversaw the construction of over 5,000 dwelling units which today house more than 20,000 people. Sensitive to the problems of families, particularly single-parent families from this work and from her tenure as the first director of New York City's Head Start program, she has also had significant experience with the elderly.

In her article she tackles the housing problems of both the elderly and single-parent families through her advocacy of shared housing in many forms, including the urban cooperative and the Mini Dwelling Unit which she helped develop. Her insight into the management issues involved in non-traditional housing was born of her SHF experiences.

*Celine G. Marcus* is executive director emeritus of the Lenox Hill Neighborhood Association. Actively involved with this association for 25 years, she served as its executive director from 1970 to 1982. A certified social worker, she served as executive director for both the Jewish Family Service of Long Beach, California, and the Jewish Association for Neighborhood Centers (renamed Associated YM-YWHAs of Greater New York). Active in Manhattan community affairs, she is vice president of Neighborhood Coalition for Shelter, Inc., chairman of the Health and Social Service Committee for Community Board 8, vice president of the Association for Recreation Management, Inc. (ARM), and a member of the housing and health committees of the Women's City Club of New York. Currently, she is consultant to the Department of Alumni Affairs and Development at Hunter College of The City University of New York.

Her article provides a cameo of the experiences she had in anticipating and meeting the needs of a poor elderly population seeking to remain in their neighborhood in the face of rapidly increasing housing costs.

*Jane Margolies* is a journalist living in New York City. She was a member of the Women and Housing Seminar during 1983-1984. As a Department of Education Public Service Scholar, she assisted the seminar directors in the administration of the meetings and played an active role in editing the manuscripts in this collection.

In her essay, she reports on efforts of seminar members to develop site-specific rehabilitation plans for urban housing.

*Lynda Simmons* is president and chief executive officer of Phipps Houses, a New York City nonprofit real estate, development and management company which currently has 6,400 units under its direction. During ten years as a practicing architect, she served as project director for several large New York housing complexes, including East Midtown Plaza, nationally recognized for its sensitive design. Upon joining Phipps, she oversaw the development of more than 2,000 apartments, the majority located in four projects in the Bellevue South Urban Renewal Area. She is a vice president of the Settlement Housing Fund and currently chairs its Single Room Occupancy Task Force.

Her article is drawn from a panel discussion with Carol Lamberg, executive director of the Settlement Housing Fund, and Linda Field, president of Linda Field Associates. The three women discuss their experiences as socially minded feminist professionals operating within the clearly bounded development system of New York City. They conclude that while the system can be slightly adjusted to address some current women's needs, more fundamental changes can occur only with a major re-direction of decision-makers' perspectives about the appropriate design and contents of modern shelter.

*Judith Edelman*, FAIA, is a partner in the Edelman Partnership, a New York firm involved in urban planning and historic preservation, as well as the design of private and public buildings. Edelman has won numerous awards for her work. Active in professional organizations, she has held offices in the American Institute of Architects, Architects for Social Responsibility, and was a founding member of the Alliance of Women in Architecture. She has taught at City College School of Architecture and has lectured throughout the United States and China.

In her article, she relates the 14-year history of her firm's involvement with developing 1,400 dwelling units in the Two Bridges Urban Renewal Area of New York City. In this presentation she stresses the difficulties of implementing architectural and planning goals which do not conform to the bureaucratic rules and procedures of funding agencies.

*Rebecca A. Lee*, director of economic development for the Urban Redevelopment Authority of Pittsburgh, is in charge of the city's business financing and industrial development programs. Formerly a program officer for the Local Initiatives Support Corporation, she directed the Charlotte Gardens project while director of project development for the South Bronx Development Organization.

In her article, written as the first units were being placed in the South Bronx, she outlines how this nontraditional form of construction became the answer to the demand for affordable housing.

*Michael A. Stegman* is professor and chairman of the Department of City and Regional Planning at the University of North Carolina at Chapel Hill. He is the author of *Cases in Housing Finance and Public Policy* (Van Nostrand Reinhold, 1985); *The Dynamics of Rental Housing in New York City* (Center for Urban Policy Research, 1982); *Nonmetropolitan Urban Housing: An Economic Analysis of Problems and Policies* (with Howard J. Sumka, Ballinger, 1976); and *Housing Investment in the Inner City: The Dynamics of Decline* (MIT Press, 1972). He also has written many articles on national low-income housing policy and programs. From 1979 to 1981 he served as deputy assistant secretary for research at the U.S. Department of Housing and Urban Development. He has consulted on a wide range of housing issues.

His presentation explores the intricacies of housing subsidies and explains how budgetary and political considerations offset the form of the subsidy after reviewing the differences between one-time capital grants, which make the development itself less costly, and continuing interest subsidy payments, which reduce the developer's borrowing costs. He summarizes the basic elements of the newly enacted rental housing production and rehabilitation programs contained in the Housing and Urban-Rural Recovery Act of 1983. He concludes with a discussion of the challenges these new programs pose to communities dedicated to expanding the supply of low-income housing.

# List of Exhibits

# Preface

This collection of essays tackles three issues: how to define gender-related needs, how to plan responsive projects and programs, and how to design implementation strategies. It provides a comprehensive view of housing analysis directed to women.

The volume is a product of the Ford Foundation-Hunter College Women and Housing Seminar, co-chaired by Donna E. Shalala, president of Hunter College and former HUD assistant secretary for policy development and research; Frances Levenson, former deputy commissioner for housing sponsorship of the New York City Housing Development Agency and currently vice president for urban housing, Goldome Bank; and Eugenie Ladner Birch, associate professor of urban planning, Hunter College. Authors of its twenty richly illustrated essays include architectural historians Dolores Hayden and Gwendolyn Wright, housing analyst Michael A. Stegman, architects Judith Edelman, Michael Mostoller, and Theodore Liebman, developers Lynda Simmons, Clara Fox, and Carol Lamberg, environmental psychologist Susan Saegert, community organizer Jan Peterson, South Bronx Development Office project director Rebecca Lee, and planner Jacqueline Leavitt.

Although the seminar initially looked at women's physical environment, i.e. their individual dwelling units, it soon became evident that this was a far too limited vision. Design issues could not be addressed without a fuller appreciation of larger planning questions. At first, seminar participants considered these as defining the client group and then creating support services as well as shelter to meet the clients' demands. Later, they realized that this view was also too narrow. They saw that the fundamental issue was income. Thus they touched upon the deeper societal concerns of equity in employment, child-welfare customs, and basic governmental funding practices for housing. This book is the result of the seminar activities.

Before investigating this product, a brief outline of the organization and workings of the seminar is useful. The seminar had two levels. For the academic years, 1981-1982 and 1983-1984, two classes, each having fifteen Hunter College students, mainly planning degree candidates, met weekly. Once a month they were joined by twenty-five to thirty carefully selected practitioners to meet in seminar sessions with invited speakers. These sessions were always lively and frequently controversial. At the end of each semester the students presented solutions to their major assignment (a project which differed from year to year) to the practitioners who acted as jury members. One year they redesigned a multifamily building and created implementation strategies. Another year they forged a position statement which was adopted by the seminar members and ultimately introduced into several political arenas, including the proceedings of the Democratic Platform Committee in early summer, 1984.

For many reasons the seminar proved to be an extremely useful teaching device in the broadest sense of the phrase. Substantively, the topic challenged the participants to apply their intellects and professional skills in new directions. Procedurally, the mixture of students and experts created a symbiotic relationship where both sides learned from each other.

The choice of the controversial, little-discussed topic, gender-related housing, fit well into an educational mission of an urban institution serving a largely female constituency. This particular theme forced the participants to separate facts from values, to extrapolate information from data collected for other purposes, and to use inductive reasoning skills to support their deductive analyses. As the seminar progressed, it was apparent that all of the participants were familiar with traditional supply and demand issues such as sheltering the poor, elderly, and handicapped; they were not accustomed to casting women as a subgroup having specific housing needs. In fact, as they quickly discovered, very few professionals dealt with this particular topic despite widespread media attention to it. Thus they found themselves at the forefront of a profound social issue and were forced to synthesize their own knowledge and experience in order to grapple with it. While they were in the enviable position of being able to master the literature of the field—because there was so little of it—they also faced the concomitant frustration of not having a clear path to follow and the challenges of being creative with this subject.

The mixture of professionals and students was clearly beneficial to both sides. The students had continual access to people with a level of experience not to be found in a traditional classroom course. The professionals used this time to investigate a topic that they would not pursue in their ordinary workdays. Furthermore, the professionals, potential employers, viewed the students firsthand, a feature that has yielded some jobs to the graduates and has pushed the students into a career network which would have taken a longer time to develop had they not had this opportunity.

The most challenging aspect of the seminar was dealing with innovation. The students learned that not only are original ideas difficult to conceive but also equally difficult to execute. The professionals had to overcome an almost automatic resistance to new approaches that their years of experience and the current economic and political climate had created for them. Yet, once they moved into a more visionary mode, their contributions, criticisms, and observations lent an air of reality to the enterprise.

Clearly, several issues still need to be addressed. Ranging from affordability to location to design, the seminar members realized that these questions were not *exclusively* women's topics yet so long as they remained unresolved or unattended women would be most severely affected and less able to achieve a decent standard of living than men. Finally, the seminar members concluded that while some concerns were more urgent than others, all were deserving of more attention than they were currently receiving.

*The Unsheltered Woman*, then, traces the effects of the demographic revolution on housing policy and practice. It contributes to the literature on affordable housing and to the mounting evidence of policy implications of the gender-related gap.

# Acknowledgments

This volume has been made possible through the generosity and hard work of many. Among those to be thanked for making it possible are Mariam Chamberlain, the Ford Foundation visionary who brought sponsorship to the project; Donna E. Shalala who found time in her busy schedule to foster it; Frances Levenson whose intelligent piloting led to many a stimulating meeting; the steering committee (Judith Edelman, Clara Fox, Lois Kleinerman, Cynthia Lewis, Sybil Phillips and Lynda Simmons) who gave moral support and fine advice; the Department of Urban Affairs who scheduled it; the seminar members—practitioners and students, particularly the graduate assistants, Barbara Cohen, Irene Fanos and Jane Margolies—who made it all possible, and, finally, and not the least, all those husbands, children and friends whose Wednesday evenings were sacrificed to this effort.

# Introduction

This collection of essays is significant not only for women, but also for housing policy in America. It is significant because, until now, very little research has focused on gender policy issues. Why not? Because to do so requires a whole new way of thinking.

I remember the difficulties we had at the U.S. Department of Housing and Urban Development in the late 1970s when we sought to develop a women's policy agenda. Finding feminists and other supporters of women in the department was easy. Getting managers and researchers to think creatively and sensitively about ways in which the department's programs and policies affect women was very difficult. We ended by asking each other to forget our training and experience and, instead, to imagine we were the department's clients—most of whom were, and are, poor women.

We could have used this collection of essays at that time. It discusses basic demographic issues and trends in household formation, using census information to reveal which groups in the country and in New York City have housing problems. The essays then turn to the needs of special groups of women; the classification alone helps us to be more sensitive. Elderly women, working-class women, professional women—married and single—are all potential customers of appropriately designed and executed new or renovated units. Later essays investigate locational and design issues related to women's concerns: a model case study in Denver; highrise housing in New York City; neighborhood housing for the elderly in Manhattan.

Although much of the content concerns itself with New York City, the book is relevant to policy analysts in all parts of the nation. The problems of New York City are unusually severe, but as the rest of America is learning, they are increasingly common in other areas of the country.

Where and by whom a new idea is developed or used is less important than the fact that it exists. As a woman and a feminist deeply committed to creating housing and developing communities that meet the needs of all Americans, but particularly those Americans whose needs have not yet been fully explored or understood—poor women, elderly women, working women, single women—I welcome this volume and congratulate its authors.

Donna E. Shalala
President, Hunter College
Co-Chair, Hunter College Women and Housing Seminar

# PART I

# Identifying the Unsheltered Woman and Her Needs

"We need a new vision that helps women and communities to adjust to the overwhelming changes in the patterns of labor and living that have overtaken us in the past few decades."[1] So wrote Donna E. Shalala, HUD assistant secretary for policy development and research in the spring of 1980. A year later, as president of Hunter College, Shalala continued to promote this idea in the academic arena. With Ford Foundation support, she decided that Hunter College would sponsor a Women and Housing Seminar to address gender-related questions. This collection is drawn from that experience.

Some pioneering research has been done in this area, much of it sponsored by Shalala at HUD. *How Well Are We Housed?* (1980), *Measuring Rental Practices Affecting Families with Children: A National Survey* (1980), massive studies on mortgage discrimination, and surveys of the quality of community life have all added substantive research and discussion to the issue of housing as it relates to women. The Ford Foundation-Hunter College project furthers this seminal work. It brings together the best minds in New York City, long a center of housing reform, and the younger imaginations of Hunter College graduate students. It aims to make concrete proposals about how dwellings can be more appropriately designed and built to meet the changing needs of women. The contributors to this volume, as well as others including Martin Levine, deputy assistant director of the Human Resources Community Development Division, Congressional Budget Office; Cushing Dolbeare, executive director, National Low-Income Housing Coalition; and Anthony Gliedman, commissioner, New York City Department of Housing Preservation and Development, participated in the effort.

The first step when looking at the issue of women and housing is to define the target group. As is well known, America's 116 million females are not a

## EXHIBIT I.1
### Females in American Households

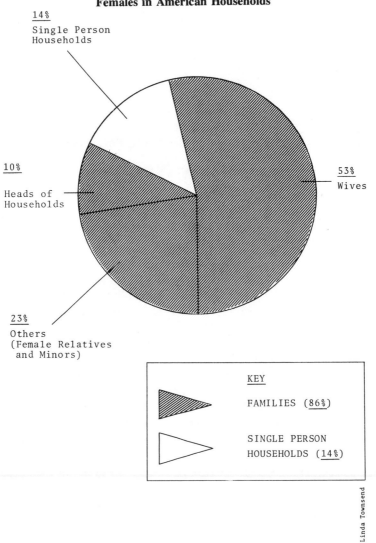

10%

Heads of
Households

53%
Wives

23%
Others
(Female Relatives
and Minors)

KEY

FAMILIES (86%)

SINGLE PERSON
HOUSEHOLDS (14%)

Linda Townsend

*Source:* George Masnick and Mary Jo Bane, *The Nation's Families, 1960-1990* (Cambridge, Mass., 1980).

monolithic mass; they are a diverse group which can be categorized according to several factors, including age, household composition, employment, and life-cycle position (marital status and presence of minor children). For example, approximately 22 percent of the nation's females are under 15 years of age, 45 percent are in their childbearing years, 20 percent are middle-aged, and about 13 percent are elderly.

**EXHIBIT I.2**
**Population of Four Categories of Women**
**(in thousands)**

| Category | Number | Percent |
|---|---|---|
| Single working women | 12,000 | 22 |
| Women in dual-career families | 25,500 | 46 |
| Female heads of households | 9,400 | 17 |
| Elderly women (single or without spouse) | 8,300 | 15 |
| TOTAL | 55,200 | 100 |

*Source:* George Masnick and Mary Jo Bane, *The Nation's Families, 1960-1990* (Cambridge, Mass., 1980) and U.S. Bureau of the Census *General Population Characteristics,* Washington, D.C.: U.S. Government Printing Office, 1982.

Looked at another way, 86 percent of the nation's 91 million adult women live in families; about 50 million women are wives (53 percent of the women); about 20 million are relatives living with families (23 percent); and 9 million women are heads of households (10 percent). The remaining 12 million (14 percent of all women) live as single householders (See Exhibit I.1). Half of all married women, a third of the female heads of household, and a third of the single women are in the labor force. Finally, of these workers, half of married women and two-thirds of female heads of household have children under the age of eighteen.[2]

Although women as a whole have housing concerns in common, the extreme problems of some can best be determined only by looking at subgroups. This book will focus on four: single working women, women in dual-career households with and without children, female heads of households, and elderly women. These four groups constitute about 55 million people or more than 60 percent of the nation's adult female population (See Exhibit I.2).

This collection is less explicitly concerned with the traditional nuclear, single-career family because it assumes the needs of these families will be satisfied by solutions already at work in the housing market. In contrast, it focuses on the selected groups in the belief that they will expand in the future. It asks several questions, ranging from the predictive (how will women be distributed in the selected classes in the future?) to the analytical (do women have housing needs which are currently not met?).

Many authors provide answers to these and other questions. Demographic research by Susan Cotts Watkins, of the University of Pennsylvania, predicts that the dramatic shifts in household and labor-force statistics of the past 30 years will probably continue (Chapter 1). According to her analysis, there will be a decline in single-career, married-couple families and an increase in female heads of households, the female elderly, and dual-career families, especially those with children.

Despite these trends, little research about their effects on housing demand has been undertaken. Thus the issue of gender-related needs is difficult to define.

When questions are posed in relation to income and other demographic characteristics, many problems emerge. Eugenie Ladner Birch, of Hunter College, employs HUD and census data measuring quality and tenure status to draw a statistical picture of women and their housing (Chapter 2). She argues that for many
women, low incomes place them in dwellings which are often physically inadequate, for which they pay a disproportionate amount of their earnings. She also
documents lower than average rates of homeownership.

Two following reports study the most severely impacted groups, female heads
of households and the elderly. Evelyn S. Mann, of the New York City Department of City Planning, outlines the growth of the single-parent class, shows
where most were living within the boroughs of New York, and speculates about
their shelter-related needs (Chapter 3). May Engler and Roberta R. Spohn use the
1980 *Housing and Vacancy* survey data to illuminate the plight of the elderly
renter in New York City (Chapter 4). They show how, in a central city where
two-thirds of the units are rented, a substantial group of renters, elderly females
living alone, are increasingly hard pressed to afford their housing. Engler and
Spohn argue that while a partial remedy, the Senior Citizens Rent Increase Exemption program, offers some relief to this group, it is not sufficient. Additionally, Engler and Spohn maintain that older women, particularly the frail, have
unique shelter needs which can only be met through the creation of special designs and living arrangements.

Together these studies demonstrate that poor women, particularly female
heads of families and elderly singles, have two clear needs: 1) decent, affordable
housing, and 2) opportunities for expanding ownership. They underline the fact
that in today's world poor women simply do not have the resources to meet these
requirements.

By examining the question of unmet needs from the perspective of lifestyle,
additional gender-related concerns are uncovered: those related to design.
Women have been forced into units tailored for the traditional nuclear family—
one where women assume primary responsibility only for childcare and housekeeping. Olivia Schieffelin Nordberg and *Savvy* magazine point to another group
who have unmet housing needs: executive women. Represented in a 10,000 response national survey, they are a new breed whose heavy work schedules have a
distinct effect on the quality of their personal and professional lives. The implications of this survey for housing market analysis are vast, particularly in the definition of service facilities and locational criteria for shelter for women of all economic classes (Chapter 5).

Barbara Behrens Gers, editor of *Housing* magazine, has recently analyzed the
results of a national buyers survey (Chapter 6). This research excluded New York
City and concentrated on consumer preferences in other regions. Gers found that
while the single-family dwelling is still very much a part of the American dream,
its design is changing to respond to the economic and social profile of contemporary purchasers. Susan Saegert of The Graduate School of the City University

of New York and New York City architects Theodore Liebman and R. Alan Melting offer a contrasting approach to traditional market research. These three describe how the city of Denver planned a project to provide downtown housing for moderate income working women (Chapter 7). The results of the Denver research yielded proposals for central city, mixed-density family projects. Finally, Elizabeth Mackintosh of the New York City Department of City Planning shares her study of urban highrises (Chapter 8). Demonstrating that the provision of community space, inside and outside of buildings, is essential to "satisfying" design, she argues that the increases in the number of dual-career families could stimulate demand for centrally located, affordable units incorporating these features.

Defining the "unsheltered woman" and her needs is a complicated task. For many, gender is a determining factor for social and economic, not biological, reasons. Regardless of the roots of the condition, the point is that a significant number of women are not being housed as well as they could be. Furthermore, women are not the only victims of inadequately met housing demand. Their families suffer as well. Thus, the first part of this volume provides a variety of sources of information for understanding which women are ill-housed and why their shelter is substandard or inadequate. While much of the material is based on the New York City experience, the conceptual approaches employed by the authors certainly can be replicated in other regions of the United States.

## NOTES

1. Donna E. Shalala, "Introduction," in Catharine R. Stimpson (ed.), *Women and the American City* (*Signs*, vol. 5, no. 3), p. 53.

2. U.S. Bureau of the Census. *Money Income of Households, Families and Persons in the United States: 1981* (Washington, D.C.: U.S. Government Printing Office, 1983); U.S. Bureau of the Census. *General Population Characteristics, Chapter B* (Washington, D.C.: U.S. Government Printing Office, 1980).

# 1

# Living Arrangements in the 1980s

Susan Cotts Watkins

In the United States as in other societies, living arrangements are closely linked to family membership. In the 1980s as in the past, Americans are most likely to live with those to whom they are related by blood or marriage; conversely, they have rarely shared their homes with those to whom they are not related. Moreover, the relatives with whom they live are usually limited to members of the conjugal family: husbands and wives, parents and children.

The long-standing expectation is that spouses will live together until the marriage is broken by death or divorce, that children will live with one or both of their parents at least until they reach a conventionally defined age of adulthood, and that two related married couples will not live together except under unusual circumstances. The greatest degree of flexibility in living arrangements is available in the interval between reaching adulthood and forming one's own family and following marital disruption. During these years, individuals choose between living with relatives, living alone, or living with others to whom they are not related.

These social rules express both the opportunities and the constraints that are associated with age and marital status. They apply to both men and women, but they do so with different results for the living arrangements of the two sexes. Membership in a family is the consequence of birth and death, marriage and marriage dissolution. Since the levels and age patterns of mortality, marriage and divorce are different for men and women, the first step toward understanding the variation in living arrangements of men and women is to appreciate the effect of disparities in the age and marital status composition of the male and female populations.

In this introductory chapter, then, we consider in detail the importance of these factors for living arrangements of women and men in the 1980s. We briefly trace trends in mortality and fertility which together determine the age composition of the population. Then we look at trends in family formation and dissolution, emphasizing the differences in male and female patterns of marriage and marital dissolution. Subsequently, we focus on the living arrangements of men and women in 1980 in order to evaluate what part of those differences is due to simple differences in demography and what part must be left for other kinds of explanation. Although this analytic approach could be applied to the population categorized in additional ways, for example, to examine differentials in living arrangements among races or ethnic groups, or among urban and rural residents, here we consider only the distinctions by gender for the total U.S. population, using primarily published tabulations for the March 1980 Current Population Survey.

The age composition of any population is primarily the consequence of past trends in fertility and mortality; of the two, fertility usually has the greater impact on the relative sizes of the various age groups, for example, the proportion of the population that is under 18 or over 65.

In the United States (as well as in the countries of Western Europe) the long-term trend in fertility has been downward. In 1800 on average women bore about seven children; by 1900 this average had fallen to about 3.5; and by 1980 it was 1.8. The only major interruption in the long-term trend was the period just following World War II when fertility rose. Subsequently, the particularly sharp declines in fertility reduced the proportion of the population in the younger years and increased the proportion in the older ages. Since children under 18 are highly likely to live with relatives, one can expect the proportion of the population that lives in families in the coming decades to be responsive to future trends in fertility. The elderly population will increase in numbers; the proportion of the population over 65 in future years will depend both upon trends in fertility and further improvements in the mortality of the elderly.

Since the sex ratio at birth is nearly equal (about 103-105 male births for every 100 female), the age composition of the male and female populations considered separately is primarily the result of their differential mortality. In most contemporary Western societies, women survive the rigors of life better than males. The most recently published life table for the United States shows that the differences between men and women are greatest in young adult life, from ages 15-40 (National Center for Health Statistics, 1980, p. 5.9). These differentials are due to genetically based factors determining survival rates and to differences in the environments in which men and women live, including expectations of the proper behavior—such as smoking or daring driving—of men and women (Waldron, 1983).

As with fertility, the long-term trends to mortality have been moving steadily downward; both sexes have benefited from improvements in life-enhancing aspects of the environment. They have, however, benefited differentially. For cohorts born in 1900 the expectation of life at birth for males was 51.1 years; in

1980 it was 69.7; for females the figures are 57.8 and 77.6 respectively (Schoen et al, 1984). Differentials between male and female mortality have thus increased slightly during this century, from 6.7 years to 7.9.

Although the overall changes in the age composition of men and women are primarily due to changes in fertility, the differences in survival chances of men and women lead us to expect that as age increases, there will be more women alive than men. If living arrangements vary by age, one would expect that male and female living arrangements would reflect their different age compositions, the outcome of their differential mortality.

The marital status composition of the U.S. population reflected in marriage, marital dissolution, and remarriage rates, has been more volatile than fertility or mortality patterns. Two variables are important in understanding this phenomenon: age at marriage and proportion ever marrying. Around 1900, marriage age was at a historical high both for men and women. It then began a steady decline, reaching a nadir in the 1940s and 1950s. More recently, it has risen again (Schoen et al., 1984). Although grooms are on average slightly older than their brides (about 3 years in 1900, about 2 in 1980), the trends have been very similar for both sexes, suggesting either that the causes of the trends are similar for both, or that one sex is directing traffic in the marriage market.

Similar trends have characterized the proportion never marrying of both men and women. For the birth cohorts of the late nineteenth century, about 12 percent of the men and about 8 percent of the women who survived to age 15 never married; for those born in the mid 1930s, only about 4 percent of men and 3 percent of women who survived to age 15 never married (Schoen et al, 1984). As the age of marriage rises, it is reasonable to expect that the proportion never marrying will also rise.

In the past decades the proportion of marriages dissolved by death has declined, while the probability that a marriage will be ended by divorce has, of course, increased substantially. The former reflects the decline in mortality rates; the latter, the change in divorce customs. In 1867, the first year for which such calculations can be made, about 5 percent of the marriages contracted ended in divorce (Preston and McDonald, 1979). Today nearly 50 percent of marriages will end in divorce. Accompanying the trend to greater divorce has been a decrease in the age at divorce. For women it has fallen from nearly 38 for those born around 1900, and is projected to be about 33 for those born in 1980; it is slightly higher for males, who marry at older ages (Schoen et al, 1984).

Both males and females have been and are more likely to remarry after divorce than after the death of a spouse. Although men and women are, of course, equally likely to divorce, males are more likely than females to remarry following divorce, and to remarry sooner. Differences in remarriage and mortality rates lead women to spend more years post-married—widowed or divorced—than men. Given the greater flexibility of living arrangements for those who are not

**EXHIBIT 1.1**
**Person Years Lived by Marital Status, 1900 and 1980**

| | Number of Adult Years | | Percent of Adult Lifetime | |
|---|---|---|---|---|
| **Marital Status** | **1900** | **1980** | **1900** | **1980** |
| Currently married | 24.9 | 37.6 | 52.8 | 59.2 |
| Post-married | 7.5 | 14.7 | 15.8 | 23.1 |
| Single (never-married) | 14.8 | 11.2 | 31.4 | 17.7 |
| Total adult years | 47.2 | 63.5 | | |

*Note:*
   Adult years are those after age 15, given survival to age 15.
   Percent of adult lifetime is years lived in marital status/total years lived after age 15.
   The probability of surviving to age 15 was .65 in 1800, .77 in 1900, and .99 in 1980.

*Source:* Watkins, Susan, Jane Menken and John Bongaarts, 1984.

currently married, from this perspective women would seem to have more lati-
tude in their living arrangements than men. However, the lower income of widowed and divorced women, and their greater assumption of responsibility to their
children, also implies greater constraints on this choice.

   One way to summarize the combined effects of changing mortality, fertility,
and marriage on women's family membership is to compare the number of adult
years (over 15) and the proportion of total adult lifetime spent single, currently
married, and post-married, under the demographic conditions of different eras.
In so doing an important question is posed: Has the shift in the source of marital
dissolution from death to divorce substantially affected the number of years
women spend in marriage, or following it? To answer this question it is possible to use available data in conjunction with computer simulation techniques
(details of the procedure are given in Watkins et al, 1984). The answer is reveal-
ing. The left-hand panel of Exhibit 1.1 shows that current cohorts of American
women are spending, on average, about seven more years post-married (following widowhood or divorce) than they did in 1900. It also shows, however, that
they are spending nearly 13 more years married, on average, than did women
under the demographic conditions of 1900. Thus, in contrast to the past, current
cohorts of females live far more years in the married state than they did in the
past. This is happening despite the fact that contemporary marriages are subject
to dissolution from two sources. Improvements in adult mortality are responsible.

   Because improvements in mortality have lengthened the span of adult life, it is
reasonable to ask also how the demographic changes have affected the *percent* of
adult lifetime in these categories. The right-hand panel of Exhibit 1.1 shows that
the percent for both the currently married and the post-married has increased, although it has fallen for the single. Whatever might be said about the declining

**EXHIBIT 1.2**
**Living Arrangements by Sex, 1980**

|  | Total | | Male | | Female | | Ratio of Males to Females |
|---|---|---|---|---|---|---|---|
|  | No. | % | No. | % | No. | % |  |
| *Total Population 15+* | 168,198 | 100.0 | 80,128 | 100.0 | 87,980 | 100.0 | |
| *Living in Families* | 142,193 | 84.5 | 68,677 | 85.6 | 73,516 | 83.6 | .93 |
| Married, Spouse Present | 97,530 | 58.0 | 48,765 | 60.8 | 48,765 | 55.4 | 1.00 |
| Others* | 44,663 | 26.5 | 19,912 | 24.8 | 24,751 | 28.1 | .81 |
| *Not Living in Families* | 26,002 | 15.5 | 11,539 | 14.4 | 14,463 | 16.4 | .80 |
| Alone | 17,816 | 10.6 | 6,793 | 8.5 | 11,023 | 12.5 | .62 |
| With Unrelated Others | 8,186 | 4.9 | 4,746 | 5.9 | 3,440 | 3.9 | 1.38 |

*Note:*
*In this exhibit and those that follow, "Others" refers to all related individuals sharing a household except those which include the spouse of the individual.

*Source:* Calculated from Table 6 of the Current Population Reports, Series P-20, No. 365, U.S. Department of Commerce.

significance of marriage, both the number of years and the proportion of total lifetime spent in marriage have increased. These figures, then, provide a historical perspective from which to view living arrangements of men and women in the 1980s.

The importance of family status for living arrangements is emphasized by classifying the living arrangements of all adults (defined as those over 15) in a simple but significant manner: whether they live 1) in families; 2) with a spouse; 3) with relatives other than a spouse; 4) alone; or 5) with unrelated others. These categories are exhaustive, in that they include the living arrangements of all Americans over the age of 15, but some familiar labels are not there. Single-parent families, for example, are not given special attention, but rather grouped, as are children over 18 living with their parents and households of siblings, grandparents, and more distant relatives, in the category "living in families." Cohabiting couples are also not singled out for attention.[1] From the point of view of the census, cohabiting couples are classified as unrelated persons sharing living quarters (landladies and lodgers, for example).

The categories used in this analysis were chosen to emphasize the fact, evident from Exhibit 1.2, that the majority of the U.S. population lives with those to whom they are related.

In 1980, 84.5 percent of those over 15 lived in family households, most of them in one which included a married couple—in other words, with at least their spouse. If cohabitation were considered a form of marriage, the percentage of

**EXHIBIT 1.3**
**Sex Ratios by Age, 1980**

**Males/Females**

| | |
|---|---|
| Under 15 | 104.6 |
| 15-19 | 103.4 |
| 20-24 | 100.1 |
| 25-29 | 98.5 |
| 30-34 | 98.0 |
| 35-44 | 96.2 |
| 45-54 | 92.5 |
| 55-64 | 88.7 |
| 65-74 | 76.7 |
| 75+ | 55.1 |

*Source:* See Exhibit 1.2

those living in families is even higher. Those who are not living in families are more likely to live alone than with unrelated others. On the basis of these aggregate data, it would seem that when we cannot live in families, we prefer living alone to living with those with whom there is no family relationship.

Exhibit 1.2 also shows the differences in living arrangements between men and women. In general, the similarities are more striking than the differences: 1) both men and women live in family households, predominantly those that include a married couple; 2) about the same proportion of each sex live in family households that do not include their own spouse; and 3) for each sex the ordering in terms of the percentage distribution in each category is 1) married, spouse present, 2) other relatives, 3) living alone, and 4) living with unrelated others. As will be seen later, the vast majority of men who are living in families, but who are not currently married, are single, and thus probably living with their parents; women have larger proportions of divorced, widowed, or married but spouse absent, and are thus probably living with their children. Whatever the composition of the family household, however, it is clear that most Americans, both male and female, live with relatives, that relatively few of either sex live alone, and that extremely small percentages live with those to whom they are not related.

Overall, then, the differences in the living arrangements of men and women are small. Notable contrasts emerge when looking at those who do not live in families: women are more likely not to be living in families than men. If they are not living in families, they are more likely to be living alone than men—12.5 percent of all adult women, and 8.5 percent of all adult men live alone. When considering only the population of those who are not living in families, the differences are even more striking: 59 percent of the adult male population and 76 percent of the female propulation are living alone. The differences are sum-

**EXHIBIT 1.4**
**Living Arrangements by Age and Sex, 1980**
(numbers in thousands)

| | 15-19 | | 20-24 | | 25-29 | | 30-34 | | 35-44 | | 45-54 | | 55-64 | | 65-74 | | 75+ | |
|---|---|---|---|---|---|---|---|---|---|---|---|---|---|---|---|---|---|---|
| | No. | % | No. | % | No. | % | No. | % | No. | % | No. | % | No. | % | No. | % | No. | % |
| *Males* | *10,159* | *100.0* | *9,801* | *100.0* | *9,076* | *100.0* | *8,270* | *100.0* | *12,296* | *100.0* | *10,962* | *100.0* | *9,870* | *100.0* | *6,549* | *100.0* | *3,234* | *100.0* |
| *In Families* | 9,741 | 95.9 | 7,675 | 78.3 | 6,970 | 76.8 | 6,812 | 82.4 | 10,859 | 88.3 | 9,731 | 88.8 | 8,776 | 88.9 | 5,627 | 85.9 | 2,490 | 77.0 |
| Married, Spouse Present | 220 | 2.2 | 2,730 | 27.9 | 5,366 | 59.1 | 6,008 | 72.6 | 9,943 | 80.9 | 8,979 | 81.9 | 8,130 | 82.4 | 5,200 | 79.4 | 2,190 | 67.7 |
| Other | 9,521 | 93.7 | 4,945 | 50.5 | 1,604 | 17.7 | 804 | 9.7 | 916 | 7.4 | 752 | 6.9 | 646 | 6.5 | 427 | 6.5 | 300 | 9.3 |
| *Not in Families* | 417 | 4.1 | 2,125 | 21.7 | 2,106 | 23.2 | 1,460 | 17.7 | 1,437 | 11.7 | 1,231 | 11.2 | 1,098 | 11.1 | 924 | 14.1 | 746 | 23.1 |
| Alone | 103 | 1.0 | 816 | 8.3 | 1,075 | 11.8 | 841 | 10.2 | 933 | 7.6 | 799 | 7.3 | 792 | 8.0 | 759 | 11.6 | 678 | 21.0 |
| With Unrelated Others | 314 | 3.1 | 1,309 | 13.4 | 1,031 | 11.4 | 619 | 7.5 | 504 | 4.1 | 432 | 3.9 | 306 | 3.1 | 165 | 2.5 | 68 | 2.1 |
| *Females* | *10,110* | *100.0* | *10,246* | *100.0* | *9,357* | *100.0* | *8,561* | *100.0* | *13,042* | *100.1* | *11,670* | *100.0* | *11,034* | *100.0* | *8,549* | *100.0* | *5,411* | *100.0* |
| *In Families* | 9,649 | 95.4 | 8,486 | 82.8 | 7,914 | 77.2 | 7,780 | 75.9 | 12,262 | 94.0 | 10,556 | 90.5 | 8,904 | 80.7 | 5,356 | 62.7 | 2,606 | 48.2 |
| Married, Spouse Present | 752 | 7.4 | 4,306 | 42.0 | 6,075 | 59.3 | 6,228 | 60.8 | 9,939 | 76.2 | 8,749 | 75.0 | 7,404 | 67.1 | 4,114 | 48.1 | 1,197 | 22.1 |
| Other | 8,897 | 88.0 | 4,180 | 40.8 | 1,839 | 17.9 | 1,552 | 15.1 | 2,323 | 17.8 | 1,807 | 15.5 | 1,500 | 13.6 | 1,242 | 14.5 | 1,409 | 26.0 |
| *Not in Families* | 459 | 4.5 | 1,759 | 17.2 | 1,442 | 14.1 | 781 | 7.6 | 779 | 6.0 | 1,114 | 9.5 | 2,129 | 19.3 | 3,194 | 37.4 | 2,805 | 51.8 |
| Alone | 102 | 1.0 | 648 | 6.3 | 753 | 7.3 | 482 | 4.7 | 524 | 4.0 | 891 | 7.6 | 1,919 | 17.4 | 3,036 | 35.5 | 2,665 | 49.3 |
| With Unrelated Others | 357 | 3.5 | 1,111 | 10.8 | 689 | 6.7 | 299 | 2.9 | 255 | 2.0 | 223 | 1.9 | 210 | 1.9 | 158 | 1.8 | 140 | 2.6 |

*Source:* See Exhibit 1.2.

marized in the last column of Exhibit 1.2, where the ratio of males to females in each category is most divergent for those living alone (.62) and for those living with unrelated others (1.38).

Evident differences between the living arrangements of men and women might be due to differences in the degree to which they find living with relatives attractive or unattractive, or perhaps in the control of economic resources which permit choice among various living arrangements. On the other hand, the previous discussion of demographic patterns suggests that if the propensity to live in some kinds of living arrangements rather than others varies by age and marital status, part of the contrast may be due to differences in the age and marital status distributions of men and women.

Differences in the age composition of the male and female populations are shown in Exhibit 1.3. In the first two decades of life, there are more men than women. Subsequently, the population becomes increasingly female, such that by the oldest age group, those 75 and older, there are currently about two females for every male. Moreover, at each given age, women can expect to live longer: a woman of 50 has, on average, 30.5 more years to live, a man has only 25.6 years (National Center for Health Statistics, 1980, p. 5.9).

The impact of age on living arrangements can be seen in Exhibit 1.4.

Differences are greatest at the younger ages, when men are less likely to be married than are women, and at the older ages, when women are less likely to be married than are men; in the age group 65-74, nearly 80 percent of the men are living in families that consist of at least a married couple, but only about half of the women are; differences become even more extreme in the oldest age group. Under 1980 mortality conditions, slightly more than 50 percent of the female population will live beyond age 80. At these advanced ages, women are highly likely to have lost their spouse by death and highly unlikely to remarry; their children are fully grown adults with their own families.

It is interesting to consider how much of the difference between the living arrangements of men and women is due simply to the differences in the age composition of the two populations. What would the living arrangements of women look like if nothing were changed but their mortality rates; in other words, what if there were the same proportion (but not the same number) of men and women in each age group? The results of such a calculation are shown in Column 3 of Exhibit 1.5, with the figures for men (Column 1) and for women (Column 2) taken from Exhibit 1.2 for comparison.

Changing the age structure of the female population so that it is equivalent to that of males makes small but interesting differences in the percent of women in each category. The percent living in families, either with spouse or with other relatives, increases, and the percent not living with families decreases. Each of these changes makes the living arrangements of women more similar to those of

## EXHIBIT 1.5
### Living Arrangements Standardized for Age and Marital Status, 1980
(in percent)

|  | Males (1) | Females (2) | By Age (3) | By Marital Status (4) | By Both (5) |
|---|---|---|---|---|---|
| *Living in Families* | 85.6 | 83.6 | 84.9 | 88.8 | 88.3 |
| Married, Spouse Present | 60.8 | 55.4 | 55.9 | 60.8 | 60.8 |
| Others | 24.8 | 28.1 | 29.0 | 28.0 | 27.5 |
| *Not Living in Families* | 14.4 | 16.4 | 19.0 | 11.2 | 11.7 |
| Alone | 8.5 | 12.5 | 11.1 | 7.1 | 7.3 |
| With Unrelated Others | 5.9 | 3.9 | 4.0 | 4.1 | 4.4 |

*Source:* See Exhibit 1.2.

men, although men still demonstrate a higher propensity to live in families and a lower propensity to live alone than do women.

Before considering Columns 4 and 5 of Exhibit 1.5, let us consider the effect of marital status on living arrangements. As Exhibit 1.6 shows, the proportion of the adult female population that is widowed and divorced is greater than the corresponding figures for men, a higher proportion of whom are single or currently married. Within each marital status category, however, there are significant differences in the living arrangements of the two sexes: for example, more widowed women (62 percent) than widowed men (55 percent) live alone.

Just as it was possible to consider what the living arrangements of women would be if they had the same distribution as men, it is also possible to ask what these arrangements would be if women had the same marital status distribution as men. Column 4 of Exhibit 1.5 shows the results. Figures are taken from Exhibit 1.2 for comparison. Standardizing for marital status reverses the direction of differences in living arrangements between men and women; instead of a smaller proportion of women living in family households, there is a larger proportion than for men, with most of the change being in the category "married, spouse present." The proportion living with relatives other than a spouse continues to be higher than for males, but the proportion living alone or with other relatives is lower than the equivalent figures for males.

The joint effects of age and marital differences between men and women are summarized in Column 5 of Exhibit 1.5, which shows the living arrangements women would have if they had both the same age and marital distributions as

**EXHIBIT 1.6**
**Living Arrangements by Marital Status and Sex, 1980**
**(numbers in thousands)**

|  | Total | | Male | | Female | |
|---|---|---|---|---|---|---|
|  | **No.** | **%** | **No.** | **%** | **No.** | **%** |
| *Married, Spouse Present* | 97,530 | 58.0 | 48,765 | 60.8 | 48,765 | 55.4 |
| In Family Households | 97,530 | 58.0 | 48,765 | 60.8 | 48,765 | 55.4 |
| *Married, Spouse Absent* | 5,269 | 3.1 | 2,093 | 2.6 | 3,176 | 3.6 |
| In Family Households | 3,072 | 1.8 | 734 | 0.9 | 2,338 | 2.7 |
| In Non-family House- |  |  |  |  |  |  |
| holds | 2,197 | 1.3 | 1,359 | 1.7 | 838 | 10.0 |
| Alone | 1,498 | 0.9 | 880 | 1.1 | 618 | 0.7 |
| With Unrelated Others | 699 | 0.4 | 479 | 0.6 | 220 | 0.3 |
| *Widowed* | 12,451 | 7.4 | 1,972 | 2.5 | 10,479 | 11.9 |
| In Family Households | 4,649 | 2.8 | 721 | 0.9 | 3,928 | 4.5 |
| In Non-family House- |  |  |  |  |  |  |
| holds | 7,801 | 4.6 | 1,251 | 1.6 | 6,550 | 7.4 |
| Alone | 7,314 | 4.3 | 1,095 | 1.4 | 6,219 | 7.1 |
| With Unrelated Others | 487 | 0.3 | 156 | 0.2 | 331 | 0.4 |
| *Divorced* | 9,711 | 5.8 | 3,875 | 4.8 | 5,836 | 6.6 |
| In Family Households | 4,681 | 2.8 | 1,133 | 1.4 | 3,548 | 4.0 |
| In Non-family House- |  |  |  |  |  |  |
| holds | 5,029 | 3.0 | 2,741 | 3.4 | 2,288 | 2.6 |
| Alone | 3,377 | 2.0 | 1,726 | 2.2 | 1,651 | 1.9 |
| With Unrelated Others | 1,652 | 1.0 | 1,015 | 1.3 | 637 | 0.7 |
| *Single* | 43,236 | 25.7 | 23,512 | 29.3 | 19,724 | 22.4 |
| In Family Households | 32,261 | 19.2 | 17,324 | 27.6 | 14,937 | 17.0 |
| In Non-Family House- |  |  |  |  |  |  |
| holds | 10,975 | 6.5 | 6,188 | 7.7 | 4,787 | 5.4 |
| Alone | 5,627 | 3.3 | 3,092 | 3.9 | 2,535 | 2.9 |
| With Unrelated Others | 5,348 | 3.2 | 3,096 | 3.9 | 2,252 | 2.6 |

*Source:* See Exhibit 1.2.

men. Looking at Columns 1 and 2 shows that a higher proportion of men than women live in families, and a smaller proportion live alone. If, however, the female population is standardized for both age and marital status, Column 5, the figures tell a different story: a higher proportion of women than men would live in family households and a lower proportion of women than men would live alone or with unrelated others. The differences are generally rather small. Since the direction is reversed, however, they are significant.

For which categories does standardization of age, of marital status, or both make the most difference? If the distinction is between the proportion living in families and those not living in families, differences between the proportion of men and women in this category are least when age alone is taken into account and greatest when marital status alone is taken into account. In the category "living alone," taking age into account reduces some of the differences between males and females, but taking marital status into account reduces them even more. In both the categories "living in families, other" and "living with unrelated others," the differences between men and women are least when both age and marital status are controlled.

When both age and marital status are controlled, women still have a higher proportion in the category "living in families, other." Some of this discrepancy is because after a divorce children of an age to be living at home are more likely to live with their mother than with their father. About half of the current divorces do not involve children under 18; of the half that do, most lead to the formation of a single-parent household with the parent as the householder—in 1982, only 16 percent of the parent-child groups shared the home of someone else (Glick, 1984). Of these single-parent households (8 percent of all households in 1982), about 90 percent are headed by females (Glick, 1984). Further evidence for the importance of parental status for living arrangements comes from Pampel's examination of changes in the propensity to live alone between 1960 and 1976 (Pampel, 1983). This analysis used individual-level data, which permitted distinguishing between unmarried (single, widowed, or divorced) individuals living with children and those without. It also controlled statistically for income, education, participation in the labor force, and race as well as age and marital status. The results showed that while there were statistically significant differences between men and women in the change in the propensity to live alone for the population of unmarried individuals, these differences became statistically insignificant when the analysis was confined to those unmarried persons who were not living with related children. Thus, it is reasonable to conclude that if unmarried women and men were equally likely to live with their children, the differences in male and female living arrangements are less than when only age and marital status are taken into account.

Racial differences in living arrangements were not considered in this analysis. However, differences in age and marital status in explaining differences in male and female living arrangements suggest that in comparing the sources of differences in these arrangements by race, one would certainly want to consider the different demographic patterns of the black and white populations. Since blacks have substantially higher rates of marital disruption (both from death and from divorce, including separation) than whites (Cherlin, 1981), it is expected that the distribution of the black population by living arrangements would show the effects of these differences. It should also be noted that since the distribution of the population by marital status and by age is distinct in urban and rural populations,

one would expect differences in male and female living arrangements in urban
and rural areas.

In general, the best prediction of the future is the past. Currently the living arrangements of men and women are similar; and, the categories in which they
differ reflect different demographic patterns. A recent analysis of changes in the
number of households in the United States between 1970 and 1980 found that the
effect of changes in marital status predominated over the effect of age composition in accounting for these changes (Sweet, 1984). It may be that there will be
changes in the desirability of various living arrangements, absent the opportunities and constraints associated with age and marital status, or in the income
necessary to achieve preferred arrangements. Some have argued that the past decades have witnessed an increased preference for living alone (Beresford and
Rivlin, 1966; Kobrin, 1976); others found preferences did not change, but the income with which to purchase autonomy changed (Michael et al, 1980). Yet it
seems clear that the fundamental social rules which result in the vast majority of
the population living in family households are unlikely to change much, since a
large proportion of these family households include a married couple. Whatever
changes do occur are unlikely to affect significantly the propensity of married
couples to live together. Thus, flexibility in the future will remain where it has
been in the past, in the proportions living in families without a married couple,
alone, or with unrelated others; differences between male and female living arrangements will continue to reflect, as they do now, differences in age and especially in patterns of marriage, divorce, remarriage, and the responsibilities for
children.

## NOTE

1. In some respects, cohabitation appears to be similar to marriage: an adult male and female share
a household, with all the responsibilities that sharing entails, and may share a budget. In other respects, particularly legally, cohabitation continues to be distinguished from marriage, and confers
neither all of its advantages nor all of its responsibilities.

## REFERENCES

Beresford, J.C. and A.H. Rivlin. "Privacy, poverty and old age." *Demography* (1966) 3:247-58.
Cherlin, Andrew. *Marriage, Divorce, Remarriage.* Cambridge, MA: Harvard University Press,
    1981.
Glick, Paul C. "American household structure in transition." *Family Planning Perspectives* (1984)
    16 (5): 205-11.
Kobrin, F.E. "The fall in household size and the rise of the primary individual in the United States."
    *Demography* (1976) 13: 127-38.
Michael, Robert T., Victor R. Fuchs and Sharon R. Scott. "Changes in the propensity to live alone:
    1950-1976." *Demography* (1980) 17 (1): 39-56.
National Center for Health Statistics. *Life Tables. Vital Statistics of the United States, 1978.* Volume
    II, Section 5. Washington, D.C.: U.S. Department of Health and Human Services, 1980.

Pampel, Fred C. "Changes in the propensity to live alone: Evidence from cross-sectional surveys, 1960-1976." *Demography* (1983) 20 (1): 433-48.
Preston, Samuel H. and John McDonald. "The incidence of divorce within cohorts of American marriages contracted since the Civil War." *Demography* (1979) 16 (1): 1-26.
Schoen, Robert, William L. Urton, Karen Woodrow and John Baj. "Marriage and divorce in 20th century American cohorts." Working Papers in Population Studies, School of Sciences, University of Illinois at Urbana-Champaign, 1984.
Sweet, James A. "Components of change in the number of households, 1970-1980." *Demography* (1984) 21(2):129-40.
U.S. Bureau of the Census. *Current Population Reports*, Series P-20, No. 365. Washington, D.C.: Department of Commerce, 1981.
———. "Provisional estimates of social, economic and housing characteristics." *1980 Census of Population and Housing*, Supplementary Report. Washington, D.C.: Department of Commerce, 1982.
Waldron, Ingrid. "Sex differences in illness incidence, prognosis and mortality: Issues and evidence." *Social Science Medicine* (1983) 17 (16): 1107-23.
Watkins, Susan Cotts, Jane Menken and John Bongaarts. "Continuities and changes in the American family." Paper presented at the annual meeting of the American Psychiatric Association, Los Angeles, CA, May 6-11, 1984.

# 2

# The Unsheltered Woman: Definition and Needs

Eugenie Ladner Birch

One-third of the nation has a housing problem. Twenty-three million households are ill-housed. They are a diverse group—the elderly, families with children, and single people of all races. Most significantly, they tend to be women. More than 40 percent of the group—or ten million—are female householders.[1] Females head about 27 percent of all American households today; yet, they are disproportionately represented among those experiencing housing problems. In fact, numerically, they are the largest subgroup of the poorly sheltered population.[2]

Recent data issued by the U.S. Department of Housing and Urban Development and the Bureau of the Census provide evidence of American housing deficiencies. Included in today's definition of a housing problem are two issues: housing quality and tenure status.

The housing quality concept employs three criteria to form an index which sets the minimum standard for decent housing in America. The criteria are: the physical adequacy of a dwelling, the extent of crowding, and the level of affordability. (The technical definition of these measures is discussed in a later section.)

Tenure status identifies a householder as an owner or renter. In America, 65 percent of all housing units are owner-occupied. Certain groups have yet to achieve this level of ownership. For example, only 48 percent of the nation's female householders are homeowners. One-fifth of them are elderly, mostly widows whose husbands' income purchased their homes. In 1981, women constituted more than 40 percent of all renters, an historic high; four years ago, female householders were only 32 percent of renters.[3]

When housing quality measures are correlated with tenure status for all house-

**EXHIBIT 2.1**
**Distribution of U.S. Households by Type, 1950-1980**
**(in percent)**

|                 | 1950          | 1960          | 1970          | 1980          |
|-----------------|---------------|---------------|---------------|---------------|
| All households  | (N=43,554)    | (N=52,799)    | (N=63,799)    | (N=82,368)    |
| Family          | 89.2          | 85.1          | 80.7          | 73.2          |
| Non-Family      | 10.8          | 14.9          | 19.3          | 26.8          |

*Source:* U.S. Bureau of the Census. *Census of Population.* Washington, D.C.: U.S. Government Printing Office, 1950, 1960, 1970, 1980.

holds, renters tend to be among the more poorly housed. For example, 30 percent of all renters are cost-burdened,[4] and 15 percent live in physically inadequate shelter. In contrast, in the homeowner group, only 8 percent are cost-burdened, and 6 percent live in physically inadequate housing. For women, these correlations are different. Across the board, all female householders have a higher incidence of housing quality problems than the general population; this phenomenon is true for homeowners as well as for renters. For example, the national figures for homeowners' cost-burden (8 percent) and physical inadequacy (6 percent) contrast dramatically with the same data for female homeowners: 17 percent are cost-burdened—two times the national rate—and 32 percent live in physically inadequate shelter—five times the national rate.

This evidence adds a new dimension to understanding American housing conditions. It suggests that gender is an important factor in identifying and elaborating housing issues. This paper explores why gender has become an essential analytical variable. It also details additional characteristics of the female population and its housing problem. In particular, it outlines housing conditions for different groups of women—single parents and the elderly. It contrasts the women's situation with minority groups usually selected for attention by analysts. Finally, it traces these phenomena as they occur in the nation and in a locality, New York City, chosen for its extreme manifestations of the problems discussed.

## AMERICAN HOUSEHOLDS: THEIR COMPOSITION AND LOCATION

While the housing problem has long been associated with women's concerns, its definition as a gender issue has been articulated within the context of the conventional family structure. Early housing advocates such as Jacob Riis and Edith Elmer Wood documented that women, particularly mothers, bore the brunt of inadequate shelter. Yet the women these reformers were concerned with were usually part of conventional families.[5]

As their successors recorded and assessed housing quality in America, they too

**EXHIBIT 2.2**
**Households in the United States, 1950-1980**
**(in thousands)**

|  | 1950 | 1960 | 1970 | 1980 |
|---|---|---|---|---|
| All households | 43,554 | 52,799 | 63,799 | 82,368 |
| Family | 38,838 | 44,905 | 51,456 | 60,309 |
| Female-headed | 3,594 | 4,422 | 5,500 | 9,082 |
| Percentage | 9.0 | 9.7 | 10.7 | 15.3 |
| Non-Family | 4,716 | 7,895 | 11,945 | 22,059 |
| Female | 3,048 | 5,179 | 7,882 | 12,780 |
| Percentage | 65.9 | 66.7 | 65.5 | 57.9 |
| Total Female | | | | |
| Households | 6,642 | 9,601 | 13,382 | 21,862 |
| Percentage | 15.1 | 18.2 | 20.9 | 26.6 |

*Source:* U.S. Bureau of the Census. *Statistical Abstract of the United States, 1982-83.* Washington, D.C.: U.S. Government Printing Office, 1984.

regarded the nuclear household—mother, father and children—as the norm. Consequently, their solutions were premised on the collective belief that they were treating a family housing problem.[6]

Until about 1950, they may have been correct. However, about that time major changes in household composition began to occur. As Exhibit 2.1 indicates, the traditional family household, while still a majority, became a smaller proportion, and the non-family, single-person household experienced dramatic growth.

Adding the gender factor to the analysis, Exhibit 2.2 demonstrates that women are increasingly heads of households. They have historically dominated the non-family class; now there are many more than formerly. Additionally, the female-headed family moved from 9 percent to 15 percent of all families.[7] Thus, in 1980, the 27 percent female-headed households constituted 22 million households. Growth rates of these households (Exhibit 2.3) demonstrate the extent of this demographic transformation. While female households more than doubled in the last generation, the non-family household, composed largely of single, elderly women who are 48.5 percent of the group, experienced the most dramatic expansion.

In New York City the picture differs from the national pattern, but it is probably characteristic of other northern industrial cities. As Exhibit 2.4 demonstrates, in 1950 the distribution of New York City households is exactly the same as in the nation. By 1960, however, this similarity begins to diminish. By 1980, the pattern is dramatically different. While non-family households are 25 percent of the countrywide total, they are over 33 percent of the city's total.

**EXHIBIT 2.3**
**Growth Rates of Female Households in the United States, 1950-1980**
**(in percent)**

|  | 1950-60 | 1960-70 | 1970-80 | 1950-1980 |
|---|---|---|---|---|
| All households | 21.1 | 23.6 | 29.8 | 89.1 |
| Family | 15.7 | 14.5 | 17.3 | 55.3 |
| Female-headed | 25.7 | 25.0 | 65.5 | 152.6 |
| Non-Family | 65.9 | 52.6 | 85.7 | 367.7 |
| Females | 67.7 | 50.0 | 64.1 | 319.3 |
| Total Female Households | 45.5 | 38.5 | 64.7 | 229.1 |

*Source:* U.S. Bureau of the Census. *Statistical Abstract of the United States, 1982-83.* Washington, D.C.: U.S. Government Printing Office, 1984.

**EXHIBIT 2.4**
**Distribution of New York City Households by Type,**
**1950-1980**
**(in percent)**

|  | 1950 | 1960 | 1970 | 1980 |
|---|---|---|---|---|
| All households | (N=2,359) | (N=2,654) | (N=2,837) | (N=2,792) |
| Family | 89.6 | 78.3 | 72.1 | 63.4 |
| Non-Family | 10.4 | 21.7 | 27.9 | 36.6 |

*Source:* U.S. Bureau of the Census. *Census of Population.* Washington, D.C.: U.S. Government Printing Office, 1950, 1960, 1970, 1980.

In turning to a more detailed analysis of household composition (Exhibit 2.5), subtle differences begin to appear. The proportion of single females in New York non-family households is quite similar to that in the nation. In contrast the percentage of female-headed families is much larger than in the country as a whole. Thus a comparison of the percentages of female householders shows that in New York City, they are almost 40 percent of the total while across America they are only slightly more than 25 percent of all households.

Finally, in looking at the growth rates of the different New York City household components (Exhibit 2.6), the results in terms of women as householders are not as dramatic as for the nation. In part, this phenomenon can be accounted for by the fact that the increase in the number of female householders, particularly female family heads, began to occur at least ten years earlier in this city than in the nation, and the number grew steadily in the following decades. In addition, the higher ratio of New York female householders can be attributed to the slow rate of household formation in New York City and to the absolute decline in urban households. These phenomena are not duplicated in the nation where

**EXHIBIT 2.5**
**Households in New York City, 1950-1980**
**(in thousands)**

|  | 1950 | 1960 | 1970 | 1980 |
|---|---|---|---|---|
| All households | 2,359 | 2,654 | 2,837 | 2,792 |
| Family | 2,113 | 2,052 | 2,044 | 1,770 |
| Female-headed | 239 | 276 | 354 | 466 |
| Percentage | 11.3 | 13.4 | 17.3 | 25.8 |
| Non-Family | 246 | 602 | 793 | 1,022 |
| Females | NA | 353 | 489 | 604 |
| Percentage | NA | 58.6 | 61.6 | 59.1 |
| Total Female | | | | |
| Households | 444 | 630 | 843 | 1,070 |
| Percentage | 18.8 | 23.7 | 29.3 | 38.3 |

*Source:* U.S. Bureau of the Census, *Census of Population*. Washington, D.C.: U.S. Government Printing Office, 1950, 1960, 1970, 1980.

**EXHIBIT 2.6**

**Growth Rates of Female Households**
**in New York City, 1950-1980**
**(in percent)**

|  | 1950-1960 | 1960-1970 | 1970-1980 | 1950-1980 |
|---|---|---|---|---|
| All households | 12.5 | 6.9 | −1.6 | 18.4 |
| Family | −2.9 | −0.4 | −13.4 | −16.2 |
| Female-headed | 15.5 | 28.3 | 31.6 | 95.0 |
| Non-Family | 144.7 | 31.7 | 32.6 | 315.5 |
| Females | NA | 38.5 | 23.5 | NA |
| Total Female Households | 41.9 | 33.8 | 26.9 | 141.0 |

*Source:* U.S. Bureau of the Census. *Census of Population*. Washington, D.C.: U.S. Government Printing Office, 1950, 1960, 1970, 1980.

household and family formation increased, but at a slower rate than for female householders.

The New York City picture is representative of patterns in much of urban America, particularly in the northeast and north central regions. Exhibit 2.7 shows the proportion of female households in America's fifteen most populous cities. Chicago, Philadelphia, Detroit, and Washington, D.C., are remarkable for their concentration of female-headed families. In the fast-growing sunbelt cities—Dallas, Houston, and Los Angeles—the number of female family heads is closer to the national figure but nonetheless is higher. Women still head one-

**EXHIBIT 2.7**
**Household Composition of Most Populous Cities in the United States, 1980***
(in thousands)

| Place | All Householders | Family | | Non-Family | | All Female Householders | |
|---|---|---|---|---|---|---|---|
| | Total | Total | %Female Head | Total | %Female Head | Total | %of all Households |
| United States | 82,368 | 60,309 | 15.3 | 22,059 | 57.9 | 21,862 | 26.6 |
| New York | 2,792 | 1,770 | 25.8 | 1,022 | 59.1 | 1,061 | 38.3 |
| Chicago | 1,094 | 712 | 30.7 | 381 | 55.6 | 431 | 39.4 |
| Los Angeles | 1,137 | 699 | 24.5 | 437 | 50.7 | 393 | 34.6 |
| Philadelphia | 620 | 415 | 31.5 | 204 | 61.5 | 256 | 41.4 |
| Houston | 603 | 394 | 20.5 | 208 | 46.5 | 177 | 29.5 |
| Detroit | 433 | 291 | 36.6 | 142 | 52.5 | 181 | 41.8 |
| Dallas | 355 | 224 | 22.9 | 130 | 54.1 | 122 | 34.4 |
| San Diego | 312 | 196 | 20.8 | 116 | 51.0 | 100 | 32.0 |
| Phoenix | 285 | 203 | 16.8 | 81 | 52.3 | 76 | 27.0 |
| Baltimore | 281 | 188 | 37.0 | 92 | 58.3 | 124 | 44.0 |
| San Antonio | 259 | 194 | 20.2 | 64 | 59.0 | 77 | 29.9 |
| Indianapolis | 260 | 181 | 21.2 | 78 | 57.7 | 83 | 32.2 |
| San Francisco | 299 | 141 | 26.2 | 158 | 49.9 | 115 | 38.5 |
| Memphis | 230 | 164 | 27.5 | 65 | 58.3 | 83 | 36.3 |
| Washington, D.C. | 254 | 135 | 41.6 | 118 | 57.3 | 124 | 48.9 |
| City total | 9,214 | 5,907 | | 3,296 | | 3,402 | |
| (% of nation) | 11.2 | 9.8 | | 14.9 | | 15.6 | |

*Note:*
*Cities are listed according to population.
*Source:* U.S. Bureau of the Census. *General Social and Economic Statistics.* Washington, D.C.: U.S. Government Printing Office, 1980; J.T. Markin. *The Book of City Rankings.* New York, 1983.

**EXHIBIT 2.8**
**Location of Female Householders in the United States, 1980**
(in thousands)

| | Total U.S. Households | Total in SMSAs | | Urban | | Rural | |
|---|---|---|---|---|---|---|---|
| | | | | Inside Central Cities | Outside Central Cities | | |
| | | Number | % | % of SMSA | % of SMSA | Number | % |
| *All female householders* | 21,723 | 16,336 | 72.6 | 52.4 | 47.6 | 5,886 | 24.8 |
| All U.S. householders | 83,527 | 57,869 | 68.2 | 46.2 | 54.0 | 27,789 | 30.8 |
| *Female-headed families* | 9,403 | 6,833 | 72.6 | 52.8 | 47.2 | 2,750 | 27.3 |
| All U.S. families | 61,019 | 40,612 | 66.6 | 39.1 | 60.9 | 20,407 | 33.4 |
| *Female non-family households* | 12,320 | 9,503 | 77.1 | 52.1 | 47.9 | 2,817 | 22.9 |
| All U.S. non-family households | 23,913 | 17,257 | 72.7 | 49.5 | 50.5 | 6,656 | 27.8 |

*Source:* U.S. Department of Commerce, Bureau of the Census. *Money Income of Households, Families and Persons in the United States, 1981; General Population, U.S. Summary, 1980.* Washington, D.C.: U.S. Government Printing Office, 1981.

**EXHIBIT 2.9**
**Location of Female Householders in New York State, 1980**
**(in thousands)**

| | Total New York State | | Total in SMSAs | | Urban | | Rural | |
|---|---|---|---|---|---|---|---|---|
| | Number | | Number | % | Inside Central Cities % of SMSA | Outside Central Cities % of SMSA | Number | % |
| All female householders | 2,123 | | 1,967 | 92.6 | 69.0 | 31.0 | 185 | 8.6 |
| All State householders | 6,345 | | 5,753 | 90.6 | 57.2 | 42.8 | 592 | 9.4 |
| Female family heads | 999 | | 936 | 94.0 | 67.9 | 32.1 | 86 | 8.6 |
| All families | 4,468 | | 4,032 | 90.2 | 51.4 | 48.6 | 407 | 9.1 |
| Female non-family heads | 1,126 | | 1,031 | 91.6 | 69.9 | 30.1 | 99 | 8.8 |
| All non-families | 1,877 | | 1,721 | 92.0 | 70.7 | 29.3 | 179 | 9.5 |

*Note:*
Totals may not add up evenly because of rounding of numbers
*Source:* U.S. Bureau of the Census. *General Social and Economic Characteristics, New York State.* Washington, D.C.: U.S. Government Printing Office, 1980.

**EXHIBIT 2.10**
**New York City Share of State's Urban Female Householders, 1980**
**(in thousands)**

|  | Number | Percent State Total |
|---|---|---|
| *Total NYC Female householders* | 1,077 | 50.6 |
| Total State Female householders | 2,125 | |
| *NYC Female Family heads* | 466 | 46.6 |
| State Female Family heads | 999 | |
| *NYC Female Non-Family heads* | 604 | 53.6 |
| State Female Non-Family heads | 1,126 | |

*Source:* U.S. Bureau of the Census. *General Social and Economic Characteristics, New York State.* Washington, D.C.: U.S. Government Printing Office, 1980.

fifth of the families in these cities. Under the non-family category, only two cities exceed the national percentage for female heads of households. In fact, most have a substantially lower proportion than is found in the country as a whole.

Cumulatively, these more populous cities contribute more female householders (almost 16 percent of the nation's total) than households (only 11 percent of the total); yet, together, they shelter less than one-fifth of the female group. This situation leads to the question: where do the nation's female householders live?

In fact, the majority of female householders, as Exhibit 2.8 demonstrates, live in metropolitan areas. In both categories, family and non-family, they are slightly more urban than the general population. They also show a tendency to be more concentrated in central cities than do other American households. This is especially true of female-headed families. Within the metropolitan areas, however, female householders do not live exclusively in central cities. Almost one-half of the metropolitan female householders live in the suburbs. Thus the concerns of female householders include a variety of issues which are tied to location. Among them is the equity question of whether female-headed families are more concentrated in central cities by choice and the quality questions about what kinds of dwellings and services different groups of women need in their respective locations.

The New York State pattern is quite different from that of the nation (Exhibit 2.9). In this highly urbanized state all householders are overwhelmingly concentrated in metropolitan areas. In general terms, the settlement pattern of female householders parallels this dominant trend. However, a closer examination of the data reveals one important deviation. Female-headed families are more concentrated in central cities than are other family types.

In fact, half of the state's female householders live in New York City. Their concentration in one city has important implications for state and local housing policy.

**EXHIBIT 2.11**
**Household Income in the United States, 1980:**
**Comparison of Female Householders and Married Couples**
**(in percent)**

| Income ($) | Total Householders | | Female Householders | | Married Couples | |
|---|---|---|---|---|---|---|
| | (N=83,527) | | (N=21,775) | | (N=49,630) | |
| under 5,000 | 10.5 ⎫ | | 26.6 ⎫ | | 2.9 ⎫ | |
| 5,000- 9,999 | 14.9 ⎬ | 40% | 27.8 ⎬ | 72% | 8.7 ⎬ | 24% |
| 10,000-14,999 | 14.4 ⎭ | | 17.9 ⎭ | | 12.3 ⎭ | |
| 15,000-19,999 | 12.3 | | 11.1 | | 12.5 | |
| 20,000-24,999 | 11.4 | | 7.1 | | 13.2 | |
| 25,000-29,999 | 9.7 | | 3.9 | | 12.3 | |
| 30,000-34,999 | 7.6 ⎫ | 27% | 2.1 ⎫ | 6% | 10.3 ⎫ | 38% |
| 35,000+ | 19.3 ⎭ | | 4.0 ⎭ | | 27.7 ⎭ | |
| Median Income | $19,074 | | $8,931 | | $25,106 | |

*Source:* U.S. Department of Commerce, Bureau of the Census. *Money Income of Households, Families and Persons in the United States, 1981.* Washington, D.C.: U.S. Government Printing Office, 1983.

## INCOME AND AGE OF U.S. HOUSEHOLDERS

An analysis of the distribution of income among households is essential to a full appreciation of gender-related housing issues. Female householders are poor. Their median income of $8,931 is less than half of the national figure ($19,074) and only 35 percent of married couples' ($25,106). Furthermore, almost 75 percent of the female householders have incomes under $15,000, while only one-quarter of the married couples fall into this category (Exhibit 2.11). At the other end of the scale, only 6 percent of the female householders earn enough to purchase a new home having today's $93,000 median price tag. In contrast, almost 40 percent of the married couples can undertake such an obligation.

The income distribution patterns in New York City, broken down according to tenure status, confirm the national pattern: female householders are poor. There are some differences among the women: owners are better off than renters. Nonetheless, a comparison of the median income of female householders and married couples reveals substantial differences: women who own their homes have less than half the median income of married couple owners; female renters earn only about 40 percent as much as husband/wife renters (Exhibit 2.12). Overall, the percentage of female householders earning under $15,000 is high—ranging from 57 percent (owners) to 79 percent (renters)—while the percentage of married couples at this income level is dramatically lower (19 percent of all owners and 43 percent of the renters).

**EXHIBIT 2.12**
**Distribution of Income in New York City, 1980:**
**Comparison of Female Householders and Married Couples by Tenure**
**(in percent)**

| | Owners | | | Renters | | |
|---|---|---|---|---|---|---|
| | All Householders (N=651,612) | Female Householders (N=146,698) | Married Couples (N=446,252) | All Householders (N=2,136,918) | Female Householders (N=930,791) | Married Couples (N=767,827) |
| 5,000 | 7.4 | 20.0 | 2.7 | 23.6 | 38.7 | 8.1 |
| 5,000-9,999 | 10.8 | 20.7 | 7.0 | 20.2 | 23.9 | 16.3 |
| 10,000-14,999 | 11.7 | 16.4 | 9.9 | 16.9 | 16.3 | 17.4 |
| 0-14,999 | 29.9 | 57.1 | 19.6 | 60.7 | 78.9 | 42.8 |
| 15,000-19,999 | 12.7 | 12.9 | 12.6 | 12.9 | 10.2 | 15.9 |
| 20,000-24,999 | 13.4 | 9.9 | 14.7 | 9.2 | 5.8 | 13.5 |
| 25,000-34,999 | 20.6 | 10.9 | 24.4 | 9.5 | 4.7 | 15.8 |
| 35,000+ | 23.2 | 8.7 | 28.6 | 7.5 | 2.6 | 13.1 |
| median income | $25,512 | $12,533 | $26,023 | $11,590 | $7,400 | $17,395 |

*Source:* U.S. Department of Commerce, Bureau of the Census. *Advance Estimates of Social, Economic and Housing Characteristics.* Washington, D.C.: U.S. Government Printing Office, 1983.

**EXHIBIT 2.13**
**Age Distribution and Median Income of American Female Householders, 1980**

| Age | Female head of family (N=9,403) | | Female single person (N=13,051) | |
|---|---|---|---|---|
| | **Percent** | **Median Income** | **Percent** | **Median Income** |
| 15-24 | 8.3 | 4,879 | 8.1 | 8,334 |
| 25-34 | 25.9 | 8,113 | 14.3 | 13,768 |
| 35-44 | 24.2 | 12,595 | 6.2 | 13,828 |
| 45-54 | 17.2 | 14,680 | 6.7 | 10,264 |
| 55-64 | 11.3 | 14,001 | 16.2 | 8,593 |
| 65+ | 13.1 | 12,429 | 48.5 | 5,625 |

*Source:* U.S. Department of Commerce, Bureau of the Census. *Money Income of Households, Families and Persons in the United States, 1981.* Washington, D.C.: U.S. Government Printing Office, 1983.

Returning to the national arena, female householders distributed by age categories and correlated with income reveal expected patterns (Exhibit 2.13). Sixty percent of female heads of families are in their childbearing years, and almost half of the single-person households are over sixty-five. In these groups the poorest are the female heads of families. Note the range of their median incomes: from $5,000 to $12,000. (The precarious position of many of these women is underscored by the fact that most are supporting one or more minor children in their homes. In fact, the average size of a female-headed family is more than three people.) The elderly, who constitute almost half of the female single-person households, are also among the poorest of the householders. With less than a $6,000 median income, they are in a precarious situation. Half have less than $500 per month to cover all their expenses, including increasing health care. These income figures have obvious implications for housing analysis.

The New York City age distribution and median income data in Exhibit 2.14 reveal three major differences from the national pattern. First, female family heads in the city are younger: there are almost twice as many female family heads in the youngest age group. Second, this New York City group is extremely poor—75 percent are below the poverty line—and can be expected to have severe problems in providing decent homes for themselves and their children. Finally, the elderly single-person female-headed household has a median income which is 15 percent lower than its counterpart in the nation. In a city where housing costs are notoriously high, these women are likely to have great difficulties affording shelter.

## HOUSING QUALITY

Measuring housing problems demands examination of the quality of individual dwelling units. Annual surveys by the U.S. Department of Housing assess qual-

**EXHIBIT 2.14**
**Age Distribution and Median Income of**
**New York City Female Householders, 1980**

| | Female head of family (N=462,933) | | Female single person (N=549,636) | |
|---|---|---|---|---|
| Age | Percent | Median Income | Percent | Median Income |
| 15-24 | 17.7 | NA | 4.5 | 7,969 |
| 25-34 | 24.9 | NA | 16.1 | 12,845 |
| 35-44 | 24.1 | NA | 8.9 | 13,194 |
| 45-64 | 29.4 | NA | 28.0 | 8,513 |
| 65+ | 12.5 | NA | 45.2 | 4,784 |

*Note:*
Although income data for female householders by age is not available, over 41 percent of female heads of family fall under the poverty threshold which in 1979 ranged from $4,723 for a two-person family to $7,412 for a four-person family.
*Source:* U.S. Bureau of the Census. *Metropolitan Housing Characteristics, New York-New Jersey SMSA.* Washington, D.C.: U.S. Government Printing Office, 1983.

ity with several indicators. The Department measures physical adequacy with a survey of systems (plumbing, electrical, heating) and facilities (kitchens and bathrooms); the presence of crowded units (more than one person per room); and the existence of excessive costs (more than 30 percent of income for rent, or 40 percent of income for mortgage and maintenance, or 30 percent for maintenance on a non-mortgaged home).

As Exhibit 2.15 indicates, about 33 percent of all American dwellings are problem-ridden. *Female householders occupy over 40 percent of these problem-ridden dwellings.* Looked at another way, women live in only one-third of the nation's homes, but they are disproportionately represented among those inhabitants of units considered substandard.

Notably, and predictably, women are most affected in the cost-burden category. With over one-third of them paying more than they should for their shelter, they constitute half of all those having this hardship. Their low income accounts for their presence here. Their high representation among those living in physically inadequate dwellings is also related to their poverty. For many, all their earnings can purchase is substandard housing.

## THE MORE SEVERELY IMPACTED WOMEN: THE SINGLE PARENT AND THE SENIOR CITIZEN

Among female householders, two groups stand out as requiring separate analyses: the single parent with children under age eighteen and the elderly female household head. The groups are isolated for two reasons. First, although they occupy 15 percent of the nation's housing stock, they live in a quarter of the

**EXHIBIT 2.15**
**Housing Quality in the United States, 1981**
**(in thousands)**

|  | All | Female Households | Female Households as % of Problem |
|---|---|---|---|
| Occupied units | 83,203 | 22,603 | |
| Total with a housing problem | 23,137 | 9,686 | |
| percent | 27.8 | 42.9 | 41.8 |
| Physically inadequate | 7,749 | 2,760 | |
| percent | 9.3 | 10.1 | 35.6 |
| Crowded | 2,489 | 469 | |
| percent | 3.0 | 2.1 | 18.8 |
| Cost-burden | 12,899 | 6,618 | |
| percent | 15.5 | 29.3 | 51.3 |

*Source:* Special tabulations based on 1981 National Housing Survey, U.S. Department of Housing and Urban Development, Washington, D.C.

**EXHIBIT 2.16**
**Housing Quality of the Female-Headed**
**Family and the Elderly Female**
**(in thousands)**

|  | Total | Female-Headed Households with Children Under 18 | Elderly Female-Headed Households |
|---|---|---|---|
| Occupied units | 13,169 | 5,856 | 7,313 |
| percent | | 44.4 | 55.3 |
| Total with a housing problem | 5,973 | 3,162 | 2,811 |
| percent | 45.4 | 53.9 | 38.4 |
| Physically inadequate | 1,647 | 861 | 786 |
| percent | 12.5 | 14.7 | 10.8 |
| Crowded | 380 | 365 | 15 |
| percent | 0.3 | 6.2 | 0.2 |
| Cost-burden | 3,946 | 1,936 | 2,010 |
| percent | 29.9 | 33.1 | 27.5 |

*Source:* Special tabulations based on 1981 National Housing Survey, U.S. Department of Housing and Urban Development, Washington, D.C.

## EXHIBIT 2.17
### Housing Quality of Impacted Female Heads of
### Household Who Rent, 1981
### (in thousands)

|  | Total Impacted Households | Female-headed Families with Children Under 18 (Renters) | Elderly Female-Headed Households (Renters) |
|---|---|---|---|
| Occupied units | 6,304 | 3,639 | 2,665 |
| Total with a housing problem | 4,010 | 2,464 | 1,546 |
| percent | 63.6 | 67.7 | 58.0 |
| Physically inadequate | 992 | 669 | 323 |
| percent | 15.7 | 18.4 | 12.1 |
| Crowded | 288 | 285 | 3 |
| percent | 4.6 | 7.8 | 0.1 |
| Cost-burdened | 2,730 | 1,510 | 1,220 |
| percent | 43.3 | 41.5 | 45.8 |

*Source:* Special tabulations based on 1981 National Annual Housing Survey, U.S. Department of Housing and Urban Development, Washington, D.C.

units experiencing housing problems. Second, they are two of society's most economically vulnerable groups. They have extremely low median incomes ($9,210 for the single parent and $4,757 for the elderly women) and little likelihood of changing their incomes without external support, such as daycare provisions allowing mothers to work, or pensions or insurance for the senior citizens. Of the two groups, the single parent has the most difficulties with her housing (Exhibit 2.16). In fact, by comparing data from Exhibit 2.16 with that of Exhibit 2.15, it can be seen that she is twice as likely as other households in the United States to have a housing problem.

Analyzing housing quality among renting single parents and elderly women uncovers even more startling conditions. The female householders of this group (Exhibit 2.17) are more than twice as likely as other American households to have a housing problem. In addition, they are three times more likely to be cost-burdened than are the other groups.

Female-family householders with minor children are the most problem-ridden group among those living in substandard shelter in the United States. While the comparisons drawn in Exhibit 2.18 are somewhat misleading because female householders are not extrapolated from the comparison groups, the analysis is useful for its measurement of the severity of impact.

Given the high incidence of female householders living in inadequate housing,

**EXHIBIT 2.18**
**Female Heads of Household with Minor Children**
**Compared to Other Groups***
**(in thousands)**

|  | Females with Children Under 18 | Blacks | Hispanics | Elderly |
|---|---|---|---|---|
| Occupied units | 5,856 | 9,025 | 4,346 | 16,906 |
| Total with a housing problem | 3,162 | 4,620 | 2,235 | 4,786 |
| percent | 53.9 | 51.2 | 51.4 | 28.3 |

*Note:*
*Groups are not mutually exclusive.
*Source:* Special tabulations based on the 1981 National Annual Housing Survey, U.S. Department of Housing and Urban Development, Washington, D.C.

policy makers should single them out for special attention. Included in this population should be the very low-income mother with children who rents. This group constitutes one-third of the female family householders with children. Over 53 percent of them have a housing problem.

Moving this analysis to the local level poses some difficulties. HUD data for housing quality is incomplete; it lacks cost-burden statistics for homeowners. Using the Bureau of the Census housing counts provides an adequate substitute although there are some definitional differences among variables. For example, unlike the HUD physical inadequacy index, the Census data measure only the ab-sence of plumbing, not other systems, and its cost-burden data differ slightly (see footnote to Exhibit 2.19). Given these caveats, the housing-quality measures pre-sented here can be used for general comparative purposes but, in fact, are under-stated.

Bearing these limitations in mind, Exhibit 2.19 provides evidence of a repeti-tion of the national pattern, although in a more exaggerated form. In New York City over 40 percent of all households have a housing problem, while 56 percent of the female households are afflicted. In all categories of quality measurement, women are heavily represented (one-third or more) among those having a given characteristic. Of particular note is the cost-burden issue. Almost half of the female householders pay too much for their units, a phenomenon that, on the one hand, is not surprising considering their low incomes; but, on the other hand, it is remarkable considering the presence of rent control in many female householder units.

Also important in the New York City data is the higher than usual incidence of housing problems. (While only 29 percent of the nation's households live in sub-standard shelter, 42 percent of New York City households do.) In part, these

**EXHIBIT 2.19**
**Housing Quality in New York City, 1980**

|  | Total Households (in thousands) | Female Households (in thousands) | Female House- holds as Percent of Total |
|---|---|---|---|
| Occupied units | 2,788 | 1,077 | 38.6 |
| Total with a housing problem | 1,169 | 606 | |
| percent | 41.9 | 56.3 | 51.8 |
| Lacking plumbing for exclusive use* | 97 | 37 | |
| percent | 3.4 | 3.4 | 38.1 |
| Crowded† | 216 | 62 | |
| percent | 7.7 | 5.7 | 28.7 |
| Cost burden‡ | 856 | 507 | |
| percent | 30.7 | 47.1 | 59.2 |

*Notes:*
 *This measure is substituted for the HUD "physically inadequate" category; it undercounts the problem.
 † This measure counts more than 1.01 persons per room as crowded.
 ‡ This measure is composed of (1) a renter paying 30 percent or more of her income for rent, or (2) a homeowner paying 37 percent of her income for mortgage and maintenance, or 30 percent or more for maintenance.
 *Source:* U.S. Bureau of the Census, *Metropolitan Housing Characteristics*. Washington, D.C.: U.S. Government Printing Office, 1983.

phenomena may be attributed to the higher number of female householders living in New York City.

To focus on special female householder populations, the data permits the singling out of renters and within them only the elderly. (The incidence of housing problems among single parents with children is not possible to ascertain from published information.) Nonetheless, Exhibit 2.20 demonstrates that female renters are a far higher proportion than the general renting population experiencing substandard shelter. Interestingly enough, there are significant differences in the range of housing problems encountered. For example, one-fifth of the general population lives in overcrowded conditions. Female householders do not share as significantly in this condition as others, such as married couples, do. (The former constitute 31 percent of those having this problem—the highest incidence, of course, being among women in the childbearing ages—while the latter comprise 64 percent.) Renters constitute the majority of householders in New York City, a phenomenon discussed below. Therefore, the high level of housing problems in this renting group is a serious policy issue.

**EXHIBIT 2.20**
**Housing Quality of Female Households**
**and Elderly Females Who Rent, New York City, 1980**
**(in thousands)**

| | Total Renters | Female House-holders | Elderly Female Heads of House-hold |
|---|---|---|---|
| Occupied units | 2,136 | 930 | 248 |
| Total with a housing problem | 1,093 | 571 | 154 |
| percent | 51.2 | 61.4 | 62.1 |
| Lacking plumbing for exclusive use* | 84 | 27 | 7 |
| percent | 3.9 | 2.9 | 2.8 |
| Crowded† | 185 | 57 | 2 |
| percent | 19.8 | 6.1 | 0.8 |
| Cost burden‡ | 824 | 487 | 145 |
| percent | 38.6 | 52.4 | 58.5 |

*Notes:*
   * This measure is substituted for the HUD "physically inadequate" category; it undercounts the problem.
   † This measure counts more than 1.01 persons per room as crowded.
   ‡ This measure is composed of (1) a renter paying 30 percent or more of her income for rent, or (2) a homeowner paying 37 percent of her income for mortgage and maintenance, or 30 percent or more for maintenance.
   *Source:* U.S. Bureau of the Census. *Metropolitan Housing Characteristics*. Washington, D.C.: U.S. Government Printing Office, 1983.


**EXHIBIT 2.21**
**Tenure Patterns of U.S. Households Compared**
**to Female Households, 1981**
**(in thousands)**

| | All | Female Households | Female Households as a % of All Households |
|---|---|---|---|
| Total | 83,203 | 22,603 | 27.2 |
| Owner | 54,631 | 10,899 | |
| percent | 65.4 | 48.2 | 19.9 |
| Renter | 28,842 | 11,704 | |
| percent | 34.6 | 51.8 | 40.6 |

   *Source:* Special tabulations based on 1981 National Annual Housing Survey, U.S. Department of Housing and Urban Development, Washington, D.C.

**EXHIBIT 2.22**
**Tenure Patterns of Selected Groups\* of U.S. Households, 1981**

|  | Total | % All Households | Owner | % All Households | Renter | % All Households |
|---|---|---|---|---|---|---|
| Female | | | | | | |
| households | 22,603 | 27.1 | 10,899 | 20.0 | 11,704 | 40 |
| percent | | | 48.2 | | 51.8 | |
| Black | | | | | | |
| households | 9,025 | 10.8 | 3,902 | 7.2 | 5,123 | 17 |
| percent | | | 43.2 | | 56.7 | |
| Hispanic | | | | | | |
| households | 4,346 | 5.2 | 1,822 | 3.3 | 2,524 | 8 |
| percent | | | 41.9 | | 58.1 | |
| Elderly | | | | | | |
| households | 16,906 | 20.3 | 12,390 | 27.6 | 4,516 | 15 |
| percent | | | 73.2 | | 26.7 | |

*Note:*
  \*These groups are not mutually exclusive.
  *Source:* Special tabulations based on 1981 National Annual Housing Survey, U.S. Department of Housing and Urban Development, Washington, D.C.

## TENURE PATTERNS: WOMEN AND OTHER GROUPS

Female householders are less likely to be owners than are American households in general. The divergence is wide. In 1981, 65 percent of all householders owned their own homes. In contrast, only 48 percent of the female householders were owners. The obverse side of the picture is women's status as renters. Today they constitute 40 percent of all American renters. Four years ago, in 1980, they were 32 percent of all renters. They have grown to be a larger proportion because other households have increased their share of ownership faster than women have.

Compared to other groups usually considered deprived in American society, women are only marginally better off. They own their homes with more frequency than minorities. This favorable position is attributed to their presence among the elderly which itself exceeds the national pattern of homeownership. This latter population is frequently comprised of widows whose spouses' income purchased their housing.

New York City provides a distorted example of the national tenure patterns. Since three-quarters of its housing stock is rented, the only measure used is the comparison of levels of female ownership with the general level of ownership. Again, women have a significantly lower level—only about 14 percent are owners in a city that has a 23 percent rate of ownership.

**EXHIBIT 2.23**
**Tenure Patterns in New York City Households, 1980**
**(in thousands)**

|  | **All Households** | **Female Households** | **Female Households as a % of All Households** |
|---|---|---|---|
| Total | 2,786 | 1,076 | 38.6 |
| Owner | 651 | 146 |  |
|    percentage | 23.3 | 13.6 | 22.4 |
| Renter | 2,135 | 930 |  |
|    percentage | 76.6 | 86.4 | 43.5 |

*Source:* U.S. Bureau of the Census, *Metropolitan Housing Characteristics, New York.* Washington, D.C., 1984.

**EXHIBIT 2.24**
**Tenure Patterns of Selected New York City Households,* 1980**
**(in thousands)**

|  | **Total** | **% All Households** | **Owner** | **% All Households** | **Renter** | **% All Households** |
|---|---|---|---|---|---|---|
| Female |  |  |  |  |  |  |
|   households | 1,076 | 38.6 | 146 | 22.4 | 930 |  |
|     percent |  | 13.6 |  |  | 86.4 | 43.5 |
| Black |  |  |  |  |  |  |
|   households | 635 | 22.8 | 109 | 16.7 | 526 |  |
|     percent |  | 17.2 |  |  | 82.8 | 24.6 |
| Hispanic |  |  |  |  |  |  |
|   households | 449 | 16.1 | 44 | 6.7 | 405 |  |
|     percent |  | 9.8 |  |  | 90.2 | 18.9 |
| Elderly |  |  |  |  |  |  |
|   households | 633 | 22.7 | 169 | 25.9 | 464 |  |
|     percent |  | 26.7 |  |  | 73.2 | 21.7 |

*Note:*
*Groups are not mutually exclusive.
*Source:* U.S. Bureau of the Census. *Metropolitan Housing Characteristics.* Washington, D.C.: U.S. Government Printing Office, 1984.

The New York City data also provides an illustration of women's tenure position relative to other groups. As in the nation, female householders are underrepresented among owners. In fact, after Hispanics, they have the lowest rate of ownership in the city. This condition is all the more important when one realizes that they are a numerically large group.

Disaggregating the data on female householders is possible at the metropolitan

**EXHIBIT 2.25**
**Tenure Patterns of Selected Groups**
**of New York City Female Households, 1980**
**(in thousands)**

| | Total | % All Households | Owner | % All Households | Renter | % All Households |
|---|---|---|---|---|---|---|
| All Female households | 1,076 | 38.6 | 146 | 22.4 | 930 | 43.5 |
| percent | | 13.6 | | | | 86.4 |
| Black Female households (under 65) | 311 | 11.2 | 30 | 4.6 | 281 | 13.2 |
| percent | 28.9 | | 9.6 | | | 90.4 |
| Hispanic Female households (under 65) | 188 | 6.7 | 8 | 1.2 | 180 | 8.4 |
| percent | 17.4 | | 4.3 | | | 95.7 |
| Elderly Female households (over 65) | 312 | 11.2 | 64 | 9.8 | 248 | 11.6 |
| percent | 28.9 | | 20.5 | | | 79.4 |

*Source:* U.S. Bureau of the Census. *Metropolitan Housing Characteristics, New York.* Washington, D.C.: U.S. Government Printing Office, 1984.

level. This process allows race and ethnic origins to be factored into the analysis. Comparisons among whites and minorities reveal extremely low rates of ownership, under 10 percent for both black and female householders.

The ramifications of the difference in housing tenure patterns are not as immediately obvious as quality issues. But in analyzing the spatial, economic, and, finally, intangible qualitative aspects of housing tenure in the United States, it becomes apparent that this low percentage of female homeownership represents a housing problem for women.

There are two dimensions to the location of owner-occupied and rental housing in the United States, intra-regional and inter-regional. Within a region, rental units tend to be located within urbanized areas and specifically in central cities. Of the 35 million rental units in the United States in 1980, 24 million, or 69 percent, were in urbanized areas and 15 million, or 42 percent, were in central cities. That year, 31 percent of all housing units in the United States were in central cities.

Female renter households, because of their inability to purchase housing units, are also concentrated in urban areas and especially in central cities. This is important for what it says about the degree of choice that female households have in

**EXHIBIT 2.26**
**Personal Income**
**(Constant 1972 dollars)**

|  | Percent Change 1970-80 | Percent of U.S. | |
| --- | --- | --- | --- |
|  |  | **1970** | **1980** |
| U.S. | +38.6 | 100.0 | 100.0 |
| Northeast | +18.0 | 27.0 | 23.0 |
| North Central | +29.1 | 28.1 | 26.2 |
| South | +57.6 | 26.6 | 30.2 |
| West | +56.0 | 18.3 | 20.6 |

*Source:* U.S. Bureau of the Census, *Money Income of Households, Families and Persons in the United States: 1981.* Washington, D.C.: U.S. Government Printing Office, 1982.

selecting location, neighborhood quality, and other services and attributes which should be considered in the definition of decent housing. All neighborhoods carry with them certain advantages and disadvantages. Choice in a freely functioning housing market permits a household to choose a desired bundle of services. For female householders, selection of services is severely circumscribed by where they can afford housing units.

Inter-regionally, the disparity in tenure means that female households have less opportunity to move to the economically prosperous areas of the country. It is not necessary for purposes of this article to review extensively the shifts in population and wealth taking place in this country today. An indicator of this shift is illustrated below. From 1970 to 1980, per capita income in the United States increased 24 percent. In the West and South, per capita income increased 26 percent and 31 percent, respectively. Total personal income and proportion of personal income earned in different parts of the country also changed substantially during this period, as indicated below.

Concurrently, the kinds of housing units being built to accommodate the growth are more likely to be owner-occupied rather than rental units. The proportion of owner-occupied units in the South increased from 1970 to 1980 from 64.7 percent to 67 percent. In the West it increased from 59 percent to 59.8 percent. Nationwide from 1970 to 1980 the stock of owned units increased by 30 percent and rented units increased by only 21 percent. The larger increase in owned units represents one barrier to the lower-income women's mobility.

Another limiting factor is the cost of owned units currently being built in the South and West. On a price index of new one-family houses sold in the United States, using 1977 as the base year, the cost of the sunbelt units has outstripped those of the frostbelt.

The concentration of female-headed households in rental units represents a lack of choice which has ramifications beyond the psychic satisfaction of having

**EXHIBIT 2.27**
**Price Index of New One-Family Houses**
**Sold by Region**

|      | U.S.  | North East | North Central | South | West  |
|------|-------|------------|---------------|-------|-------|
| 1970 | 55.3  | 61.5       | 58.2          | 58.7  | 48.8  |
| 1975 | 81.7  | 89.8       | 82.5          | 85.1  | 76.2  |
| 1977 | 100.0 | 100.0      | 100.0         | 100.0 | 100.0 |
| 1980 | 145.2 | 138.5      | 135.4         | 144.3 | 154.2 |

*Source:* George Sternlieb, James W. Hughes and Connie O. Hughes, *Demographic Trends and Economic Reality.* New Brunswick, NJ; Center for Urban Policy Research, 1982.

options or the opportunity of moving where economic growth is taking place. It means that these individuals are more likely to be excluded from areas with desirable bundles of services, especially higher-quality schools and lower crime rates.

The fiscal aspects of the tenure question come into play in two ways. For one, home ownership creates equity for the owner which never occurs for renters. It is the major form of wealth for most American families and provides the owner with a significant asset and with financial flexibility. An owner can borrow against its worth or can sell this asset.

In addition, payments of mortgage interest and property taxes are tax deductible, a deduction not available to renters. There are, of course, certain advantages to rental housing. These units usually take a smaller proportion of monthly income than do owned units. Also, less expense is involved when moving. The fact that female households do not have the option to make the decision as freely as other households, but are forced to rent, is the problem.

## CONCLUSIONS

One of the first questions asked in this paper was who is the unsheltered woman? The answer is clear. She is either a young mother not yet 35 with minor children, probably living in rental housing, or an elderly single person living alone in either a rented or owned unit. She is urban; yet she has an equal chance of living either in the central city or the suburbs. In contrast, if she is a New Yorker, she will probably be living in a central city and has a fifty-fifty chance of being a New York City resident. Above all, she is poor, in all likelihood having an income of less than 80 percent of the nation's median. (In fact, one in two female householders earns less than 50 percent of the median.)

These characteristics, poverty and her life-cycle position, define her prominent place among the ill-housed one-third of the nation. As a group, female householders constitute more than 40 percent of the nation's housing problem. Being a female householder means that a woman has a one in three chance of being cost-burdened and a one in eight chance of living in an inadequate dwelling. Any other American citizen, for example, has only a one in six chance of being cost-burdened. If she is a single parent, she has more than a 50 percent chance of having a housing problem. A comparison of these odds with those of blacks and Hispanics, groups generally studied by housing analysts, reveals that female householders, on the whole, are as badly off; but in spite of their numbers, which exceeds that of the other groups, they are not frequently singled out for special attention.

The poverty of female householders creates another phenomenon that is rightly considered a housing problem: low rates of homeownership. Today a female householder has less than a 50 percent chance of achieving homeowner status; a single parent has a 40 percent chance. (If she is black or Hispanic living in New York City, she has less than a 10 percent chance of owning her own home in a city where the average rate is 25 percent ownership.)

This portrait of the female householder is complete only with the recognition that she is fast becoming an important subgroup in American society. (It is beyond the scope of this paper to comment on the appropriateness of this condition other than to note that the single-person household is growing faster than the single-parent family; but each group represents about half of the population in question.) Only thirty years ago the female householder comprised 15 percent of the total—today she is approaching one-third. Her needs, particularly for low-cost, decent shelter, cannot be ignored.

How these needs should be met is the subject of a lengthy policy debate whose outlines can only be suggested here. One approach, to improve the purchasing power of the female householder, can be developed through a variety of programs ranging from the income-targeted solutions such as job training, child care, pension, and other devices to the shelter-targeted including Section 8-type arrangements or housing vouchers. Another strategy, to increase the supply of low-cost rental and ownership housing, can be implemented through programs designed to reduce the costs of construction, rehabilitation, and home purchase through any number of devices used in the past, from public housing to interest subsidy. The method is less important than the goal: to reduce the number of unsheltered women. What is lacking is the political will.

This discussion has been limited to defining American housing problems according to the availability of data which can measure preselected parameters—physical qualities, cost, and tenure status. It does not touch upon larger issues such as the suitability of the actual dwellings and their location. Since affordability is the crux of the problem, however, the data does suggest that dwellings designed for households of the past, which differ radically in composition from almost one-third of today's households, may not be appropriate. It may be that the female householder needs specially designed dwellings which meet more than shelter needs and that are so located as to address broader issues such as economic opportunity. Inherent in the latter concept is the idea that certain designs, such as intergenerational housing, might be organized to blend the physical features of shelter, the economic advantages of sharing, and the social aspects of service delivery. Thus, new designs and financial programs to implement them should be one of the demands of the unsheltered woman.

## NOTES

1. Female householders are defined by the U.S. Bureau of the Census as female heads of families and single-person households.
2. These figures are drawn from special tabulations based on the 1981 National Annual Housing Survey, Housing and Demographic Analysis Division, U.S. Department of Housing and Urban Development. The author is especially grateful to Duane McGough and Iredia Irby of HUD who patiently assembled this data.
3. Ibid., 1977.
4. Cost-burden is defined by HUD as renters paying 30 percent or more of their income for rent; or owners paying more than 35 percent of their income for mortgage and maintenance or 30 percent for maintenance of a mortgage-free unit.
5. Eugenie Ladner Birch, "Woman-made America, The Case of Early Public Housing Policy," in Donald A. Krueckeberg, *The American Planner* (New York: Methuen, 1983), pp. 149-178.
6. Grace Milgram, "The Rationale for Assisted Housing," in Congressional Research Service, *Housing–A Reader* (Washington, D.C.: U.S. Government Printing Office, 1983).
7. Anthony Downs, *Rental Housing in the 1980's* (Washington, D.C.: The Brookings Institution, 1983). The author is grateful to Carol Smolenski for her contributions to this discussion on tenure.

*3*

# Female-Headed Families
# in New York City

Evelyn S. Mann

Between 1970 and 1980 in New York City there has been more than a 47.4 percent increase in the number of female householders with related children under 18 but with no husband present. The increase of almost 100,000 such families, from 209,105 to 308,121, is corroborated by other census data such as the 59 percent increase since 1970 in the number of divorced females and an 8 percent increase in the number of separated females, ages 20 through 54. We do not have the 1980 figures yet; but in 1970, 71 percent of all families headed by a divorced female of any age had one or more children under 18 years of age. As many as 82 percent of the families headed by a separated female of any age had children under 18. Incidentally, so did 39 percent of all single female heads of households of any age. The number of never-married females, ages 20 to 54, increased by 149,923 (36.4 percent) between 1970 and 1980. This increase is partially due to the size of the baby boom cohorts and partially to the delayed age of first marriage.

Also contributing to the increase in families headed by a female with children under 18 were the 355,000 out-of-wedlock births occurring in New York City between 1970 and 1980. In 1980, this phenomenon had reached 38,567 annually, representing 36 percent of all births occurring in the city.

The future seems to point to increasing numbers of divorced or never-married females with children under 18; most of these women will be householders. Some, however, will be doubled up in the household of a relative. Although the numbers are still small, there were some 29,249 female-headed subfamilies in 1980, a 38 percent increase over 1970. In New York State, there is an increasing tendency to divorce when separated, so little, if any, increase in separated females, with or without children, is anticipated. Also, more females who used to report themselves as separated are less reluctant now to report themselves as divorced.

47

**EXHIBIT 3.1**
New York City Female Householders with Related Children Under 18,
1970 and 1980

| | 1970 | | 1980 | | Change | |
|---|---|---|---|---|---|---|
| | Number | Percent | Number | Percent | Number | Percent |
| New York City | 209,105 | 100.0 | 308,121 | 100.0 | 99,016 | 47.4 |
| Bronx | 53,535 | 25.6 | 77,417 | 25.1 | 23,882 | 44.6 |
| Brooklyn | 80,125 | 38.3 | 116,224 | 37.7 | 36,099 | 45.1 |
| Manhattan | 42,553 | 20.4 | 55,356 | 18.0 | 12,803 | 30.1 |
| Queens | 29,165 | 13.9 | 50,985 | 16.5 | 21,820 | 74.8 |
| Staten Island | 3,727 | 1.8 | 8,139 | 2.6 | 4,412 | 118.4 |

*Source:* 1970 Second Count, 1980 Summary Tape File 2B.

Families in which there is a female householder with children was the largest growing household-type segment among all families between 1970 and 1980. While similar families with children headed by an unmarried male increased by 39 percent, the total numerical increase was only 9,270.

To put this in the context of total household- and family-type change, in the decade, the city lost 48,342 (−1.7 percent) of total households (occupied housing units) but lost 286,201 (−14.0 percent) of total family households. The largest decrease, part of a national trend, was among husband-wife family households, a loss of 400,252, or one quarter of all such households as of 1970. Almost making up for the loss in family households was the 237,859 increase (30 percent) in non-family households made up of persons living alone or with non-relatives only. Very few of the non-relatives were children under 18; in fact, in the whole city, there were only 17,903 children classified as non-relatives living in either family or non-family households. Most (83 percent) of the 197,961 increase in non-family households were one-person households, the only household-size group to increase since 1970, up by 27.7 percent. Assuming that female householders with children and the increasing number of one-person households are competing for the same limited available living space, it is understandable that most landlords would rather rent to a single individual or a husband-wife family than to a family with children.

In 1980, 116,224 female householders with related children lived in Brooklyn, representing 38 percent of the city's share. Such families increased by 45 percent since 1970 (Exhibit 3.1). The second largest number, 77,417, lived in the Bronx in which the category also increased by 45 percent. Queens had a dramatic increase of 75 percent, gaining in total city share of female householders with related children, up from 13.9 percent in 1970 to 16.5 percent in 1980. Similarly, the percent of Staten Island's female-headed households more than doubled since

1970. Manhattan had the lowest percentage increase and declined in relative city share.

It should be no surprise that there is a relationship between the city's distribution of low-income families by census tract and female householders with children. The largest concentrations of the latter are in the South Bronx, University Heights, East Tremont, North Harlem, East Harlem, West Harlem, Washington Heights, the Lower East Side, Red Hook, Bedford-Stuyvesant, Crown Heights, Flatbush, Bushwick, Ocean Hill-Brownsville, Arverne-Far Rockaway, and Fox Hills in Staten Island.

What kind of housing can unmarried female householders with children afford? Those below the poverty level, 169,422 families, represent 55 percent of the 308,000 total female householders with related children. In 1980, almost 69 percent of all families below the poverty level with related children (including husband-wife families) were female-headed families, up from 59 percent in 1970. Between 1970 and 1980, female-headed families with related children under 18 and below the poverty level increased by 72 percent.

The below-poverty-level, female-headed families with related children have, on the average, a larger number of children than similar female-headed families above the poverty level. In 1970, these average numbers of children were 2.85 and 1.87, respectively. When comparable 1980 census numbers are available, the relative relationship is expected to remain the same, but because of a decline in the birth rate, there will be a slightly lower level of average children per family for both groups.

The distribution of families below the poverty level with female householders and children under 18 by borough is not too different than that of all families with female householders and children under 18 (Exhibit 3.2). Just over 40 percent of the 169,422 poverty-level families live in Brooklyn. Brooklyn had the largest numerical share of the increase since 1970, up by 27,585 such families. The next highest borough is the Bronx, with 28 percent of the total. The relative relationship among the boroughs shifted between 1970 and 1980, with losses in percentage share in the Bronx, Brooklyn, and Manhattan picked up by Queens where the group increased by about one-and-one-half times. Small numbers were gained in Staten Island, almost doubling that borough's families in the category.

The decade change in the number of women in the labor force is significant to the above discussion. The total number of women (16 years of age or over) of any marital status with children under 18 declined by 141,380 or 14 percent, while those in the labor force increased by 61,118 or 18 percent. Of those in the labor force, females with own children under 6 increased by 30,688 or 29 percent and those with own children 6 to 17 years increased by only 30,433 or 13 percent. We do not yet have this data cross-tabulated by either marital status or household type but it can be assumed that many female householders with no husband present are included in the figures cited.

**EXHIBIT 3.2**
**New York City Families Below the Poverty Level,**
**Female Householders\* with Related Children Under 18, 1970-1980**

|                | 1970 | | 1980 | | Change | |
|----------------|--------|---------|--------|---------|--------|---------|
|                | Number | Percent | Number | Percent | Number | Percent |
| New York City  | 98,685 | 100.0   | 169.422| 100.0   | 70,737 | 71.7    |
| Bronx          | 29,146 | 29.5    | 47,983 | 28.3    | 18,837 | 64.6    |
| Brooklyn       | 40,920 | 41.5    | 68,504 | 40.4    | 27,584 | 67.4    |
| Manhattan      | 19,572 | 19.8    | 30,428 | 18.0    | 10,856 | 55.5    |
| Queens         | 7,976  | 8.1     | 19,456 | 11.5    | 11,480 | 143.9   |
| Staten Island  | 1,071  | 1.1     | 3,051  | 1.8     | 1,980  | 184.9   |

*Note:*
   \*No husband present.

   *Source:* 1070 Fourth Count, 1980 Summary Tape File 3.

Married or not, there is an implication that for larger numbers of working females, the availability and cost of day care facilities and after-school activities centers are important. A recent national survey (*Current Population Survey,* June 1977) reported that 17 percent of women 18 to 44 years of age with preschool children who are not in the labor force said they would enter if satisfactory child care were available at reasonable cost. Furthermore, these mothers were shown to be in lower socioeconomic strata, making them less able to afford paid child care. Since mothers of young children have been entering the labor force in increasing numbers over the decade, and since more of these mothers are living in non-traditional family settings, the availability of child care is an acute problem. Unless there are other female family members present in the household or available nearby, the lack of low-cost day care and after-school activities facilities are disincentives to work. Further, even if available, as income goes up, day care costs are proportionately elevated and in many instances eligibility to participate in such programs is lost. Work hours are usually not flexible and a full-time job is not compatible with school attendance hours. The dangers of part-time baby sitting in lieu of professionally administered day care centers and of unsupervised latch-key children in lieu of teacher-supervised after-school centers are not lost on landlords who wish to protect their property. Instead of expanding day care center facilities, budget cuts are forcing elimination or consolidation of some facilities. After-school retention programs are also shrinking.

These are but a few of the housing and shelter-related problems faced by New York female householders with minor children and no husband. The point is that this group is a growing portion of the city's population. As such, their concerns are the city's concerns. The solutions to their problems will be possible only with a recognition of their number and with the input of government funds to carefully selected programs tailored to meet the needs of these women.

*4*

# The Elderly in New York City: Demographic Characteristics

May Engler and Roberta R. Spohn

The housing crisis facing New York City and the nation has intensified over the past decade. Affordable rentals are nonexistent for low- and middle-income people of all ages, while rent and utilities consume a higher and higher proportion of their income. For young people this has led to shared living, couples working, and delaying families or remaining with parents for longer periods. These options are not available to the elderly.

The elderly, those 65 and over, generally do not have the opportunity to supplement income or replace savings. Therefore, the amount of money they have left for other necessities after they pay their rent is likely to be more limited. The ratio of rent to income can make the difference between an old age of poverty or relative comfort. Moreover, changes in federal housing policy have eliminated money for new construction and rehabilitation of existing housing stock and have jeopardized subsidized housing such as Sections 8 and 202.

The *1980 Housing and Vacancy Survey of New York City*, conducted by the U.S. Bureau of the Census, provides data which documents the continuing and worsening plight of the elderly with regard to housing. This report, *Housing and the Elderly: Older Renters in New York City in 1980*, focuses on the current characteristics and conditions of elderly renters and brings up to date the information from 1975, which indicates that the proportion of households headed by a person 65 and over in New York City did not change between 1975 and 1980. Although the total number of households headed by elderly individuals declined slightly, from 546,000 in 1975 to 542,000 in 1980, the proportion of elderly households in the total population was about the same (20 percent) because of a greater loss of younger households.

As with the total city population, the elderly are predominantly renters. About

**EXHIBIT 4.1**
**Distribution of Renter Household Heads 65 and Over**
**by Age and Sex: 1980, 1975, 1970**
**(in thousands)**

| Age and Sex | 1980 | | 1975 | | 1970 | |
|---|---|---|---|---|---|---|
| | N | % | N | % | N | % |
| *Total* | | | | | | |
| 65 and over | 355 | 100.0 | 376 | 100.0 | 471 | 100.0 |
| 65-74 | 212 | 59.7 | 252 | 67.0 | NA | NA |
| 75 and over | 143 | 40.3 | 124 | 33.0 | NA | NA |
| *Males* | | | | | | |
| 65 and over | 154 | 43.4 | 189 | 50.3 | 263 | 55.7 |
| 65-74 | 97 | 27.3 | 131 | 34.9 | NA | NA |
| 75 and over | 57 | 16.1 | 58 | 15.4 | NA | NA |
| *Females* | | | | | | |
| 65 and over | 201 | 56.6 | 187 | 49.7 | 209 | 44.3 |
| 65-74 | 114 | 32.1 | 121 | 32.2 | NA | NA |
| 75 and over | 87 | 24.5 | 66 | 17.5 | NA | NA |

*Source:* See text.

two-thirds (65.6 percent) of all households headed by a person 65 or older were renter households. The ratio of elderly renters to elderly homeowners remains about two to one from 1975 to 1980 (356,000 renters to 186,000 owners). The following sections present the demographic and economic characteristics of elderly renter households with particular attention to their income in relation to their housing costs.

## DEMOGRAPHIC CHARACTERISTICS OF ELDERLY RENTERS

The demographic characteristics of the elderly renters with respect to age, sex, ethnicity, and other variables indicate that significant changes identified in the 1975 survey are continuing and can now be viewed as trends. Elderly households are increasingly headed by females living alone, with a greater proportion of minorities.

### Sex and Age

Over half (56.6 percent) of the elderly renter households were headed by women in 1980, up from 49.7 percent in 1975[1] (See Exhibit 4.1). In addition, four of ten (40.3 percent) of the elderly renter households in 1980 were headed by individuals 75 years of age or older, a rise from 33.0 percent in 1975. Among this older population the proportion of female-headed households is 60 percent.

**EXHIBIT 4.2**
**Distribution of Renter Household Heads 65 and Over**
**by Size of Household and Sex: 1980, 1975, 1970**
**(in thousands)**

|  | 1980 | | 1975 | | 1970 | |
|---|---|---|---|---|---|---|
| **Age and Size** | N | % | N | % | N | % |
| *65 and over* | 355 | 100.0 | 376 | 100.0 | 471 | 100.0 |
| One person | 211 | 59.4 | 196 | 52.1 | 229 | 48.6 |
| Two | 121 | 34.1 | 151 | 40.2 | 196 | 41.6 |
| Three or more | 23 | 6.5 | 29 | 7.7 | 46 | 9.8 |
| **Male** | | | | | | |
| *65 and over* | 154 | 100.0 | 189 | 100.0 | 263 | 100.0 |
| One person | 45 | 29.2 | 45 | 23.8 | 64 | 24.3 |
| Two | 92 | 59.8 | 123 | 65.1 | 162 | 61.6 |
| Three or more | 17 | 11.0 | 21 | 11.1 | 37 | 14.1 |
| **Female** | | | | | | |
| *65 and over* | 201 | 100.0 | 187 | 100.0 | 209 | 100.0 |
| One person | 166 | 82.6 | 151 | 80.7 | 165 | 78.9 |
| Two | 30 | 14.9 | 28 | 15.0 | 34 | 16.3 |
| Three or more | 5 | 2.5 | 8 | 4.3 | 10 | 4.8 |

*Note:*
Numbers and percentages may not add due to rounding.
*Source:* See text.

These changes in the composition of elderly households portend serious challenges to the housing industry and social services. Older women will have significantly lower incomes than men and be predominantly single-person households. Moreover, the 75-and-over population generally includes a larger proportion of frail individuals who are more likely to require some assistance to remain at home or to be among those requiring institutional care.

### Living Arrangements

The living arrangements of the elderly changed significantly between 1970 and 1980, with a 10.7 percent increase in the proportion of one-person households (Exhibit 4.2). By 1980, six of ten were living alone.

These overall proportions, however, mask differences between older men and women renters with respect to the proportions living alone. Women are almost three times as likely as men (82.6 percent to 29.2 percent, respectively) to report themselves in one-person households.

The increase in the proportion of elderly renters living alone, coupled with the

56                                                    *Engler and Spohn*

**EXHIBIT 4.3**
**Distribution of Renter Household Heads 65 and Over**
**by Borough: 1980, 1975, 1970**
**(in thousands)**

|                          | 1980 |      | 1975 |      | 1970 |      |
|--------------------------|------|------|------|------|------|------|
| **Borough of Residence** | **N** | **%** | **N** | **%** | **N** | **%** |
| *Total*                  | 355  | 100.0 | 376  | 100.0 | 471  | 100.0 |
| Brooklyn                 | 106  | 29.9  | 115  | 30.6  | 134  | 28.5  |
| Manhattan                | 93   | 26.2  | 106  | 28.2  | 146  | 31.0  |
| Queens                   | 88   | 24.8  | 83   | 22.1  | 87   | 18.5  |
| Bronx                    | 63   | 17.7  | 67   | 17.8  | 99   | 21.0  |
| Richmond                 | 5    | 1.4   | 5    | 1.3   | 6    | 1.3   |

*Note:*
   Numbers and percentages may not add due to rounding.
   *Source:* See text.

increase in the proportion of renters 75 and older is a clear alert to the potential need for supportive services for the elderly, particularly in their own homes.

### Length of Residence in Present Dwellings

As expected, elderly renters tend to have occupied their apartments for many years. Overall, six in ten (60.1 percent) lived in their apartments for 11 years or more.

The proportion of renters 65 and over throughout the city as a whole who moved during the five years between 1975 and 1980 was very low when compared with the under-65 population (12.8 percent and 56.3 percent, respectively). This proportion, however, represents some 45,200 elderly renters who changed their residence within New York City or moved here during that period. There is no information about residents who moved away from the city.

### Race and Ethnicity

As of 1980 the composition of elderly renters remained predominantly white (77.6 percent), significantly different from the younger population of renters in New York City, which by 1980 was 50.0 percent white. The black elderly constituted 13.6 percent of the households in 1980, and Puerto Ricans comprised 5.5 percent.

The 1980 Housing Survey data reflects those of the full Census of the Popula-

tion. Both surveys indicate the continuation of the trend toward larger proportions of minority representation among elderly renters as they age into the 65-
and-over category. This trend supports the expectation that in future years, elderly renters in New York City will be more and more like the younger renters,
that is, more heavily made up of minority group members.

## Borough Residence

There were no dramatic changes in the proportion of elderly renter households
in the citywide distribution by boroughs between 1975 and 1980 as there were
between 1970 and 1975 (Exhibit 4.3). The 1980 borough distribution of elderly
renters was virtually the same as it was for younger renters, with the largest concentration of renters in Manhattan and Brooklyn. Brooklyn ranked first in proportion of renters 65 and over, 29.9 percent; Manhattan was second with 26.2
percent; and Queens ranked third with 24.8 percent. The Bronx was fourth with
17.7 percent, followed by Staten Island with just 1.4 percent of all elderly renters
in 1980.

## Summary

Although there is a continuing increase toward more minority representation
among elderly renters 65 and over, the majority of them are elderly white
women, increasingly among the very old, 75 and older, living in one-person
households for more than a decade at the same location. These data suggest that
home maintenance, including such simple tasks as changing bulbs and opening
and closing windows overlaid with layers of paint, often requires assistance. Security becomes a greater concern for those who live alone and feel vulnerable and
defenseless. While the wear and tear of public space diminishes when a building
population is increasingly old, the need for assistance from building superinten-
dents within the apartments of the elderly will increase.

## CHARACTERISTICS OF UNITS RENTED BY ELDERLY

*The Housing and Vacancy Survey of New York City* collected data on the control status of rental units, the size of the units, and the gross rent charged for
them.

## Control Status

The decade since 1970 witnessed a dramatic decline in renter households of all
ages living in rent-controlled units (Exhibit 4.4). Six in ten (60.2 percent) were
living in rent-controlled units in 1970. By 1975, the proportion was just over

**EXHIBIT 4.4**
**Distribution of Rental Units by Control Status for**
**Total Renter Population: 1980, 1975, 1970**
**(in thousands)**

|  | 1980 | | 1975 | | 1970 | |
|---|---|---|---|---|---|---|
| **Status** | **N** | **%** | **N** | **%** | **N** | **%** |
| *Total* | 1,839 | 100.0 | 1,999 | 100.0 | 2,100 | 100.0 |
| Controlled | 274 | 14.9 | 642 | 32.1 | 1,265 | 60.2 |
| Not controlled | 1,152 | 62.6 | 1,174 | 58.1 | 617 | 29.4 |
| Decontrolled | 279 | 14.6 | 251 | 12.6 | 158 | 7.5 |
| Stabilized | 882 | 48.0 | 770 | 38.5 | 350 | 16.7 |
| Free market/ | — | — | — | — | 75 | 3.6 |
| regulated | — | — | 153 | 7.7 | 34 | 1.6 |
| SRO | — | — | 18 | 0.9 | 63 | 3.0 |
| Public | — | — | 165 | 8.3 | 156 | 7.4 |
| State/city assisted | 39 | 2.1 | — | — | — | — |
| Other | 374 | 20.3 | — | — | — | — |

*Note:*
  Numbers and percents may not add because of rounding.
  *Source:* See text.

three in ten (32.1 percent). In 1980, less than 15 percent of all renter households were living in rent-controlled units, a 78 percent decrease over a 10-year period in the major category of affordable housing for low- and moderate-income New Yorkers.

As for households headed by someone 65 or older, there has been a 38.8 percent decline in the number living in rent-controlled units since 1975—a decline of 83,000 units (Exhibit 4.5). Over the 10 years since 1970, a total of 181,000 fewer rent-controlled units were occupied by elderly renters. However, 48 percent of the rent-controlled apartments are occupied by elderly households. The one advantage elderly renters have over those under 45 years old is their length of residence in their current units. A larger proportion (36.9 percent) of 65-and-older households, therefore, are living in rent-controlled units compared to 6.6 percent of the younger group. As new cohorts of the elderly age in, they will increasingly be living in the more expensive rent-stabilized housing stock of the city.

**Size of Unit**

Over four in ten (46.5 percent) of the elderly rental households occupy three-room apartments. Another 38.6 percent live in apartments of four or more rooms, while 14.9 percent live in one- or two-room units. This distribution is virtually unchanged from 1975.

**EXHIBIT 4.5**
**Distribution of Rental Units by Control Status for**
**Renter Population 65 and Over: 1980, 1975, 1970**
**(in thousands)**

|  | 1980 | | | 1975 | | | 1970 | |
|---|---|---|---|---|---|---|---|---|
|  | N | % | % Change from 1975 | N | % | % Change from 1970 | N | % |
| *Total* | 355 | 100.0 | | 376 | 100.0 | | 471 | 100.0 |
| Controlled | 131 | 36.9 | −38.8 | 214 | 56.9 | −31.4 | 312 | 68.3 |
| Not controlled | 149 | 42.0 | 17.3 | 127 | 33.8 | 29.6 | 98 | 21.5 |
| Decontrolled | 39 | 11.0 | 44.4 | 27 | 7.2 | 28.6 | 21 | 4.6 |
| Stabilized | 110 | 31.0 | 34.1 | 82 | 21.8 | 32.2 | 62 | 13.5 |
| Free market/ | — | — | — | — | — | — | 9 | 2.0 |
| regulated | — | — | — | 18 | 4.8 | 200.0 | 6 | 1.4 |
| SRO | — | — | — | 3 | 0.8 | −400.0 | 15 | 3.3 |
| Public | — | — | — | 32 | 8.5 | 0.0 | 32 | 7.0 |
| State/city assisted | 11 | 3.1 | — | — | — | — | — | — |
| Other | 64 | 18.0 | — | — | — | — | — | — |

*Note:*
  Numbers and percents may not add because of rounding.
  *Source:* See text.

## Gross Rent

Gross rent,[2] which includes the cost of utilities, in and of itself does not really describe the plight of elderly renters as it consumes a major proportion of their incomes. This section discusses only the actual dollar amount paid by the elderly renter, and the changes in that amount that occurred since 1975. The significance of these changes is discussed in subsequent sections.

The median gross rent paid by elderly New Yorkers rose from $135 in 1975 to $212 in 1980, an increase of 57.0 percent. Although this increase was lower than that experienced by the under-65 population (62.2 percent), elderly households are more severely affected by increased housing costs because their members are no longer working and are without the possibility of adding to their incomes.

In the five years between surveys truly low rents have disappeared. Whereas 25.5 percent of those 65 and over were paying less than $100 for rent and utilities in 1975, only 11.3 percent were paying below $100 in 1980 (Exhibit 4.6). Those paying $100 to $199 were 55 percent in 1975 in contrast to 34.3 percent in 1980, while those paying $200 or more almost tripled, from 18.9 percent in 1975 to 54.3 percent in 1980.

The declining number of rent-controlled units for elderly renters in the future will result in a substantial increase in their housing costs because other housing

**EXHIBIT 4.6**
**Distribution of Gross Rents for Renter Households**
**65 and Over: 1980, 1975, 1970**
**(in thousands)**

|  | 1980 | | 1975 | | 1970 | |
| --- | --- | --- | --- | --- | --- | --- |
| **Gross Rent** | N | % | N | % | N | % |
| Total | 355 | 100.0 | 376 | 100.0 | 471 | 100.0 |
| Less than $100 | 37 | 11.3 | 93 | 25.5 | 252 | 56.6 |
| $100 - 149 | 50 | 15.3 | 126 | 34.6 | 111 | 24.9 |
| 150 - 199 | 62 | 19.0 | 76 | 20.9 | 44 | 9.9 |
| 200 - 249 | 59 | 18.1 | 31 | 8.5 ⎫ | 20 | 4.5 |
| 250 - 299 | 51 | 15.6 | 14 | 3.8 ⎭ |  |  |
| 300 or more | 67 | 20.6 | 24 | 6.6 | 11 | 2.5 |
| No cash rent | — | — | — | — | 8 | 1.8 |
| Not reported | 29 | — | 12 | — | 25 | — |
| Median | $212 | | $135 | | $93 | |

*Source:* See text.

costs are more expensive. The median gross rents for households headed by a person 65 and over by categories of housing are: controlled, $190; decontrolled, $224; stabilized (pre-1947), $211; stabilized (1947 or later), $309; and state and city assisted, $213. (There was no data for public housing.)

There is another cause for concern with respect to the cost of rental housing. There was a larger increase in median rents for older renters over the 10 years between 1970 and 1980 than in the overall cost of living for urban consumers in the New York-northeastern New Jersey area.[3] Median rents for households headed by someone 65 or older rose from $93 in 1970 to $212 in 1980, an increase of 128 percent. The Consumer Price Index for that same period rose from 110.8 to 213.0, an increase of 92.2 percent. The relationship between housing costs and the ability of individuals with limited incomes to secure other essentials of living is underscored by these figures.

## INCOME OF ELDERLY RENTER HOUSEHOLDS

Overall, the incomes of elderly renter households continued to be extremely low, with rent consuming inordinately large proportions of their limited incomes. This is particularly so for elderly renters with the lowest incomes. Moreover, although the gap between the incomes of younger and older renters (as measured by median incomes) has narrowed slightly since 1975, the median income of elderly renter households remains less than half that of the younger households.

**EXHIBIT 4.7**
**Median Income of Renter Households**
**65 and Over by Sex: 1980, 1975, 1970**

| | Median Income ($) | | | Percent Change | |
|---|---|---|---|---|---|
| **Sex** | **1980** | **1975** | **1970** | **1975-1980** | **1970-1975** |
| Male | 7,833 | 5,297 | 4,857 | 47.9 | 9.1 |
| Female | 4,968 | 3,163 | 2,204 | 57.1 | 43.5 |
| Total | 6,032 | 4,106 | 3,512 | 46.9 | 16.9 |

*Note:*
Although the housing and vacancy data was collected in 1970, 1975, and 1980, respondents were asked to provide income data for the preceding years.
*Source:* See text.

## Median Incomes

Elderly renter households had a median income of $6,032, less than half (49.3 percent) that of the population under 65 ($12,229). The median income for elderly renters increased 46.9 percent over the previous five years (Exhibit 4.7).

It should be noted that the income of elderly renters increased almost three times that of younger renters largely due to the regular cost-of-living adjustments paid to Social Security recipients. However, median incomes remain disproportionately low for the elderly even though the rate of change may be greater.

The rise in the median income of elderly renter households over the decade from 1970 to 1980 must be seen in the context of other economic changes which partially mitigated the increase. The decade which saw a 71.8 percent rise in median incomes also saw a rise of 92.2 percent in the Consumer Price Index and a 128 percent rise in rents, thus leaving the elderly renter in a worse financial position despite the increase.

As for the median incomes of elderly men and women, the gap continues to narrow, although the difference is still great. The median income for households headed by males was $7,833 while the median income for female-headed households was $4,968. In 1970, the median income for elderly renter households headed by women was 45.4 percent of the median for those headed by men. By 1975 it had increased to 59.7 percent, still a large gap, but significantly narrower. In 1980, the median income of elderly households headed by women was 63.4 percent of those headed by men. The gap continues to reflect the fact that 83.3 percent of the households headed by women consist of one person (in contrast to 25.0 percent of those headed by men) so that there is no other person to contribute income through additional Social Security benefits, wages, or other assets.

**EXHIBIT 4.8**
**Income of Renter Households 65 and Over**
**by Sex of Household Head: 1980, 1975, 1970**
**(percent)**

| | Total | | | Male | | | Female | | |
|---|---|---|---|---|---|---|---|---|---|
| Income | 1980 | 1975 | 1970 | 1980 | 1975 | 1970 | 1980 | 1975 | 1970 |
| Less than $4,000 | 24.9 | 48.8 | 54.7 | 10.2 | 32.4 | 42.6 | 36.2 | 65.5 | 69.7 |
| $4,000 - 5,999 | 24.6 | 19.5 | 13.7 | 19.6 | 24.5 | 15.2 | 28.4 | 13.9 | 11.6 |
| $6,000 - 9,999 | 24.1 | 15.6 | 15.1 | 31.5 | 21.4 | 19.2 | 18.5 | 10.1 | 9.6 |
| $10,000 or more | 26.4 | 16.0 | 16.8 | 38.7 | 21.5 | 22.8 | 16.9 | 10.4 | 9.0 |

*Source:* See text.

There are other significant differences in median incomes among groups of elderly renters in 1980. Two major groups of minority elderly 65 and over have significantly lower median incomes than do white, non-Puerto Rican elderly whose median income was $6,339. The median income of black, non-Puerto Rican elderly was $4,651, 26.6 percent lower than for white, non-Puerto Ricans. The median income of the Puerto Rican elderly was $4,061, 35.9 percent lower than the major group, while other elderly had a median income of $6,021, or 5.0 percent lower.

Inasmuch as these groups of aged with the lowest median incomes are increasing in New York City, while housing and utility costs are continuing to rise, the economic status of the city's aged will worsen. Their disposable incomes after rent and utilities are deducted will be insufficient to cover the cost of food, clothing, and medical care to an even greater extent than is now the case.

**Income Distribution**

The greatest change in the income distribution of elderly renter households was the decrease in the proportion reporting incomes at the lowest level, that is less than $4,000. For all elderly renter households the proportion was reduced from 48.8 percent in 1975 to 24.9 percent in 1980. The decrease in households at the lowest level was redistributed upward for each successive income category, even among those reporting incomes of $10,000 or more.

The differential between male- and female-headed households is clearly apparent from the income distributions presented in Exhibit 4.8. Over one-third (36.2 percent) of the female household heads had incomes below $4,000 a year, the lowest income category, compared to 10.2 percent of the males. Conversely, over one in ten of the women reported incomes over $10,000, while almost four in ten (38.7 percent) of the men fell into this category. The difference, however,

**EXHIBIT 4.9**
**Poverty Levels for Population 65 and Over, 1980**

**Size of Household**

| Level | Single 65 and Over | Couple 65 and Over |
|---|---|---|
| Poverty | $3,949 | $4,983 |
| 125% of poverty | $4,936 | $6,229 |

*Source:* See text.

in incomes between men and women should be viewed in the context of the over-all low incomes of the elderly.

## Poverty

Another way of looking at the plight of elderly renters is by viewing their incomes in terms of the poverty level. The concept of poverty level is a gross index indicating income levels below which a household is defined as poor. These levels are arrived at by taking into account certain variables such as age, size of household, and farm/non-farm residence. Poverty levels apply nationally and do not incorporate regional differences in cost of living (Exhibit 4.9).

In 1980 in New York City, the number of elderly renter households with incomes at or below the poverty level was 81,000, or 27.9 percent of all such households reporting income (Exhibit 4.10), an additional 30,000 households since 1975 or an increase of 58.8 percent. In addition to the households below the poverty level, another 57,000 households received incomes in the range between poverty and 125 percent of poverty,[4] bringing the total number of elderly renter households in this category to 138,000, an increase of 27.8 percent over the five years. Thus, four out of every ten elderly rental households are poor or near-poor.

Moreover, the number of poor elderly increased even as incomes have risen reflecting several factors: the impact of inflation; the growth of the number of minority elderly; and the increase in elderly women 75 and over.

## ECONOMICS OF RENTING FOR ELDERLY HOUSEHOLDS

Rent consumes a disproportionate amount of the incomes of elderly renters. In the past, federal guidelines set no more than 25 percent of income as the maximum that should be spent on housing by the elderly, although Section 8 now requires 30 percent of income be paid for rent. In 1980, the percent budgeted by the Bureau of Labor Statistics (BLS) nationally for gross rent for elderly low- and intermediate-income households was almost 33 percent. The amount budgeted

**EXHIBIT 4.10**
**Poverty Status of Renter Households**
**Headed by a Person 65 and Over: 1980, 1975**
**(in thousands)**

|  | 1980 | | 1975 | |
|---|---|---|---|---|
| **Poverty Status** | **N** | **%** | **N** | **%** |
| At or below 125% of poverty | 138 | 47.6 | 108 | 38.4 |
| Between poverty and 125% of poverty | 57 | 19.7 | 57 | 20.3 |
| At or below poverty | 81 | 27.9 | 51 | 18.1 |
| Total reporting Income* | 290 | 100.0 | 281 | 100.0 |

*Note:*
   *In 1980, 81.6 percent of the population 65 and over reported income. The proportion in 1975 was 74.2 percent.
   *Source:* See text.

for elderly households in New York City by BLS was 23.1 percent and 22.4 percent, respectively, largely due to rent control, rent stabilization, and the existence of public housing.

However, the elderly renter in New York City is paying a much larger proportion of income for shelter than the amount indicated in either the lower or intermediate BLS budgets.

**Rent as a Proportion of Income**

When the ratio of rent to income for elderly renter households in New York City is examined, the urgent need for affordable housing is underscored. In 1980, the median ratio of gross rent to income was 35.3 percent, unchanged from 1975. Half, or 141,000 elderly households, paid rents that were 35 percent or more of their incomes. Another quarter, 64,000 households, paid between 25 and 35.3 percent of their income for rent and utilities.

Moreover, the proportion of rent to income increases for elderly renters with the lowest incomes. Half those reporting incomes less than $4,000 pay more than 50 percent of their incomes for rent. Even for those households having income between $4,000 and $5,999, half pay between 42.5 percent and 50.0 percent of income for gross rent. (It has been noted that 79 percent of one-person elderly households are headed by women.) Only at incomes above $10,000 does rent drop below one-third of income (Exhibit 4.11).

**Standard of Living**

After rent and utilities (gross rent) are paid, what does the elderly renter have left for food, clothes, and other necessities? Overall, elderly renters in New York

**EXHIBIT 4.11**
**Median Ratio of Gross Rent to Income by Income Level of**
**Renter Households 65 and Over by Size of Household, 1980**

| | One Person | | Two Person | | Three Person | |
|---|---|---|---|---|---|---|
| Income Level | Number | Median Ratio | Number | Median Ratio | Number | Median Ratio |
| Less than $4,000 | 62,745 | 50.0+ | 5,948 | 50.0+ | 1,643 | 50.0+ |
| $4,000 - $5,999 | 54,040 | 42.5 | 19,313 | 48.7 | 1,917 | 50.0+ |
| 6,000 - 6,499 | 10,534 | 39.9 | 7,512 | 40.0 | 1,210 | 50.0+ |
| 6,500 - 9,999 | 17,774 | 35.7 | 27,227 | 33.7 | 3,827 | 33.2 |
| 10,000 - 12,499 | 8,588 | 31.6 | 13,693 | 28.3 | 1,960 | 31.8 |
| 12,500 - 19,999 | 6,689 | 20.3 | 14,387 | 20.4 | 3,133 | 21.5 |
| 20,000 - 24,999 | 1,449 | 20.0 | 5,661 | 17.9 | 2,020 | 18.1 |
| 25,000 - 34,999 | 2,978 | 20.3 | 4,492 | 17.1 | 1,828 | 14.3 |
| 35,000 or more | 2,588 | 18.6 | 4,852 | 13.1 | 1,109 | 10.0 |

*Source:* See text.

City face severe deprivations as their rents are higher and incomes lower than those budgeted by the Bureau of Labor Statistics.

In 1980, the BLS lower budget for a retired couple[5] included 32.6 percent nationally and 23.1 percent locally for gross rent. The dollar amount for New York City was $1,659 per year. The median gross rent for those 65 and over reported in the *Housing and Vacancy Survey* was $2,544 per year, or 42.2 percent of total income. On the average, elderly renter households in New York City were paying $885 more than the amount budgeted by BLS for a couple in 1980 (Exhibit 4.12), thus reducing their disposable incomes for all other expenses by nearly $70 a month.

## DISCUSSION AND CONCLUSIONS

Since 1972 New York City has attempted to protect the elderly from increases in rent through the Senior Citizen Rent Increase Exemption Program. In 1983, 71,330 renter households 62 years or older paid no rent increases if their income was $8,000 or less after taxes and their rent was one-third or more of their income. The program cost the city $44.9 million in lost real-estate taxes in 1982. While the program protects aged renters from increases, it does not reduce their rent to one-third of income. If they are paying 40 or 50 percent of income prior to eligibility for the program, they will continue to pay the same high proportion for rent. Those with low income, therefore, require a Section 8-type subsidy where the maximum rent would be no more than 30 percent of income. The Rent Increase Exemption Program has protected the elderly from subsistence living during these years of inflation, but it is no substitute for an expanded, federally

**EXHIBIT 4.12**
**Comparison of Rent and Disposable Income Between 1980 Bureau of Labor
Statistics Lower Budget for Two-Person Renter Households 65 and Over and
Median Incomes of all Elderly Renter Households in New York City**

| | NYC | | BLS Lower Budget for 2-Person Households 65 and Over | |
|---|---|---|---|---|
| **Budget Items** | **Medians** | **Percent** | **Dollars** | **Percent** |
| Total Income | 6,032 | 100.0 | 7,196 | 100.0 |
| Gross Rent | 2,544 | 42.2 | 1,659 | 23.1 |
| All other expenses | 3,488 | 57.8 | 5,537 | 76.9 |

*Source:* See text.

supported rent subsidy program which would limit rents to no more than one-third of income.

Analysis of rent levels of 62-64 year-olds by type of rent-regulated status suggests that rent will become an even greater drain on incomes as this population retires. With the phasing out of rent control, more and more aged will be living in the post-1947 rent-stabilized portion of the housing stock. The median contract rent (no utilities costs included) for male-headed households 62-64 years of age was $385.69 per month, and for females it was $270.93. For those 65 and over the median rents were $293.24 for males and $274.77 for females. The 62-64 males had a median rent/income ratio of 35 percent, and for the 65 year olds it was 37.36 percent. For women the median rent/income ratio was 28.75 percent for the younger cohort and 35.54 percent for the 65 and over. Since the younger groups are more likely to have some work income, the full impact of reduced income and high rent will not occur until this age group retires.

Both the Housing and Vacancy Survey and the 1980 Census reveal that the number of male-headed households between 60-64 years of age decreased significantly between 1970 and 1980. While there have been no studies of the cause of out-migration of older New Yorkers, it may be that the high rent/income ratio even prior to retirement has been a strong contributing factor to this move out. New York City raised the eligibility for the rent increase exemption to $10,000 a year as of August 1, 1982. This would permit a household paying $276 or more with an income of $10,000 to pay no increase in rent. While the $10,000 maximum eligibility level will cover nearly three-quarters of the male-headed households, and 83 percent of the female-headed households, for the newly retired and eligible, particularly those living in rent-stabilized units, income devoted to rent will result in a substantially decreased standard of living.

It should be noted that elderly renters have no protection under the rent exemption program if they live in decontrolled housing. There were 39,000 renters 65 and older who live in buildings with less than six units. The median contract rent for these tenants was higher than those in pre-1947 rent-stabilized housing. This portion of aged renters will grow as this housing stock increases. There is also a small, but generally very low-income, group of elderly renters who live in buildings which pay no taxes to the city. When rents are increased in these buildings either to ensure adequate maintenance or after renovation, the elderly renter is not eligible for an exemption. There is, therefore, a continuing problem to protect these elderly renters while insuring the maintenance of the housing stock.

The city of New York has, through its Rent Exemption Program, provided the least expensive, most clearly defined shelter subsidy program in the country for its elderly renters. However, the data from this study portends a growing housing crisis for the elderly in decades to come. With a decrease in federal rent subsidies, the near elimination of Section 202, and the phasing out of rent control, there will be no low-rent housing available. Older tenants will have to remain in higher-rent housing although incomes are reduced in retirement. Relocation to smaller apartments for widows and the frail will be impossible. For the growing numbers of very old and frail who require special housing, there will be no additional units built.

While the plight of the elderly renter is particularly acute in New York City, the housing crisis for the aged is nationwide. Decent housing at affordable rents is a basic human need for all ages. There is no way that the private housing market will be able to meet this need. There must be a reversal of the current federal housing policy to provide both the subsidies to construct and rehabilitate housing. A comprehensive federal housing policy aimed at meeting the needs of all Americans should also produce appropriate and affordable housing for the elderly whose specific needs include assistance with housing costs as well as specially designed housing with supportive services.

## NOTES

1. The drop in the actual number of women-renter household heads may be attributed to various explanations, such as the influence of the out-migration early in the decade or simple sampling error.

2. Gross rent is used in this discussion, rather than contract rent (which excludes the cost of utilities), because it provides a more comprehensive perspective of housing costs which are unavoidable for the renter. Sections of this report dealing with the ratio of rent to income are also based on gross-rent data.

3. Income and cost-of-living data are for the previous year: 1970 data refer to 1969 totals; 1975 to 1974 totals; and 1980 to 1979 totals.

4. The 125 percent of poverty level, also described as "near poor," sets the dollar threshold 25 percent higher than the poverty level. The number of households in this category includes those whose incomes were below the poverty level and those with incomes above poverty but below 125 percent of poverty.

5. The BLS lower budget for a single retired person is 79 percent that of a couple.

5

# Executive Women:
# Results of the *Savvy* Survey

Olivia Schieffelin Nordberg

Do woman managers want a health spa on the apartment house roof? Are they home long enough to cook, or would they trade kitchens for kitchenettes and larger closets? Do they entertain, and would they be interested in a sky lounge, a separate party area that could be reserved by anyone in the building? Or would they prefer a pool?

We do not know.

More than any other women in American history, this new professional elite can afford what they want in the way of housing, yet we have done very little research on their housing needs. In the absence of specific studies, however, we have learned something about the values and behavior of women executives and their trade-offs between home and office that have important housing implications.

The findings described here are from a self-administered, mail-back survey originally published in *Savvy* magazine, a national monthly with a circulation of 225,000 and substantial newsstand sales, which describes itself as "the magazine for the executive woman."

The main editorial thrust of *Savvy* is a slight variation of the superwoman theme: you can do it all—home, husband, children, and upwardly mobile, self-fulfilling career. Many of the articles consist of sensible advice on specific job-related topics, such as how to ask for a promotion, how to survive a difficult boss, and how to deal with an outside consultant. The questionnaire, announced as "The *Savvy* Survey on the New Executive Lifestyle," appeared in the August 1981 issue, bound into the magazine. By October, 10,000 *Savvy* subscribers had mailed it back, a 4.4 percent response rate. A sample of almost 2,500 was selected as the data base. The final article appeared in the March 1982 issue of the magazine.

## THE *SAVVY* SAMPLE

This sample has enormous limitations. It is entirely self-selected, consisting only of *Savvy* subscribers who chose to complete and return the questionnaire, using their own stamps and envelopes. The sample is not representative of American women, of American working women, or even of *Savvy* readers, since it reflects only subscribers, not newsstand purchasers. Furthermore, among the subscribers, the sample is doubtlessly biased toward the eager beavers, those who wanted the editors of the magazine to know what they were doing and how they felt about it. An indication of the strong identification these women feel for the magazine is that about one-third ignored the promise of anonymity and identified themselves by including their business cards, letterheads, or home-return addresses on the envelope with the completed questionnaire.

Despite these substantial limitations, the sample is of interest because it gives insight into the behavior of what might be considered a pioneering group: younger women who are making a full-time career commitment in largely professional, technical, and managerial jobs, a category of jobs that, according to the Bureau of Labor Statistics, accounts for 35 percent of the net increase in women's employment over the last five years.

Compared to most American women, in general the *Savvy* respondents are substantially better educated, earning more, more likely to be white, and less likely to be married or have children. They represent, by some of these measures, an elite: 72 percent have four or more years of college compared to 20 percent of all U.S. women aged 25-34. Their median total household income is more than twice that of all U.S. households in 1979—$37,000 compared to $16,000. All of them are working, 97 percent of them full-time, 98 percent of them out of the home. The mean age of the sample is 34.5.

## PURPOSE OF THE SURVEY

The survey was designed as a statistical follow-up to an anecdotal report in *Savvy* presenting hour-by-hour diaries of one working day in the lives of five professional women. The gist of the report was that the five women interviewed did not have much time left from their professional commitments for their personal lives, which took many forms. One was married and had two teenagers, one was currently engaged, another was married with three young children including an infant, and two, both married, had decided not to have any children, at least for the time being. They all worked very long hours, even those with children.

The behavior of these working women did not follow the pattern of past trends in relationships between female labor-force participation and marital status and fertility, whereby women worked full-time until marriage, part-time after marriage, and not at all once the first child arrived. Was this traditional pattern changing? Would the survey findings based on 2,500 women confirm the anecdotal evidence, based on five women, that work behavior varied little by marital status and fertility?

To explore these questions required returning to the underlying explanation of traditional patterns of withdrawal from the labor force, derived from the image of the nuclear family, a practical division of labor, and theories of role strain, namely that the more demands on a woman at home, the less time would be available to her at the office.

The sample was divided into three groups, representing what were hypothesized to be commitments at home of an increasingly demanding nature and, therefore, theoretically, allowing decreasing amounts of time for work: the singles, the wives, and the mothers.

To outline the three groups briefly, the singles, comprising 40 percent of the sample, are by definition not currently married and have no children under the age of 18 living at home. The wives, 30 percent of the sample, are by definition currently married but have no children under 18 at home. The mothers, another 30 percent of the sample, two-thirds of whom are currently married, have at least one child under 18 at home.

The three groups are mutually exclusive. Some of the singles and some of the wives have children, but they are older than 18, not at home, or both. The groups differ very little by other demographic measures. By age, the singles are younger; by education, the mothers are less educated. But the similarities are more important than the differences. For example, the proportion with a graduate degree is one-third for each group.

The objective of the classification was to separate women by current demands on their time at home. A mother with a child under 18 was assumed to have to give more time and attention to that child than a mother with a child over 18. A wife was assumed to need or want to spend more time at home than a single woman, whether never married or divorced. The point was to test whether the singles, having the most time available, would work at the most demanding jobs, be able to commute the longest to those jobs, put in longer hours on a daily basis, travel more often for their jobs, and for this effort, earn more; and conversely, whether mothers, with the least hypothesized time available, would choose occupations such as teaching that would give them longer vacations, shorter hours, and less overnight travel. Wives without children at home were hypothesized to fall between the singles and mothers.

## PROFESSIONAL COMMITMENT

Do such traditionally crucial demographic characteristics as marital status and fertility affect the jobs of this elite sample?

**EXHIBIT 5.1**
**Professional Commitment:**
**Objective Measures, *Savvy* Sample**
**(in percent)**

| | Total | Single | Wives | Mothers |
|---|---|---|---|---|
| *Occupation* | | | | |
| Professional manager | 55 | 54 | 53 | 57 |
| Professional non-manager | 25 | 24 | 28 | 24 |
| Non-professional | 20 | 22 | 18 | 19 |
| Total | 100 | 100 | 100 | 100 |
| N | 2371 | 956 | 679 | 736 |
| *One-way Commuting Time Yesterday* | | | | |
| Under 30-minutes | 72 | 75 | 67 | 74 |
| 30-59 minutes | 22 | 19 | 25 | 22 |
| 60 minutes or more | 6 | 5 | 8 | 4 |
| Total | 100 | 100 | 100 | 100 |
| N | 2335 | 945 | 677 | 713 |
| *Approximate Time Given* | | | | |
| *to Work Yesterday,* | | | | |
| *at Home and in the Office* | | | | |
| 6 hours or less | 7 | 6 | 6 | 9 |
| 7-9 hours | 64 | 64 | 67 | 63 |
| 10-12 hours | 25 | 26 | 25 | 24 |
| 12 or more hours | 4 | 4 | 3 | 4 |
| Total | 100 | 100 | 100 | 100 |
| N | 2385 | 961 | 682 | 742 |
| *Percent Reporting They have* | | | | |
| *Job-Related Overnight Travel* | | | | |
| *at Least Once a Month* | | | | |
| Percent | 25 | 28 | 22 | 24 |
| N | 2412 | 969 | 695 | 748 |
| *Annual Personal Income* | | | | |
| Under $15,000 | 14 | 11 | 11 | 19 |
| $15,000-$24,999 | 40 | 39 | 42 | 39 |
| $25,000-$39,999 | 34 | 38 | 36 | 30 |
| $40,000 and over | 12 | 12 | 11 | 12 |
| Total | 100 | 100 | 100 | 100 |
| N | 2414 | 971 | 696 | 747 |

Five major variables served as objective measures of work behavior: current occupation, length of time for a one-way commute yesterday, approximate time given to work yesterday at home and at the office, incidence of job-related overnight travel once a month, and personal annual income.

The findings are summarized in Exhibit 5.1. The first measure, occupational choice, is largely unaffected by commitments at home. Of each group, over half are professional managers, about a quarter are professional non-managers, and under a quarter are non-professionals. The differences among the groups are not statistically significant. Mothers do not disproportionately choose professions characterized by shorter hours and longer vacations.

The second measure, amount of time spent commuting one way yesterday, varies little between the two groups hypothesized to be at opposite ends of the spectrum, the singles and the mothers. Wives spend the longest amount of time commuting, perhaps because they live with a husband who has a job in the opposite direction. Over two-thirds of all three groups take less than half an hour to get to work.

The next measure, the approximate number of hours given to work yesterday, both at home and in the office, is perhaps the most critical index of professional commitment. Although mothers are more likely to work shorter hours, the overwhelming proportion, about two-thirds of each group, reports working seven to nine hours, or an eight-hour day. A relatively high proportion, over a quarter of each group, works a prodigious ten or more hours a day, regardless of whether there is a young child, a husband, or no one at home.

The fourth measure of time away from home is the proportion having to travel overnight at least once a month because of their job. This might also be interpreted as an indication of level of job responsibility. There is no particular trend. Although singles are most likely to travel, mothers travel more than wives. The differences are very small: 22 percent of the wives travel, 24 percent of the mothers, and 28 percent of the singles.

The last objective measure of professional commitment is the fruits of all the time spent away from home, namely personal earnings. If the data in Table 1 are taken at face value, 40 percent of the sample earn between $15,000 and $24,999, 34 percent earn between $25,000 and $39,999, and 12 percent earn over $40,000. Mothers are overrepresented in the lowest-income groups, under $15,000, and singles are overrepresented in the higher income groups, but the differences, though statistically significant, are small—no more than 8 percent.

The similarity in earnings is consistent with the relative absence of differences in the measures of work commitment discussed above. If singles, wives, and mothers are working at similar sorts of jobs for similar amounts of time at similar levels of responsibility (using overnight travel as an indicator of responsibility), they ought to earn similar amounts of money, and they do.

Data on the mothers alone, not presented in the exhibits, show that two other demographic variables, both measuring increasing role demands at home— number of children under 18 at home and age of the youngest child under 18— have no statistically significant relationship with any of these variables, except hours worked: mothers of teenagers spend the most time at their jobs.

In summary, differences in work behavior among these working women by

**EXHIBIT 5.2**
**Professional/Personal Trade-offs:**
**Subjective Measures, *Savvy* Sample**

|  | Total | Singles | Wives | Mothers |
|---|---|---|---|---|
| Percent reporting they are "somewhat" or "very" satisfied with their current job | 77 | 72 | 77 | 82 |
| Percent answering "yes" to the question "When you were originally thinking about the type of work you would like to do, did you consider how the time demands of work would affect your personal life generally?" | 51 | 43 | 53 | 58 |
| Percent agreeing that "My personal life is more important to me than my professional life." | 51 | 38 | 58 | 60 |
| Percent reporting they had not had enough time over the past year for: | | | | |
| reading for pleasure | 51 | 44 | 53 | 55 |
| just relaxing | 52 | 42 | 49 | 57 |

marital and parental status do not emerge from the *Savvy* survey in any clearcut or strong way.

## PROFESSIONAL/PERSONAL TRADE-OFFS

What do these working women think about their situation? Four subjective measures were used to determine perceived trade-offs between professional behavior and personal values. The first is a direct question concerning job satisfaction. The second is a retrospective assessment of the impact of time demands on career choice. The third is a reading of current priorities, measured by proportions agreeing with the statement that "My personal life is more important to me than my professional life." The fourth and last is a question about whether respondents felt they had had enough time in the last year for two specific leisure activities, reading for pleasure and just relaxing, two measures of leisure that do not cost much, unlike the theater or vacations, and are easily available to all, regardless of income or location.

Exhibit 5.2 summarizes the results for the singles, the wives, and the mothers in the *Savvy* sample. On the first measure, 82 percent of mothers are satisfied with their current job, 77 percent of the wives, and 72 percent of the singles. When asked, second, "When you originally were thinking about the type of work you would like to do, did you consider how the time demands of work would affect your personal life generally?," a majority of the mothers (58 per-

**EXHIBIT 5.3**
**Quality of Personal Life:**
**Subjective Measures, *Savvy* Sample**

| | Total | Singles | Wives | Mothers |
|---|---|---|---|---|
| Percent reporting they are "very happy" in their love relationship | 50 | 38 | 61 | 50 |
| Percent answering "yes" to the question, "All in all, balancing personal against professional satisfactions and considering other aspects of your life that we have not discussed here, are you content?" | 75 | 70 | 82 | 75 |

cent) and a minority of the singles (43 percent) report that they had gone through such a thought process. Third, the statement, "My personal life is more important to me than my professional life," elicits agreement from 60 percent of the mothers, 58 percent of the wives, and 38 percent of the singles. Last, a majority of mothers (57 percent), compared with a minority of singles (42 percent), say that they have not had enough time in the past year for just relaxing.

The same pattern appears on all four measures of trade-off. Mothers (with the highest demands at home) are significantly most likely, and singles (with the fewest demands at home) least likely to value their personal life, to claim it had a role in their original career choice, to be satisfied with their job, and to feel they have too little leisure. The percentage differences are quite substantial, up to 22 points. Thus, in these more subjective measures of the tug between home and career, the very same marital and parental statuses that had no impact on objective aspects of professional commitment, such as type of job, hours worked, and earnings, are all important.

## QUALITY OF PERSONAL LIFE

Man does not live by bread alone, and neither, it was assumed, does woman. Thus, the emotional quality of the personal lives of these executive women was briefly analyzed in Exhibit 5.3.

The first effort was the inspiration of the editors of *Savvy* magazine, namely the question, "Are you happy in your love relationship?" The analysis includes those singles and currently unmarried mothers who reported a love relationship, as well as the wives. As other studies have shown, the wives, those women who by definition have a husband but no children under 18 at home, are most likely to be "very happy" in love: 61 percent of the wives, compared with 50 percent of the mothers and 38 percent of those singles with a love relationship.

The other attempt to get an overall measure of the general well-being of the three groups was the final question of the survey, the "Is it all worth it?" question, phrased as, "All in all, balancing personal against professional satisfactions, and considering other aspects of your life that we have not discussed here, are you content?" Again, contentment is significantly related to marital and parental statuses: 82 percent of the wives, 75 percent of the mothers, and 70 percent of the singles say yes.

## SUMMARY

Increasing demands at home, in the form of a husband and children under the age of 18, do not appear to have a strong bearing on how much time young women executives give to work. Added dimensions at home do, however, in the form of a husband or child, affect working women's perceptions of trade-offs between work and home and their evaluation of the quality of their personal life. Although mothers are most satisfied with their jobs, and singles have the most time to read and relax, wives without young children at home are most likely to be content overall, balancing personal against professional satisfactions.

The conclusion of these findings is that these professional women, like the five whose daily diaries had initially struck me, have a strong dedication to their careers, superseding other commitments, such as marital or parental, and remain constant as they move into and out of various demographic categories. Gone are the days when marriage meant changing jobs and a first birth meant quitting work.

These are serious and committed young women, different from other young women: 82 percent of them characterize themselves as "very ambitious," 78 percent are not interested in the option of working shorter hours if it means less pay and a reduced chance of promotion, 73 percent have a job that "requires working late, bringing work home or working overtime at least once a week," and 21 percent report they went into the office the past weekend to work. While their very seriousness is a problem in that they are not representative of most young women—to return to the original warning about the self-selection of the sample—that commitment to career, regardless of personal events in their lives, is what makes them interesting.

Interpretation of these data is difficult. Do the lives of these women show much balance between their professional and private roles? Many of them have given up a lot personally for jobs that only 51 percent report have "ample opportunity for upward mobility." The happiest among them are the wives, yet 52 percent are not currently married. The next happiest are the mothers, yet 22 percent claim to be worried about the biological clock—"That I will have to decide whether to have children before I am ready to." While the traditional satisfactions of the roles of wife and mother still have force, these professionals, 29 percent of whom report they worked 10-12 or more hours yesterday, simply do not seem, at least currently, to have *time* to be wives and mothers in the traditional sense. It is hard to avoid the feeling that they may be, temporarily at least, taking their careers *too* seriously—more seriously than the husbands and fathers take theirs perhaps—and in the process of overcompensation are assuming what used to be exclusively masculine work values and behavior.

The original premise of the relationship between female labor-force participation and marital and fertility status was that the more demands there were on a woman at home, the less time would be available to her at the office. It seems that a reversal has taken place. Whether for economic, psychological, or fertility reasons, things are beginning to operate the other way around: the more demands there are on a woman at the office, the less time is available to her at home.

Other data from the survey, not presented here, shows that what little time there is at home is devoted to the same series of household and child-raising tasks that were a woman's job before she took on a "real job." Indeed, the greater the obligations at home, the more likely these elite women are to fulfill them after work themselves. For example, 45 percent of the singles report doing the most recent food shopping themselves, compared to 51 percent of the wives, and 59 percent of the mothers.

What does this mean? How do such findings regarding work and domestic patterns of women relate to broad housing issues?

Overall, the *Savvy* survey overwhelmingly reaffirms other evidence that a dramatic reorientation of priorities is taking place among American women, particularly the more educated. Whether they are committed to their job because they like the work, or they need the income, or both, is irrelevant. The point is that they are committed, single, married, with or without children.

Housing plans that assume such commitment will be more realistic and practical than those based on prior trends. Women who work full-time have different needs from those who do not, for example, adequate commuting facilities, perhaps including provision for parking a car; nighttime outdoor lighting; convenient shopping and services open before and after work; methods whereby daytime deliveries can be received and properly disposed of; 24-hour maintenance available from a trusted source who can enter a dwelling in the absence of the dweller; ways to make a dwelling easily monitored for intrusion, fire, and freezing pipes when the owner is away; some provision, be it a local service or an extra bedroom with a separate entrance, for child-care support; and space for an office at home for evenings and weekends.

In short, women no longer give up everything personal to sustain a professional life, or abandon everything professional for a private life. Indeed, the very meaning of the terms professional and personal may be changing. Although it goes beyond the data to speculate, this may be true not only for women, as they struggle to find a genuine balance between work and home, but also for men. Should that be so, these observations would apply to housing needs of all Americans, regardless of sex.

# 6

# Housing Preferences:
# Changes and Patterns

### Barbara Behrens Gers

Changing demographics and lifestyles, the twists and turns of the economy, and the whims of fashion—all play a role in the housing market, just as in any other market. So it is essential for builders to know who their potential customers are and what their preferences may be before they commit to the time- and capital-consuming process of planning a single-family subdivision or condominium complex. That is why *Housing* magazine has provided its readers with various in-depth consumer studies, including an annual survey of buyer preferences. Conducted yearly since 1978, this survey has been carried out on a national level, in cooperation with Walker & Lee, a California-based real-estate firm.

In 1981, *Housing* surveyed 2,237 people as they visited builders' model homes—a sample chosen because members of this group are most likely to be thinking seriously about what they want in their housing and would be aware of what is actually available in the housing market. These homeshoppers filled out questionnaires consisting of more than two dozen multiple-choice questions, asking for such information as the shoppers' household size and type, income level, housing needs, and perhaps most important, housing expectations.

They were surveyed in eight representative metropolitan areas—Dallas, Denver, Chicago, Kansas City, Los Angeles/Orange County, Miami, San Diego, and Washington, D.C. Significantly, New York City is not on this list. It was omitted because the kind of housing in Manhattan—high rises and lofts, for example—is so far out of line with the patterns prevalent in most areas of the country that New Yorkers' expectations are of little interest to homebuilders in the rest of the nation.

What is of interest to builders—and their prospective buyers—is the single-family suburban home, still the most popular type of housing in the United States. Two-thirds of the people *Housing* surveyed were shopping for a detached house on its own lot. The others were looking for a unit in a multifamily building, an apartment, townhouse, or luxury condominium. The smaller size of the attached-housing sample is a direct reflection of the proportionately smaller amount of such housing for sale in many of the cities surveyed.

Overall, the shoppers were a diverse group. The largest subgroup was families, with an average of two children or less. As one might expect, they were seeking a single-family home in most cases—making up 54 percent of the detached-house shoppers and only 31 percent of those looking for an attached dwelling. Even though they made up the majority of the single-family shoppers, their share of this category still leaves quite a large proportion—46 percent—for other types of buyers.

Young couples, for example, make up 21 percent of the single-family house shoppers surveyed. Ninety-two percent of them are two-income households, suggesting that young couples still desire the traditional single-family home, although some traditional sex roles may have changed.

When households shopping for detached housing are compared to those in the market for an attached house, a difference in income is apparent. Young couples shopping for attached housing tend to be less affluent, although in 88 percent of the cases both husband and wife are working, and the income gap has been widening over the years. For the most part, these couples do not already own a piece of real estate they can sell to meet the larger downpayment and higher maintenance and carrying costs of a single-family home. In many cases, therefore, it is not so much housing preference as lack of income and/or capital that forces many households to seek attached housing: the main reasons they gave for wanting to buy were being tired of renting and wanting the tax benefits of ownership and a hedge against inflation.

Although many young couples are looking for attached housing because they cannot afford single-family homes, older couples whose children have left home are seeking attached housing for positive reasons. This is the group the housing industry calls "empty nesters." Not retirees, these older couples are generally still working and, in fact, 54 percent of those surveyed consist of two-income households. They said they want relief from the responsibilities of single-family ownership, such as maintaining the yard, so they can have more time for themselves. For this group, an attached dwelling is a preference, rather than an economic necessity. In fact, many will buy rather expensive attached homes.

In addition to less affluent couples and empty nesters, singles were shopping for multifamily units; they make up 17 percent of the attached-housing shoppers, split in half between men and women. Singles also make up 7 percent of the single-family market. Since there is only one paycheck, they tend to show household incomes a little lower than those of other groups. But the single buyer is not disadvantaged by any means; about half already own a house or condominium, a phenomenon which shows the importance real estate has assumed as an investment.

Females dominated a small subgroup of the sample, single-parent families: 87 percent of the single-parent households in the attached-housing category were headed by women, as were 72 percent of the single-family, single-parent shoppers. However, they were still a small proportion of the total sample, making up only 3 percent of the single-family homeshoppers and 5 percent of the attached-housing shoppers.

Another small subgroup was unrelated individuals shopping together. Such unrelated buyers made up 2 percent of the single-family sample and about 6 percent of the multifamily sample.

From their answers to the survey's questions, it was possible to get a good idea of what shoppers want when it comes to house size, number of rooms, and types of rooms. Regarding home size, for instance, the survey revealed that people are lowering their expectations, probably because of increased housing costs. Over the last three years, the amount of square footage shoppers say they expect in a home has gone down from nearly 2,000 to about 1,900 square feet, a loss roughly equivalent to one bedroom. (A typical 1,900 square-foot detached house might contain two or three bedrooms, living room, family room, dining room, kitchen, and two bathrooms.) The median square footage that attached-house shoppers said they expect was 1,482 square feet.

However, shoppers probably will not be able to afford even the reduced amount of space they want. Most builders currently are producing many single-family homes as small as 1,200 to 1,500 square feet in order to keep them affordable. And attached units are often much more compact, with units sized under 1,000 square feet very common.

Questions on the survey addressed this disparity between what shoppers say they want and what is available to them. For instance, they were asked where they would be willing to sacrifice space if square footage had to be cut in order to keep down housing costs—another way of asking shoppers to rank rooms in a home in order of their importance.

The results showed that shoppers are least willing to compromise on space in the kitchen. In fact, in both years this questions was asked, there was consensus among different household types and among shoppers from different parts of the country that the kitchen was the first priority.

After the kitchen, shoppers say the private, personal areas—master bedroom and bathrooms—are most important. The master bedroom ranked second only to the kitchen when shoppers indicated where they were most unwilling to give up space. And they wanted not only square footage, but architectural excitement as well. As an indication of how important the master suite is, over half the shoppers surveyed said they would pay an extra $2,500 to have a balcony or patio off their master bedroom.

Shoppers surveyed also agreed that bathrooms were of high importance. In fact, since last year there has been an increase in the number of bathrooms that shoppers say they want. Hardly any household in the sample, whether shopping for a detached or attached house, was interested in less than two bathrooms. Most single-family detached-home shoppers want at least two and one-half baths, and they are interested in luxury features such as double-basin vanities, oversized tubs, and skylights.

While master bedrooms and bathrooms are increasingly prized, other rooms have become less important in shoppers' eyes. For one thing, since families and households have gotten smaller, fewer bedrooms are needed. Most shoppers did not need more than one or two in addition to the master suite. The majority of the single-family shoppers wanted only two or three bedrooms altogether, and three quarters of the multifamily shoppers wanted only two or three. In addition, with the exception of the master bedrooms, shoppers probably will accept bedrooms that are rather scaled down in size.

Another room deemed less important is the formal dining room. What is interesting is that opinions about the importance of the dining room did not vary by household type, but by city. Thus, while people in Chicago and Miami are less willing to give up dining room space, people in Denver, Dallas, and Kansas City are more willing to. The low ranking generally of the dining room is in tune with what builders are offering—typically, a dining area that is part of an extended, open living area.

A place where most shoppers are very willing to give up space is the breakfast nook—the extra eating space in a kitchen. In fact, it can be minimized or eliminated altogether. The den was another room not highly valued. However, it is likely that many shoppers will use one of the rooms labeled "bedroom" on the builder's plans as a den, furnishing it with a daybed so that it can double as a guest room. As houses become smaller, people are not only lowering their expectations about the amount of space they will have, they also are making rooms serve dual purposes.

Finally the room least important to shoppers—where they say they are most willing to give up space—is the bonus room, a term for the type of space found in a finished basement. However, in another question, 60 percent of the shoppers said they would pay extra to get bonus space—an attic, basement, oversized garage, etc. Solving this apparent contradiction was their answer to an additional question—nearly 80 percent of them would want this space unfinished in order to keep down the cost. Over half the shoppers also said they would pay $200 to get detailed architectural plans showing them how they could expand their homes in the future. These responses may reflect the fact that while shoppers are lowering their expectations about the amount of space they will be able to afford in a new home, they feel that in the future they will be able to enlarge it. The dream of the big, single-family home is still very strong.

# 7

# Working Women:
# The Denver Experience

Susan Saegert, Theodore Liebman,
and R. Alan Melting, A.I.A./A.I.C.P.

Historically, one tradition in American housing policy has sought to achieve two goals: (1) equal access to resources by all consumers, and (2) the creation of better human communities based on freeing individuals from constricting stereotypes. The women's movement shares these goals. For this reason, the housing field serves as an excellent vehicle for the interjection of feminist goals into public policy.

In both the housing and the women's movements, however, the political reality of decision-making often leads to focusing on one goal at the expense of another. Consequently, seemingly compatible goals can become incompatible as advocacy groups seek to shape politically feasible programs. When problems are formulated in terms of equal access to a resource, solutions tend to prohibit discrimination and emphasize economic equality. When problems are articulated in terms of community-building, strategies tend to address a broader range of issues and center attention on a particular geographic space and specific groups of interacting people. In the short run, the divergence between the two approaches comes about because the first focuses on independently defined human needs—employment, housing, income, health care, and leisure—set within the existing social, institutional, and physical environment, while the second looks comprehensively at society and seeks to reorganize the whole environment. In all likelihood, neither approach will be sufficient alone to achieve either the broader goals of social justice or the narrower objectives of decent housing.

Nowhere have these phenomena been more dramatically illustrated than in Denver, Colorado. In January, 1980, the Denver Housing Authority provided us with the opportunity to address feminist goals of access to housing, jobs, and services within a new community as part of an effort to provide new strategies for urban development in Denver. The project unfolded in several phases. At first, a multi-disciplinary team analyzed different options for development in the central section of Denver. The increasing number of women and working parents in the workforce led them to emphasize a vision of the future city that would combine residential, commercial, and recreational space for a mix of incomes and household compositions. In this phase, workshops with city leaders, officials, and representatives of community groups and development interests were held to evaluate this city form against alternatives. No consensus emerged.

A second phase of qualitative and quantitative research began in the summer of 1980. Sponsored by a consortium of public agencies, private corporations, and foundations, the team studied several questions: Who wants to live in the city? How big was the market for this kind of urban housing? What features and services would be most important to future residents? What kind of households and other characteristics would prospective residents have? The team employed a variety of methods to answer these questions. This paper describes the project and the outcomes of the studies. It uses the feminist goals described above as a framework.

The interjection of gender-related issues occurred in the first phase when project team heads Theodore Liebman and R. Alan Melting posed the following question for the Denver Housing Authority: How does the entrance into the workforce of large numbers of women, including mothers of young and school-age children, change the requirements of urban design? To answer this question they assembled a multi-disciplinary team that included an environmental psychologist, Susan Saegert, who had done substantial work in the evaluation of urban and suburban living from the point of view of women. Saegert's research suggested that many women were forced to choose living environments all of which required sacrifice. The suburbs were seen as good for family life but limiting their personal development. Living in a central city, they had more opportunity for career development, satisfying social relationships, and cultural enrichment. However it also meant enduring cramped living conditions, inaccessibility of play space for young children, and fear of crime. Neither urban nor suburban forms suited the needs and desires of these women. The Denver project presented the opportunity to explore this hypothesis more fully and to try to develop more fulfilling alternatives. The team assisting Liebman and Melting also included legal specialists in economic development Stadtmaurer and Bailkin; ecological consultant R.T. Schadelbach; and a local urban designer, Richard Farley.

## HOUSING DEVELOPMENT STRATEGIES: DENVER—THE 1980s

In 1980, Denver was the scene of dramatic physical and economic changes. The city was experiencing enormous growth in the work force. At the same time, its residential population was shrinking. It was down 5.7 percent between 1970 and 1978. In some cases, housing units were lost to commercial uses. In others,

Exhibit 7.1—In 1980, Denver offered the possibility of living in a single-family home only minutes from the downtown.

buildings that had been converted from single-family homes to multifamily housing were being returned to their original use. While several large multifamily apartment buildings were under construction, the Denver City Planning Department estimated comparatively little expansion of the residential population. The growing work force would probably not become residents, but commuters.

Most of the employment growth was focused on a small section of the city known as downtown Denver. In 1977, the work force in this area numbered 82,300. By 1981, 100,000 people worked in the area. That same year, the Planning Department revised its projections for the downtown work-force size for 1985 to 143,000—a 24 percent increase over a year earlier. Employment in Denver as a whole was expected to increase from 212,700 to 255,000. General population estimates for Denver predicted that its 1977 base of 523,000 would grow to 560,000 in 1985. If all these estimates were correct, the entire growth in the work force could be attributed to new downtown workers.[1]

Physically, Denver reflects this statistical portrait and reveals disjunctions between old and new districts. The center is distinguished by block after block of new highrise office buildings. Separated only by streets, parking lots, and construction sites from the superblock highrises, single-family homes and one-story multifamily units ring the downtown (Figure 7-1). For the moment in 1980, Denver offered the possibility of living in a single-family home on a tree-lined street in a city neighborhood minutes away from downtown offices. The well-maintained parks in the neighborhoods further added to the sense of space and livability.

What of the future? Extrapolating from present trends of downtown office and suburban housing development, expansion of the downtown area would displace the residential neighborhoods. Suburban development seemed to provide the path of least resistance both in terms of land and construction costs and local development history. Yet, the concerns that Liebman and Melting brought to the study suggested that the households of the future would fit uncomfortably with the segregation of home from work place. It was into this breach that the researchers cast their strategies. They chose to engage in strategic planning, a methodology that takes into account the variety of actors by attempting to harmonize their different pursuits.

The goal of their housing strategies centered on meeting a variety of housing needs while taking advantage of the city opportunities. The approach stressed responsiveness to the context. Areas within the downtown required a variety of solutions; different housing markets required varied responses. The changing economic climate required a range of approaches to financing.

**Program of Work**

The team participants engaged in three levels of analysis. They examined physical factors, demographic and market characteristics, and implementation strategies. They then brought this material to the public in 20 workshops in the spring of 1980. In order to identify locations for downtown housing, Liebman and Melting made analyses of neighborhood context, land-use patterns, traffic, parking and mass transit, existing community services, recent development, vacant land, public land and building condition, land values, and the architectural, historical value and character of the downtown area.

At the same time, Saegert analyzed demographic data from the Denver Planning Office, the Denver Office of Policy Analysis, and the Denver Regional Council of Governments. She compared these findings to the data on regional and national trends from national sources. To the extent possible, she disaggregated data by sex of head of household, household composition, and income. Her approach allowed the team to go beyond stereotyped assumptions about housing markets to include analysis of groups usually ignored. In addition, she conducted group interviews with about 100 local residents, including residents of the downtown area, the city neighborhoods, and the suburban ring. Realtors and development personnel also were interviewed.

Finally, Bailkin delineated various markets and public-sector financial packages. He projected economic impacts and cost factors of various strategies. Mechanisms included public assistance programs, financing and/or operating subsidies, and zoning strategies.

In the workshops held in spring, team members began briefing over 50 groups and individuals with potential roles in downtown development. The workshops explored different "futures" for downtown Denver based on the information gathered in the foregoing research.

## Emergence of the Strategies

As different members of the team developed their analyses and consulted with each other, they began to develop a picture of the future choices open to Denver. The sense that the city was changing rapidly brought both an excitement about the development of new urban forms and puzzlement concerning the viability of non-traditional patterns of residential and work-place mixtures. Much of their work involved helping those who would contribute to the future of the city imagine alternatives to suburban development.

While this paper emphasizes the aspects that most directly addressed women's needs, the team learned through workshops that the majority of public- and private-sector actors involved did not view Denver's future from this perspective. Many received the idea of people wanting to live in a dense urban setting with skepticism. Although they acknowledged the problems presented for working parents by existing segregation of home, work place, and child care, they thought that the idea of children living downtown was neither very plausible nor desirable. Interestingly, most people did think that single parents would benefit from downtown housing. On the whole, however, most workshop participants did not distinguish women's needs as being different from those of men.

The members of the development community spoke of the market for downtown housing primarily in economic terms. Thus, gender entered into their analysis by virtue of women's employment. They saw two-earner households, particularly those without children, as prime candidates for downtown housing. In the developers' view, such consumers could pay high prices, did not need much space, desired proximity to work, and sought to enjoy the cultural and entertainment offerings of the city. They referred to these couples as "empty nesters," those whose children were grown up, and "young professionals," those who did not yet, and perhaps never would, have children. Further, the critical factors were income and absence of children. Developers also saw very well-paid executives as a target market whether or not they were married or their spouses worked. Thus, from the team's point of view, the very households that might benefit most from spatial proximity of work, home, and services were ignored by the developers.

Finally, only a few of the public officials, corporate executives, developers, and financiers saw housing as a necessary component of a viable downtown. Their most frequently expressed concern about the separation of housing and work place was their fear that businesses would begin to relocate in the suburbs as a way of assuring accessibility for the work force. They singled out clerical workers, most of whom were women, as particularly problematic because these employees often had domestic responsibilities combined with less money to spend on transportation and paid child care.

The workshops and the informal contacts leading up to them allowed discussion of a wide range of options. Prior to the workshops, the team had conducted group and individual interviews with a broad spectrum of Denverites. The opinions and concerns expressed in these interviews helped them formulate issues for the workshops. Some of the key points to emerge were:

(1) Many developers of downtown housing and office space were unsure about the depth of a market for downtown housing, its profitability compared to office-space development, and the characteristics of both the market and marketable housing.

(2) Realtors confirmed the idea that many of those seeking housing in Denver did not fit the working-husband-wife-at-home-with-children pattern most suited for suburbia. Working couples with and without children, single parents, divorced parents whose children sometimes lived with them and sometimes did not, singles, unmarried couples, and a variety of households based on the economic necessity of sharing housing all presented housing needs not particularly well met by existing housing (except sometimes in city neighborhoods). These different household types also provided new challenges for the design of housing.

(3) Interviews with groups of people who worked in Denver revealed a variety of people with strong interest in city living. Their enthusiasm often was coupled with uncertainty about what kind of living environment downtown Denver could or would provide in the future. Some people drew on images of Manhattan or San Francisco; others thought of Chicago, Toronto, or even European cities. Most were sure that none of these images really fit.

The team also discovered a core of urban pioneers who already were living in restored housing and loft space very near the center as well as a few residents of the newly constructed highrises in the urban renewal area. Those living downtown already found the experience stimulating and sometimes trying due to lack of grocery stores and other facilities.

The strong relationship of women with housing began to appear in these group interviews. As contacts were made with local civic and community groups, women volunteers expressed excitement about the new urban forms the team was exploring. They eagerly organized the interview sessions, found participants, and provided space and equipment. Without this spontaneous and effective help, the team could never have met with the variety of people that it did. Another indication of women's keen interest in new relationships between home and work can be seen in the much greater attendance at the group interviews of women. Men were quite willing to be interviewed in their professional roles, but did not volunteer readily to speak about their personal needs in housing.

(4) As workshop participant lists were developed through contacts with city officials, leaders of downtown civic and business organizations, and influential busi-

Exhibit 7.2—Workshop participants discuss strategies for downtown development.

nessmen, names of people to speak for women's needs in housing did not surface. Through an intensive networking effort, the team was able to gather a group of about 40 or 50 women in Denver who had a special interest in the topic, including planners, public officials, architects, developers, realtors, and women in business. In addition, women who ran projects to help women obtain mortgage credit, to provide high quality child-care, to shelter battered women, etc., also participated in meetings and interviews. Special workshop sessions were held for representatives of these groups. While this arrangement of workshops underlines the absence of a self-conscious voice for women's perspectives in the development community, the meetings and workshops led to the formation of an organization called Women for Downtown Housing. It formed committees to explore policy and development projects, and invited speakers, including major downtown developers and active public officials, to address the group.

   In the workshops, participants evaluated the concept of downtown housing in a variety of forms. They viewed slides of urban residential environments suggesting how other cities have provided comfortable, attractive city housing and recording the alternatives in Denver at that time. Drawing on statistics and on the interviews, they explored the market potential for different population groups and household types. They discussed public policy approaches to facilitate residential development. They employed land-use and land-cost analysis to examine the potential of different sites. Throughout the workshops, the team linked images of urban housing not currently existing in Denver to the needs of different kinds of households with children and to the physical and financial arrangements needed to insure accessibility to the housing for a heterogeneous population (Figure 7-2).

In the end, Liebman and Melting recommended strategies for downtown housing that differed dramatically from previous studies of the market for downtown housing. Their revised market study called for 64 percent of the 10,470 units to be targeted for families. In architectural renderings of the future housing, the sizes of apartments, scale of development, mix of housing types, open-space design, and facilities responded to the needs of a diverse population. In addition, they assessed locations for development in terms of nearness to existing schools and play facilities. Finally, Liebman and Melting phased the development to provide space for 1,000 to 5,000 families during the first five years. This pace allowed for 66 percent of the units constructed during the first phase to be for families. (Of course, they could not insure that households with children would occupy these units. Couples or anyone who could afford the additional space could buy or rent.)

But the idea of providing housing suitable for children contrasted strongly with the kind of housing being built at that time in the city's main urban residential development, Skyline Urban Renewal Area. There most of the buildings were towers sited directly on the street with little access to services and no consideration for children's needs. The one low-rise development that also showed attention to open space was affordable only for upper-income households. In contrast, the Liebman and Melting strategies designated over 75 percent of the units as affordable by middle-income households. The physical form and location of the suggested housing combined with its volume would change the course of Denver's development from a city that segregated places for work and adult leisure from places for domestic life and child rearing.

## AFTER THE STRATEGIES

The new city that would support both nurturing and production has not been built yet. During the course of Liebman and Melting's work, changes in the federal administration altered the financial and political climate of development. Prior to Reagan's election, the financial feasibility of the plan had not been tested and proven successful. During his administration he reduced financing schemes that might have made the development feasible. Furthermore, the development community in Denver was never totally convinced.

The workshop did, however, lead to a demand for a more detailed study of the market for downtown housing. Initially, the Housing Authority of the City and County of Denver commissioned this research. Later, United Bank of Denver,

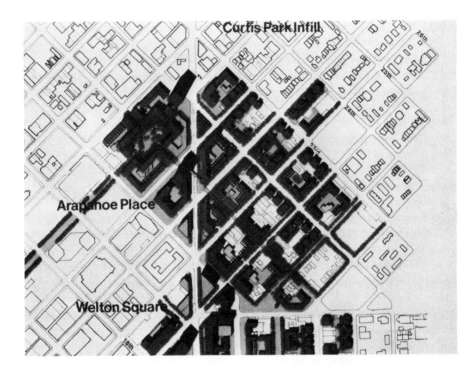

Exhibit 7.3—The Arapahoe Place proposal was an example of low- to moderate-income housing incorporating services and play areas to make the development suitable for family living.

Piton Foundation, Central Bank of Denver, Empire Savings Bank, Midland Federal Savings and Loan, Public Service Corporation of Colorado, Colorado Housing Finance Authority, and the City and County of Denver supported the final survey of the downtown workforce. Susan Saegert undertook this project. Her goal was to sample representatively the downtown workforce and to determine the extent of demand for different kinds of housing, including urban housing. In the survey, she paid extensive attention to the kinds of design features, activity spaces, environmental qualities, and local services different household types would require.

She developed the research in three phases.[2] First, she compiled a comprehensive list of downtown employers to be sampled representatively. (She decided to obtain respondents through employers to increase the return rate on the questionnaire, and to allow her to analyze respondents according to the type of business or other institution they represented. Thus, if she found a particular type of firm to be primarily responsible for growth of the downtown workforce, then she could look at responses for that industry separately.) Second, she engaged in intensive qualitative interviewing with employees from a representative spectrum of the workforce. Third, she administered a survey to employees of 53 companies and institutions in downtown Denver. In total, 2,631 persons responded to the survey.[3] Of the companies and institutions asked to cooperate, 88 percent agreed. The questionnaire return rate was 43 percent.

In the 40 intensive interviews, many issues concerning women's access to urban housing and the suitability of urban housing for children were discussed. Downtown living attracted women for the reasons expected: greater access to work, closeness to a variety of activities, and perceived suitability for alternative lifestyles. Many unmarried women also expressed great concern about the affordability of city housing coupled with a rejection of suburban alternatives.

The specific vision of life held by the women affected the kind of housing and neighborhood they desired. One category of respondents wanted fairly standard apartment housing. They accepted highrise living. They emphasized low maintenance and the convenience of walking to work. Of the four people in this group, three were single women. Two women, divorced and in their mid-fifties, were executive secretaries and saw downtown as a place that offered experiences different from their earlier lives as suburban wives and mothers. The third was a young woman, a bank teller, who mainly wanted a roof over her head and an affordable mode of transportation. The fourth, a young male professional, married to a committed female professional, saw the highrise apartment as compatible with their work-centered lives.

Three other professionals, two single women and a single mother, described very clearly what they wanted in housing and stated that it was not available. They stressed (1) proximity to work and other downtown facilities; (2) a sense of open space either because of the view, nearness to park, yard, terrace, or common grounds; (3) architectural interest; (4) low maintenance; and (5) good investment potential. The unmarried women had sold single-family houses to buy condominium apartments. The single mother who had risen to the top of her profession, nursing, was hampered by the fact that her income would never approach that of many similiarly advanced male professionals. She expressed an interest in alternative ownership forms such as a limited equity cooperative, although this form of ownership was nonexistent in Denver.

A third category of respondents, two men and one woman, desired urban living because of the social and physical diversity of this environment. The woman, a single mother of a racially mixed son, wanted to raise her child in an environment that exposed him to different kinds of people and the diversity of roles they played. The absence of children's facilities, open space, trees, and a healthy environment led her to reject existing urban options. (Other parents who were living in the city also reported that the housing options were unsuitable for children. Easy access to play spaces that could be supervised from inside the unit was a main requirement. Parents wanted children as young as two years old to be able to go outside without having to accompany them.)

However, it was not only parents of young children who rejected highrise housing. Six women and one man who stressed their desire to live near their work and other city amenities felt that only a single-family home, no matter how small, would do. All were single and employed in secretarial or lower-level managerial positions. The cost of transportation was an issue for them.

In contrast, the six respondents who preferred suburban living and unambiguously rejected any urban housing alternative were all married. Their lifestyles and their desire for a physical separation of home and work were smoothly accommodated by existing housing alternatives. Unlike all other groups, they expressed neither conflict nor ambivalence about their housing choices. Four of this group were working women (two of whom had children) who did not mention any specific problems related to living in the suburbs and working downtown.

However, 47 percent of the downtown workforce of survey respondents were sufficiently dissatisfied with their current housing status to state that they planned to move within the next five years. Ten percent of this group wanted to move to the downtown area and another 26 percent wanted to move to a city neighborhood. Many desired to change homes but stay in the same area. Downtown was the only area in which most of those who targeted the area for their next move were not already living there.

Of those expecting to move and wanting centrally located housing, single women dominated. Single women living alone comprised only 11 percent of the sample, but nearly 20 percent of those wanted to move to centrally located housing. Single men (6.9 percent of the sample) comprised 14.3 percent of those wanting to move to centrally located housing. Single mothers were also over-represented (6.5 percent as compared to 4.3 percent in the sample). Unmarried adults living together were the only other household type in which the proportion of respondents wishing to move downtown or nearby exceeded the sample proportion (16.9 percent versus 13.3 percent).

These figures do not mean, however, that the market for downtown or centrally located housing is confined to unmarried adults, mostly without children. While only 11.7 percent of those wanting to move to centrally located housing were married and had children under 18 years old (compared to 21.1 percent of the sample), another 9.1 percent of those attracted to this area lived in households containing a married couple, children under 18, and other adults (compared to 7.3 percent of the sample). We do not understand the composition of these households very well. They could include couples with children living with parents or other adults and older children living with their parents who have siblings in the younger age group.

Another non-traditional type of household was attracted to centrally located housing: unrelated adults with children under 18 (7.8 percent were attracted to centrally located housing versus 6.3 percent of the population). If we include single mothers, we find that the largest number of households actively wanting centrally located housing in the next five years includes those with children under 18 (34.9 percent of all those wanting centrally located housing).

It appears that marriage rather than the existence of children under 18 years old contributes most strongly to preferences for less urban housing. This intriguing finding suggests that feminist architectural historians' claim that the lure of the suburbs is more ideological than functional may continue to be true. Or it may reflect the greater resources married couples can call on to overcome the greater demands on time and money made by suburban single-family housing occupancy. If both spouses work, they can afford to hire more help, own more cars, or spend more on transportation. If one spouse does not work outside the home, the couple can better cope with the demands of spatially spread out daily activities. In both cases the demands of home maintenance can be shared.

While marriage may make suburban home occupancy more desirable, it also would make it easier to afford newly constructed city housing. The largest percent, 57 percent, of all of those who wished to move downtown but expected to be unable to do so were single females living alone. Still, 63 percent of the respondents in households of married adults with children also felt blocked from moving downtown. Two-thirds of the single mothers said they could not move downtown now even though they wanted to. Single mothers were the only group that cited inability to find suitable housing as frequently as financial reasons. Single females living alone were disproportionately represented among those giving as their reason for not moving inability to afford other housing.

The findings suggest that housing and urban design as well as other aspects of environmental quality deter households with children from moving to centrally located housing even when the costs are bearable. It is particularly interesting that single mothers stated that housing suitability was as important as cost in deterring them from moving to downtown housing. Single mothers' median income was reported to be in the $20,000 to $29,000 range as compared with a median household income for married parents of $30,000 to $49,000. Single adults, both male and female, reported the same median income as single mothers although the average for those without children was lower (single mothers, average income, $33,290 versus singles alone, average income, $24,140). Neither medians nor means showed much difference between the earnings of single women and men in this sample of people wanting to move to centrally located housing. (A complete demographic analysis is limited by the small sample size, especially for single mothers wanting to move to downtown housing.) Unmarried adults living together with children had the lowest median income reported: $15,000 to $19,999. This finding may indicate that the sharing of a household was based more on economic necessity than on preference. Unmarried male-female couples without children reported a median income of $20,000-$29,999. Same-sex roommates without children reported an even higher median income of $30,000-$49,999. (All are medians for the sample wanting to move to centrally located housing only.)

Over two-thirds of those who wanted to move to centrally located housing wanted to buy. Of these, 47.2 percent specifically stated that they would like to buy a condominium, 25.2 percent specified a house, and 4.9 percent stated a preference for co-op ownership. (At the time the study was conducted, we could discover no existing cooperatively owned housing in Denver.)

Single women made up the largest percent of any household type interested in buying condominiums. They also were the largest group interested in renting apartments. While respondents' lack of familiarity with co-op ownership makes it hard to interpret findings about this option, those who favored this alternative were mainly married with children. Among people attracted to downtown housing, single mothers expected to make higher downpayments for their income level but expected to pay less monthly. Couples with and without children expected to pay proportionately more of their incomes for housing as the income category went up.

Of those who wanted downtown housing, 14 percent required one bedroom, 54 percent required two bedrooms, and 25 percent needed three bedrooms. Only singles living alone were willing to accept one bedroom but frequently expressed preferences for two. Household composition had a stronger effect than income on stated number of bedrooms required. While singles were more willing to accept one bedroom at all income levels than other households, the number of bathrooms depended more on income.

Households pretty much agreed that they required the following features in their homes: separate kitchens, garage space, laundry facilities, and a balcony, terrace, or patio. Only the last feature differentiated downtown movers from others expecting to move. Regardless of where people wanted to move, they also agreed in their ranking on which of 32 optional features were most important: large bedrooms, soundproofing, a washer/dryer in the unit, and a large kitchen or extra storage space (tied).

Lower-income households and couples with children and single mothers expressed preferences for lower buildings. The strongest preferences for highrise buildings were among households making $50,000 without children who wanted to move downtown. On a number of different measures, people with higher incomes seemed to find highrise buildings more acceptable. Even parents with incomes over $30,000 saw low- or mid-rise apartments as relatively good places to raise children whereas lower-income groups did not. Generally, people with higher incomes expected multifamily housing to be less stressful and a better financial investment and to give them more control over their housing than did lower-income people.

Two interesting issues arose concerning building preference. First, over half of the 47 percent of the sample who reported wanting to move (all destinations) stated that they would consider a range of building types and that they had no first preference. Second, the percent of people who definitely prefer a detached house was dramatically lower than the percent now occupying detached houses. These data suggest that perhaps the availability of single-family housing rather than preference accounts for the frequency with which it has been chosen in the past. The data might also reflect a realistic assessment by prospective movers of their purchasing power in the housing market.

Respondents planning to move in the next five years wanted a wide range of shops and services located within a mile of their dwelling. Over 80 percent of the respondents wanted a bus stop within three blocks of their home, and many, especially singles and families with children, wanted to live near a rapid-transit stop. High-income households and those moving downtown were less interested in proximity to daycare. Single parents were the most interested in nearby day care, but only slightly more than other households with children. Single parents stressed proximity to a variety of facilities more than other groups. They wanted nearby convenience stores, shops for necessities, indoor recreation, and access to a park or open space. Singles without children also desired proximity to stores and other daily needs. Couples with children joined single parents in their desire for indoor recreational facilities in their housing. However, two-parent families were willing to settle for a park or open space within three blocks, whereas many single parents wanted outdoor space within the housing development or adjacent to the unit. Generally, people were not very positive about the idea of having non-residential land uses in a residential building.

People wanting to live downtown more frequently stated that they would prefer few or no children in their residential development than did those wanting to move to suburban or other areas. Those looking for new housing in city neighborhoods tended to state that some children were acceptable. Parents were more accepting of both young children and teenagers in their development than were others, regardless of where they wanted to live. Most people regardless of where they wanted to move saw elderly people as quite acceptable in housing developments. However, those looking for suburban housing were more opposed to a concentration of elderly in a development. Singles were most accepting of sharing the development with the elderly if the housing was downtown. Single parents were the most positive about having elderly neighbors.

Since the study was addressed to the feasibility of developing housing near or in downtown, we looked at people's reasons for moving to see if those who preferred downtown housing differed from others. While they were similar to others who wanted to move in that the most frequently stated reasons were a desire for a better investment and wanting to go from renting to owning, they differed in other ways. Those attracted to downtown housing were more likely to express concern about the cost of transportation, the cost of energy, and too much maintenance.

The vision of a downtown residential community presented during the strategies workshop included people of different incomes and ages, including children. The data, however, reveal that almost no one thought downtown, as it existed, was an acceptable place to raise children. Respondents saw the central city as having poor-quality public schools and a paucity of child-care arrangements. While over one-third of the households interested in centrally located housing had children, their attraction seems based on adult considerations such as proximity to work and other facilities as well as adult lifestyle issues. Downtown living was not seen as positive for children themselves.

We concluded from the survey that a market for downtown housing existed in Denver. However, for the city to move in the direction of an integration of people varying in age, income, and lifestyles, the urban form of Denver as well as the availability of services and affordable housing would need to be changed in ways that required intervention in the market forces. The research reminds us that while cities, including Denver, offer many specialized public amenities, they frequently lack the basic public features of a livable environment and support for childrearing. The development process in fact tends to decrease the quality of the urban environment as a place to live and grow. This problem is one that feminists confront when they try to envision a community that would not constrain women and men socially and physically and perpetuate a gender-based division of labor, one that historically has impoverished women economically.

## REFLECTIONS AND PROJECTIONS

The scale and process of development in Denver during 1980-81 probably made it inevitable that feminist goals would not be realized fully. Leavitt and Saegert have argued recently that women tend to build and maintain communities by starting with their ties to others, assessing their needs and working to meet them without destroying, but by saving, existing communities. The workshops represented one effort to involve many sectors of the community in the rapid and expensive process of urban development that was occurring. Probably a much more intensive and grounded effort is required. Such an effort would be a significant political phenomenon. As non-residents, as architects and social scientists, the consultants could not bring about that level of participation.

However, the ideas introduced are not dead. Since the completion of the study, a new mayor has been elected who raised as a campaign issue the need for central-city housing for all types of people and households. Liebman and Melting have designed a housing development near downtown that has gone through many phases. Initially it was to house 20 percent low- and moderate-income households and to include a daycare center and a health club for residents. At this point, the health club remains, though scaled down, but the daycare center is gone as are expectations that low- and moderate-income families will be able to afford the housing. The gardens and open spaces, however, will provide an amenity to all residents in the immediate city environment. They are hopeful that the project will break ground in the near future.

Future strategies to address the process of building a socially heterogeneous central-city community in which people live, work, and play would build on several things. First, much of the work focused exclusively on the downtown area. To rethink the form, function, and social composition of the area was a large enough task in itself. The survey filled a gap in thinking about the city by providing information about a large population who used the city intensively as workers, but not necessarily as residents. However, the constituency for a downtown community must include those who live in Denver, particularly those residing in the neighborhoods around the downtown area. The strategies developed were sensitive to the need to preserve the neighborhoods and provide an integrative transition. The physical scale, targeted housing costs for low- and moderate-income households, and the appeal to households with children all were designed for these purposes in contrast to the march of highrise office space and some highrise luxury or heavily subsidized housing that seemed to be advancing into the neighborhoods. Since 1981, the demand for downtown office space has decreased, but it has not been replaced by the building of housing. The rise in land costs based on expectations for future office buildings remains a barrier to the construction of housing.

One premise of the work was that for a city to provide opportunities for social and cultural enrichment, economically productive work, and domestic life, the population should be diverse, and the urban, physical, and social form should meet their similar and different needs. This paper focused on differences in the needs of households related to a historically gender-based division of responsibility for nurturing and economically productive work even if it has often been more of an ideal than a reality. It also discussed differential access to housing related to women's lower pay scales. Denver like most cities provides homes for people of diverse racial and ethnic backgrounds. These differences are more overtly part of the political process than gender-related issues in part because minority groups live in partially segregated, existing communities. Yet the needs for access to modestly priced housing, and for communities that support both human development and economically productive work are shared. One positive force for building a coalition directed at changing the form of the city to serve the needs of changing households better involves the public availability of services and amenities created.

Environmentalists' concerns also buttress the goals of a re-visioned community form. Housing development at greater than suburban densities mixed with the workplace and services would reduce energy needs. The environment most people feel children need for healthy development also represents a better economical balance and requires control of pollutants. The needs and desires that women have for housing and community are not women's needs, but rather shared and unmet human needs. At present, women are most affected by this lack and often most involved in daily efforts to overcome it for themselves and their families. Because of this experience, women are in a position to contribute significantly to the new vision of community form.

## NOTES

1. Of course the compatibility and precision of the different estimates make such an extrapolation impossible. But the point of the comparison seems justified.

2. At this point Kathleen Butler of Apt West then joined Saegert as the on-site coordinator of research. Paxson continued as research assistant and was joined by Selim Iltus, both of the City University of New York Graduate Center, Center for Human Environments. Their work and that of many other part-time workers made the project a success. In addition, special thanks are due to Phillip Milstein, the retired director of Downtown Denver Inc., who served as a consultant to the project. His insights, guidance, and personal generosity got the project over critical hurdles.

3. Internal analysis of the sample suggests that returns were representative. The report is available from the Denver Housing Authority.

# 8

# Highrise Family Living in New York City

Elizabeth Mackintosh

Does the urban highrise provide good shelter for families? Is it suitable for some types of families but not others? Are certain types of women more satisfied with urban highrises than others? Do men and women differ in their housing attitudes? Are some highrises designed better than others? These are some of the questions that were investigated in a research study[1] on middle-income families at three highrise sites in New York City.

When the research was first conceived in the 1970s, highrise housing for families with young children had been severely criticized. For over 15 years, theorists and researchers had been claiming that highrise housing had many negative effects on parents and children.[2] The most serious criticism leveled at highrises was that they make access to the outdoors difficult, particularly for children. Upper-floor children had to use elevators to go outside. Parents could not easily supervise their children. Past studies indicated that children who lived in upper-floor apartments were kept in more than those from lower floors or single-family houses. Research also suggested that parents with young children on upper floors were hindered in their social interaction, were more confined to their dwelling unit with their children, and were therefore more emotionally stressed. Highrise mothers were thought to feel lonely and isolated because of this confinement and because their housing provided no communal meeting spaces and discouraged neighborly contacts. Highrise buildings were also criticized for engendering a sense of social detachment and a lack of accountability leading to vandalism and crime.

Another criticism of highrise buildings was that they are antithetical to the "American dream" of homeowning. According to this view, the highrise apartment cannot satisfy a family's need to control its environment, build up equity, and present a symbol of accomplishment.

Negative research findings and observations led the governments of many countries to put restrictions on the construction of highrise housing for families with children. In the United States, housing construction guidelines for Section 8 (subsidized) housing in the Housing and Community Development Act of 1974 state: "Highrise elevator projects for families with children may not be utilized unless HUD determines there is no practical alternative" (U.S. Department of Housing and Urban Development, 1974, p. 4067). Design criteria for moderate- and middle-income, government-aided housing in New York State specify: "Whenever possible, concentrate the placement of large apartments on lower floors to maximize surveillance of outdoor space and minimize the need for children to use elevators" (City of New York, n.d., p. 13). In 1975, Clare Cooper, a well-known housing researcher, declared: "Highrise is most unsuited for families with children under five as presently designed" (Cooper-Marcus and Hogue, 1975, p. 2). The British government concluded that "It is now generally accepted that families with children should not live in highrise dwellings" (Adams and Conway, 1975, memo). In the mid-1970s, England, Denmark, and Sweden altered their construction policies accordingly.

The problem was whether or not such a full-scale condemnation of highrise buildings was justified. A review of past studies revealed that conclusions were based primarily on highrise housing that:

1. suffered from poor design qualities and facilities not inherent in this building form;
2. was situated in poor neighborhoods;
3. lacked responsive management; and/or
4. housed low- or moderate-income populations.

It was apparent that the highrise had not been given the thorough evaluation it deserved. In addition, some types of families may be more satisfied with this building form than others. Therefore the research examined the experience of middle-income families with young children in three well-regarded and reportedly well-designed highrise sites in a good neighborhood.

The three sites are on the east side of Manhattan in New York City (see Exhibits 8.1 and 8.2). One site, Stuyvesant Town and Peter Cooper Village, embodies the best in 1940s design knowledge. These developments are owned by Metropolitan Life Insurance Company and consist of 56 13- and 14-story brick buildings, housing 11,250 apartments. Stuyvesant Town was the first urban renewal project in the United States developed by private enterprise with public assistance. Stuyvesant Town and Peter Cooper Village have long waiting lists for their apartments. Their site is separated from the rest of the surrounding neighborhood, resulting in private walks and streets separated from regular traffic. The developments have many age-segregated playgrounds and extensive landscaping (see Exhibits 8.3-8.6).

Exhibit 8.1—Study area.

The second site—East Midtown Plaza—typifies the best in 1970s design theory. This 746-unit cooperative[3] is diagonally across the street from Peter Cooper Village. It was built under the 1955 New York State Mitchell-Lama Law that provided for city or state long-term, low-interest mortgages and tax exemptions. Completed in the early 1970s, East Midtown Plaza has 746 apartments in buildings 9-, 11-, 22-, 27- and 28-stories high. It has won three design awards for excellence in architecture. In addition to a street-level playground, there are three terrace playgrounds that are accessible only through the buildings (see Exhibits 8.7-8.9). Near these interior play areas are duplex units with outdoor corridors. Fifteen percent of the development's apartments are three-bedroom units. The waiting list for apartments at East Midtown Plaza became so long and the turnover so low that the development has closed the waiting list.

The third site consisted of single highrise buildings in the immediate vicinity

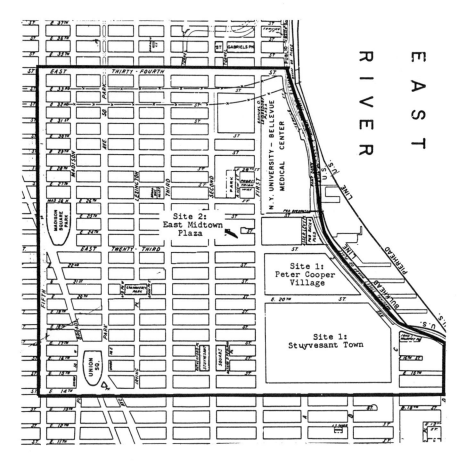

Exhibit 8.2—Study area in detail.

(within five blocks) of the other two sites. These buildings are "typical" highrise buildings without any shared facilities or common open space (see Exhibit 8.10).

The study sample consisted of 120 people (30 at Stuyvesant Town/Peter Cooper Village, 60 at East Midtown Plaza, and 30 in single buildings). Husbands and wives who had at least one young child between the ages of two and ten were interviewed and filled out questionnaires and time diaries.

Sample families all had a husband and a wife who were usually well-educated, professional, and middle income. The majority had two children. Sample parents were in their mid-thirties. All men were employed; 60 percent of the women held jobs outside the home (25 percent full-time jobs). These families lived in the same building or development for about five and one-half years. Many lived on high floors; one-third were on floors 10 through 26.

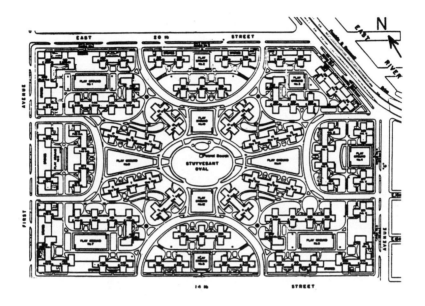

Exhibit 8.3—Site plan of Stuyvesant Town (Courtesy of Metropolitan Life Insurance Company).

## OVERVIEW[4]

Sample families as a whole were oriented to city living in multi-family housing. The majority had no intentions of moving from their present highrise homes and were highly satisfied with the city and their housing development. The majority were satisfied with their apartments, but not highly pleased. Most of the sample felt ownership of one's home was desirable, but not in the suburbs, and not necessarily in the form of a detached home.

In response to the question, "What would be your ideal home assuming finances were not a consideration?," three-quarters of the sample said some form of city home, a townhouse, an apartment in a luxury apartment house, or a larger version of their present apartment. The rest of the sample was evenly split between wanting a suburban or a rural house. It appears that most of the sample would prefer to live in the city if they could afford it.

When asked whether the suburban single-family house had any special or symbolic meaning for them, people spoke about the importance of owning a house regardless of its location. Most felt that ownership brought with it a sense of control, security, and a feeling of permanence. Some thought the suburban single-family home symbolized high status and a peak of accomplishment. About one-third felt this type of housing had no symbolic meaning. Some spoke of the suburbs as socially and culturally isolated and narrow.

Exhibit 8.4—View of Stuyvesant Town from street.

## Implications

Highrise housing should not be universally condemned or stereotyped; it can provide a satisfying housing environment. Because more people said their ideal home was in the city than those who said they were definitely staying in the city, it appears that (at least for the type of people studied) if suitable housing were provided in the city, these people might not leave for the suburbs. The sample's positive feelings about ownership indicate that cooperative and condominium buildings would be attractive to them. That the sample registered less satisfaction with their apartments than with the city or their housing development indicates that improvements in apartments are called for.

## DUAL-CAREER COUPLES

Women's employment status predicted attitudes toward housing and the city better than income, education, or age. Couples in which the woman was working outside the home (dual-career couples) preferred highrise homes because of the proximity to jobs, the excellent public transportation, and little home mainte-

Exhibit 8.5—Stuyvesant Town: internal sidewalks, play area in background.

nance. Dual-career families were more committed to remaining in the city than single-career families (61 percent had no moving plans compared to 39 percent of the couples with only the husband working). No woman working full-time said her ideal home was a suburban house. Seventy-one percent of the dual-career families felt that the commute from the suburbs was too long, compared to 50 percent of the single-career couples.

Typical comments by women working full- or part-time follow:

> [Why chose to live in Manhattan?] Well, I work and my husband works and we're ten minutes from our work by living where we are . . . And if I do have a problem when the kids are sick, I'm ten minutes from the house.

> We always thought since we both worked if we lived near where I worked then I could spend more time with the kids.

> [Consider the suburbs?] We immediately ruled that out. Because my husband's place of business is in Manhattan and I don't want him to commute—fatherless, husbandless marriage. Plus I think it is a rather horrendous pursuit to have to go through every day. And I want to keep up my career; I don't want to commute either.

Dual- and single-career couples had distinguishable opinions on city living and housing. Women working outside the home gave more importance to proximity to work as a reason for staying in the city. Dual-career couples felt that it was

Exhibit 8.6—Stuyvesant Town: basketball court, apartment buildings in background.

easier for a woman to have a job in the city. In contrast, single-career couples chose more frequently to live in Manhattan because it was familiar. They more often mentioned that the city's cultural stimulation was an advantage of city living and were bothered more about children's restricted freedom outside. Women without jobs more frequently mentioned that public schools were a problem and gave more importance to not having equity in a house and crime as reasons for leaving the city.

Dual-career families did not have higher satisfaction with the city or their apartment, but single-career couples tended to express more satisfaction with their building or development. Dual-career couples had fewer of their good friends in their building or development than single-career couples who more often described their neighbors as "warm, friendly" people. Over half the working mothers said they would like to see people more but could not because of job and/or children.

## Implications

Some people are better served than others by urban highrise housing. Couples in which the woman is working prefer highrise homes because this type of shelter satisfies their needs.[5] Therefore, it is extremely important that policy makers provide this housing form for this subgroup. Researchers and feminists have frequently stated that suburban living is disadvantageous for women because of its lack of public transportation, cultural and social isolation, and high maintenance demands.

Because the number of dual-career couples is increasing, we would expect an increased demand for urban highrise housing. More than half of all mothers with school-age children now work outside the home; a third with children under the age of three are employed. And recent research indicates that mothers who work are happier than those who do not.[6]

The finding of no difference in apartment satisfaction between employed or non-employed women or dual- or single-career couples may indicate that career-oriented people, despite their high value on urban job and social opportunities, still wish they had more adequate "homes." Planning for this group of people should therefore focus on improvements to apartment units.

## SEX DIFFERENCES

Men and women differed in their attitudes towards their housing, city living,

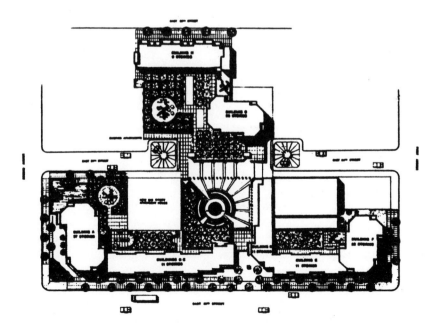

Exhibit 8.7—Site plan of East Midtown Plaza (Courtesy of East Midtown Plaza).

Exhibit 8.8—East Midtown Plaza: nine-story buildings, street-level playground in foreground.

and about what they thought were the effects of city life. Proximity to work and a good buy were mentioned more by men than women as the best features of the place where they were living. Women, on the other hand, cited as more important than men "social contacts easier" and "can walk, not drive to stores, restaurants, etc." as reasons for staying in the city. More men than women said that an effect of city living is that adults do not have the tension and inconvenience of a commute.

Reflecting their traditional role of "homemaking," women complained more than men that limited apartment space creates crowding and tension. They also said that home entertainment was harder in a city apartment. The poor quality of the city's environment (noise, dirt, pollution, lack of green, open space) also bothered women more than men. Women mentioned more negative effects of city living for both the adult and for the child. The complaint that the outside appearance of their housing was bad (that it looked like a project) was mentioned by more women than men.

There were no significant differences between men and women on satisfaction with New York City, one's housing development, or apartment, the importance and symbolic meaning of the suburban single-family home, or the ideal home.

The sample was asked, "Do you and your spouse have the same or different opinions on your housing and its location?'' Almost 60 percent of the sample said they held the same opinions as their spouse, while the rest of the sample was divided almost equally between husbands or wives feeling more pro-city.[7] Where mismatches in housing desires occurred in couples, the cases in which wives who wanted to stay in the city and husbands who wanted to move to the suburbs seemed the most difficult. Husbands in these cases wanted to own property and have a sense of permanence. Their wives, on the other hand, were usually starting or about to start a career or job and were afraid that it would be difficult to find work in the suburbs, or impossible to commute into the city and be in close touch with their children. These women also worried that their determination to find a job might fade if surrounded by suburban women who did not work. The other case, in which a woman wanted to move to the suburbs and her husband did not, usually involved a wife who wanted a more gracious lifestyle and more freedom for her children, while her husband did not want to commute and was not very interested in their housing per se. The roots of some conflicts between husbands and wives about staying in the city lay in the difference in their housing backgrounds; one partner may have grown up in a house, the other in an apartment. The following comments illustrate the intensity of the conflict between some husbands and wives:

> We do differ about it. It's a very complicated issue. Basically, he wants to have a feeling of permanence, he wants to own something. We've been renting for 17 years and we don't own any property anywhere. . . . I have a dozen reasons why I don't want to go. I really *don't* want to go. . . . I think it's going to be very hard for me to get back to work, to find a job, a good serious job. . . .

> My husband has always wanted to move to the suburbs because he is a frustrated carpenter and he looks around and he doesn't know what to do. And we always thought at some point we would be moving out because of the school situation. As it turns out there has always been this underlying tension between us. . . . About two years ago my husband turned to me and said, "You won." [East Midtown Plaza resident.]

> [Her husband.] I wanted to get out of the city. I did not want to stay. I wanted to buy a house and she did not want that because once she did that she would be isolated and she would not be able to work.

> I could very readily move to the suburbs. . . . My wife not so—she wants to live in New York City for the rest of her life; she likes the activity.

> [His wife.] To him owning property is far more important. You see, I don't care if I never own any property. . . . I never really lived in a house. It's hard to envision.

## Implications

Sex differences, reflecting traditional roles, were found in people's opinions on the positive and negative qualities of their environment. The general picture

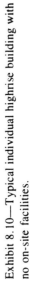

Exhibit 8.10—Typical individual highrise building with no on-site facilities.

Exhibit 8.9—East Midtown Plaza: Terrace Playground above community room on right.

the findings give is that the sample women were more bothered by their housing and the city's environment than the men but enjoyed the social contacts the city provided. Sample men, on the other hand, liked the proximity to their jobs and took more pleasure in their housing than women but worried about having enough money. These findings are reinforced by the time-budget data which showed that women spent more time inside the apartment, and more time performing "homemaker" duties, even on Sundays, than men. The home environment therefore had a greater impact on the women's lives than the men's.

As women are increasingly inclined to pursue meaningful careers (and present demographic trends indicate that this will be the case), we would expect more conflicts between husbands and wives over housing location based on the study findings. It will be interesting to see if men will assume their equal share of homemaker duties and if they do, whether or not their desire for a suburban single-family home which requires more maintenance will diminish.

## SITE DIFFERENCES

The three highrise sites attracted different types of families because each offered a unique setting. East Midtown Plaza residents had a very high proportion of dual-career families, people who grew up in apartments in the outer boroughs of New York City, and large families. The East Midtown Plaza population was most committed to the city. It had fewer moving plans and was most satisfied with New York City, its public schools, its public transportation, and the opportunities it provided for women to have jobs. The cosmopolitan East Midtown Plaza families chose their housing because it was a cooperative, it offered a sense of community, play areas, and excellent design. The development fulfilled their expectations. Satisfaction with the development and apartments was high.

The people at Stuyvesant Town/Peter Cooper Village were mostly single-career couples in traditional marriages. They represented the classic "transient" types who plan to move to the suburbs after a short stay in the city. Their ideal home was the suburban house. Stuyvesant Town/Peter Cooper Village residents felt more negatively about urban living and the city's public schools. Stuyvesant Town and Peter Cooper Village, with their insular design and extensive landscaping, were the most "suburban" of the three sites. Residents were highly pleased with their housing, which they had chosen for its convenient neighborhood, sense of community, and play areas.

Single-building residents had lived the longest in their housing and had a very high percent of employed women. Although oriented to urban living, single-building families were the least satisfied with New York City, their building, and their apartments. They had chosen their housing for its neighborhood characteristics. Of the three highrise sites, the single buildings had the least to offer in terms of facilities; the apartments were the most dense. Single-building residents had the most building-related complaints.

## Implications

People selected their housing site to match their aspirations and attitudes toward urban living. The sites, each in their own particular way, reinforced these attitudes. Yet satisfaction varied at each site, indicating that although people tried to find the most appropriate housing for their needs, some sites provided more fulfillment than others. This finding indicates that in spite of self-selection, certain physical and social features of highrise housing provide more satisfaction than others.

## NEIGHBORING AND SOCIAL BEHAVIOR

Residents in housing with on-site facilities (Stuyvesant Town/Peter Cooper Village and East Midtown Plaza) were more involved with their neighbors than people living in housing with no shared facilities (single buildings). Ninety percent of the total sample were satisfied with their relationships with their neighbors. In most cases, people who wanted a sense of community explicitly chose the development sites for that feature and those who wanted a more impersonal relationship with their neighbors chose single buildings which allowed for a more anonymous existence. For example, a single building resident stated:

> I think you get more involved in involuntary relationships in a communal life [i.e., in a development, or in a complex of buildings]. I think that is positive as well as negative, and for me it happens to be mainly negative . . . I like the sort of relationships that you can maintain with people in the city—I like sort of a combination of physical proximity with psychological distance.

In contrast, residents in the housing complexes spoke of enjoying a sense of community. In response to the question, "What is best about the place where you're living?," a Stuyvesant Town/Peter Cooper Village resident explained:

> Here I was very quickly, very easily able to not just meet people, but people that I really enjoy. And as my child grew up, he had friends immediately—there was no effort, because as soon as you are out on the playground, there are other children. He is part of an ongoing community. I think for New York City, establishing a kind of community is terribly important.

East Midtown Plaza residents spoke of a sense of community and cooperative activities:

> You get a flavor of community here, which is really incredible. It's wonderful. There are a lot of women like myself who are, let's say, older mothers who worked and are not just housewives. I really like the whole idea of the food co-op, the babysitting pools and just the feeling of community. I am very happy here.

## Implications

Communal facilities and a cooperative setting enhance residents' interactions. Individual buildings with no shared facilities allow residents to avoid undesired interaction with their neighbors. Designers should be aware of the consequences of both designs.

## CHILDREN'S ACCESS TO OUTDOOR PLAY FACILITIES

One of the most significant findings of the study was that fewer children in buildings with no on-site playgrounds (single buildings) were allowed to play alone outside than children from housing with such facilities (Stuyvesant Town/ Peter Cooper Village and East Midtown Plaza). The single-building children also had to be older than the development children before they were permitted to play outside by themselves. On weekends single-building parents spent more time both indoors and at the playground with their children.

Seventy-three percent of the residents in East Midtown Plaza said they allow their child out alone, compared to 39 percent of the Stuyvesant Town/Peter Cooper Village sample and only 14 percent of the single-building families. For the sample as a whole, the average age of children who were allowed out alone was 6.4 years old. Children permitted out alone at East Midtown Plaza were younger than at the other two sites (6.0 years old versus 7.5 years old).

Stuyvesant Town/Peter Cooper Village residents frequently spoke about how pleased they were that their developments' open space and playgrounds were separated from traffic and the general public's use. This comment from a woman living in Stuyvesant Town was typical:

> You can just walk downstairs and there are playgrounds. The kids can ride their tricycles through all the walks here; they are not on the streets. Here it's all enclosed; you can sit on a bench and they can run around the whole place, and you can still see them. You are not worried every minute they are going to dart out in front of a car.

East Midtown Plaza has one playground at street level which is open to the public and three small playgrounds at the second-floor level which are accessible only through the building. These interior play areas were extremely popular. They were intended for young pre-school children but because parents were hesitant to allow their children to use the public plaza playground, school-age children played in the interior areas as well. Children were allowed to play alone in the interior play area at a younger age than in the public plaza. Of the entire sample's children permitted to play alone outside, 19 were under six years old. Ninety-five percent (18 out of 19) were children permitted to play unsupervised in the East Midtown Plaza interior play areas. Only one child under six was permitted use of Stuyvesant Town/Peter Cooper Village facilities alone. East Midtown Plaza parents typically commented:

> I feel for the kids it is a great place, because my children have many friends right in the complex. They can go from floor to floor, at will. They can play on the second floor without feeling uptight about it. It is secure.

> We thought about a move to the suburbs but we have most of the advantages here of privacy and having independence from my five year old. She can go visit friends outside in the building and play on the second floor and I don't have to be with her all the time. I don't have to walk and sit in the playground, which I can't stand to do.

A very interesting finding is that single-building residents used the public play facilities at Stuyvesant Town/Peter Cooper Village and East Midtown Plaza. And East Midtown Plaza residents used Stuyvesant Town/Peter Cooper Village playgrounds. The developments' facilities were therefore serving not only residents but also people in the nearby neighborhood. A third of the single-building sample used East Midtown Plaza's public playground.

The question of public access to East Midtown Plaza's common open space and facilities was the most controversial issue in the development. The plaza was intended for the use of the surrounding community as well as the residents and therefore designed in an open, inviting way. Residents bitterly complained that undesirable outsiders intruded on the space. A locked fence was eventually placed across one of the entrances to the plaza to limit outsiders' access. Stuyvesant Town/Peter Cooper Village's open space and facilities are on private property; therefore access to non-residents is restricted. Over half the residents sampled there stated that this insular layout was good.

## Implications

Well-designed on-site playgrounds are essential for highrise housing with young families. The more private the facilities are, the earlier the age children will be permitted out alone. The findings indicate that highrise families would greatly appreciate and utilize many large, well-equipped, restricted-access play areas and that such playgrounds increase children's outdoor freedom.

The question of public access to housing development playgrounds is an issue that planners and designers must be sensitive to. Residents prefer their open space to be off-limits to outsiders; on the other hand, people in nearby housing without facilities need and use housing-development seating and play areas. The upkeep of the city's public playgrounds is of great importance. The better equipped and maintained the city's playgrounds are, the less the pressure will be for outsiders to use housing developments' play facilities.

## FLOOR HEIGHT

Floor height affected children's play. Ninety-two percent of the people on floors one through five said they could see their child outside from the apartment window, while only 50 percent on floors six and above said they had such visibility. Lower-floor parents more frequently allowed their children outside by themselves than higher-floor parents. Upper-floor parents spent almost one hour more with their children than lower-floor parents on a Sunday.

Upper-floor residents had less satisfaction with their development and reported apartment tension more frequently. However, they still preferred living on upper floors to lower floors. Eighty-five percent of the upper-floor sample generally preferred higher-floor living, but so did 65 percent of the lower-floor sample. People preferred upper floors for the views, the light, the quiet, and the safety. Lower-floor apartments were seen as undesirable because of their vulnerability to break-ins, dirtiness, and lack of views and light.

### Implications

The genuine advantages of lower-floor living for children's access should be publicized so that families with children can make an informed choice (if they have one) of floor location for a highrise apartment. With such knowledge, people may still give more priority to view, light, and safety. Designers should not therefore limit family apartments to lower floors but should provide a variety of alternatives. Lower-floor apartments should be designed to maximize their safety and view.

## APARTMENT DENSITY

Sample families in higher-density apartments had more complaints about space and privacy than those in lower-density situations.[8] Those with a density rating of 2 (four people in a two-bedroom apartment) or over had these complaints. High-density residents registered lower overall satisfaction with their apartments.

An additional bedroom is definitely the most needed space. When asked, "What would you use an extra 150 square feet for?," higher-density people said "another bedroom." Lower-density families gather in the living room or dining area whereas the high-density households used the parents' bedroom to gather because the living room or dining area was being used for a child's homework or play.

### Implications

The findings indicate that people living in high-density environments complained more but were not necessarily hurt by their crowded apartment living.

Because adults can escape their apartments, the effects of crowding are probably not as significant on adults as on children. Some studies have shown detrimental effects of density on children.

East Midtown Plaza, which had the lowest density of all the sites, includes two-, three-, and four-bedroom apartments. Although the bedrooms were small, they were highly appreciated and more important than additional space elsewhere in the apartment.

To avoid the possible detrimental effects of crowding and to keep middle-income families in the city, three- and four-bedroom apartments should be constructed.

## CONCLUSIONS

This study has illustrated the benefits of well-designed highrise housing for middle-income families. East Midtown Plaza and Stuyvesant Town/Peter Cooper Village were constructed under government subsidy programs for middle-income people. These programs no longer exist. Little urban multifamily housing for middle-income families is now being constructed. Middle-income families are on the waiting lists of housing developments like East Midtown Plaza and Stuyvesant Town/Peter Cooper Village for years and never get apartments. It is unfortunate that under the present national policy there is no hope that the type of housing represented by East Midtown Plaza and Stuyvesant Town/Peter Cooper Village will be built in the near future. Those middle-income population subgroups such as dual-career couples who prefer highrise apartments will suffer the most from the present national housing policies.

When highrise housing is once again constructed, it will hopefully incorporate the design features recommended in this study: on-site facilities, terrace play areas, outdoor galleries, community rooms, and three- and four-bedroom apartments. Well-designed and well-managed urban highrises not only provide an important and satisfying housing option for middle-income families, but also have a positive impact on family dynamics.

## NOTES

1. This research was funded under Grant No. MH 24795 and Grant No. 1 F32 MHO 5857-01 and -02 from the National Institute of Mental Health, United States Department of Health, Education and Welfare.

2. See: Adams and Conway, 1975; Becker, 1976; Becker, 1974; Cooper-Marcus and Hogue, 1975; Cooper-Marcus, 1974; Department of the Environment, 1973; Doxiadis, 1974; Fanning, 1967; McCarthy and Saegert, 1976; Mitchell, 1971; Morville, 1969; Newman, 1972.

3. Residents pay a small "down payment" (average $4,000 for the sample) which is like a security payment. When the apartment is sold, the resident does not benefit from the increased market value of the apartment; he or she receives only the "down payment" back.

4. The findings reported in this article are statistically significant. Analysis of variance, chi-square tests, and multiple-regression analysis were used in analyzing the data. A complete discussion of the research can be found in: E. Mackintosh, "The Meaning and Effects of Highrise Living for the Middle Income Family: A Study of Three Highrise Sites in New York City," a doctoral dissertation in

psychology, The City University of New York, 1982 (University Microfilms International, 82-12, 204).

5. People who grew up in apartments are another significant group who preferred urban living. See: Mackintosh, "High in the City," 1982.

6. D. Goleman, "Psychology is revising its view of women." *New York Times*, March 20, 1984, p. C1, and R.S. Albin, "Has feminism aided mental health?" *New York Times*, June 16, 1981, pp. C1 & C3.

7. For other study findings on husband-wife differences, see: Mackintosh, Olsen, and Wentworth, 1977.

8. Each household was given a density rating by dividing the number of persons in the family by the number of bedrooms.

## REFERENCES

Albin, R.S. "Has feminism aided mental health?" *New York Times*, June 16, 1981, pp. C1 & C3.

Adams, B. and J. Conway. "The Social Effect of Living Off the Ground." Occasional Paper, Department of the Environment Housing Development Directorate, London, England, January 1975.

Becker, F.D. "Children's play in multifamily housing." *Environment and Behavior*, 1976, *8*, 545-574.

Becker, F.D. and L.P. Friedburg. *Design for Living: The Residents' View of Multi-Family Housing.* Ithaca, New York: Center for Urban Development Research, Cornell University, May 1974.

City of New York. *Housing and Development Administration. City Mitchell-Lama Design Criteria.* Photocopied report, no date.

Cooper-Marcus, C. "Children's play behavior in a low-rise inner-city housing development." *Proceedings of the Fifth Annual Conference of Environmental Design Research Association.* Stroudsburg, Pa.: Dowden, Hutchinson and Ross, 1974.

Cooper-Marcus, C. and L. Hogue. "Design Guidelines for High-Rise Family Housing." Paper prepared for Symposium on Human Response to Tall Buildings sponsored by the American Institute of Architects and Joint Committee on Tall Buildings, Chicago, July 1975.

Department of the Environment. *Children at Play.* London: H.M.S.O., 1973.

Doxiadis, C.A. *Anthropopolis, City for Human Development.* New York: W.W. Norton and Company, 1974.

Fanning, P.M. "Families in flats." *British Medical Journal*, 1967, *18*, 382-386.

Goleman, D. "Psychology is revising its view of women." *New York Times*, March 20, 1984, p. C1.

Mackintosh, E. "High in the city." In P. Bart, A. Chen, and G. Francescate (eds.). *Knowledge for Design*, Proceedings of the Thirteenth International Conference of the Environmental Design Research Association. College Park, Maryland, 1982.

Mackintosh, E. "The Meaning and Effects of Highrise Livng for the Middle Income Family: A Study of Three Highrise Sites in New York City." Doctoral dissertation in psychology, The City University of New York, 1982 (University Microfilms International, No. 82-12, 204, Ann Arbor, Michigan).

Mackintosh, E., R. Olsen, and W. Wentworth. *The Attitudes and Experiences of the Middle Income Family in an Urban Highrise Complex and the Suburban Single-Family Home.* Report from the Center for Human Environments, The City University of New York, 1977.

McCarthy, D. and S. Saegert. "Residential Density, Social Overload, and Social Withdrawal." Paper presented at Eastern Psychological Association Conference, April 1976.

Mitchell, R. "Some social implications of high density housing." *American Sociological Review*, 1971, *36*, 18-29.

Morville, J. *Children's Play on Flatted Estates.* (English Summary) Copenhagen: Statens Byggesorsknings Institut, Report # 10, 1969.

Newman, O. *Defensible Space.* New York: MacMillan, 1972.

U.S. Department of Housing and Urban Development, Office of Low Rent Public Housing. "Housing Assistance Payments Program—New Construction, Proposed Rules." *Federal Register*, Vol. 39, No. 224, Part II. Washington, D.C.: U.S. Government Printing Office, November 1974.

# PART II

# Planning for
# the Unsheltered Woman

With the "unsheltered woman" defined according to four categories (singles, single parents, working wives, and elderly), her lifestyle can be examined and her housing requirements determined, thus forming a gender-conscious approach for planning. Clearly, the needs of all these women for housing overlap to some extent, and certain criteria apply to all four groups; children, however, are a distinguishing variable. The checklist below is a summary of these needs. It provides a framework for developing specifications for housing that would be more responsive to the needs of women within these categories.

## SUGGESTED CHECKLIST FOR GENDER-CONSCIOUS HOUSING[1]

WOMEN OF ALL FOUR GROUPS REQUIRE:

- housing located in safe, well-serviced neighborhoods;
- housing near safe, reasonably priced transportation;
- housing with access to shopping and other services;
- dwellings arranged to relieve housekeeping burdens; and
- dwellings containing flexible spaces to be used according to lifestyle.

WOMEN WITH CHILDREN REQUIRE:[2]

- housing in neighborhoods with child-oriented services;
- housing in close proximity to work places;
- dwellings with family-related amenities;
- dwellings with kitchens designed for more than one worker; and
- dwellings with adequate private space for parent(s).

---

1. Although items are arranged by category, many items are interchangeable.
2. Included are female heads-of-household and women in dual-career families.

WOMEN WITHOUT CHILDREN REQUIRE:[3]

- housing designed to accommodate sharing;
- housing incorporating security measures; and
- dwellings having safety features for the elderly.

In this section, several authors demonstrate attempts to meet these needs. They examine actual designs as well as the political and social process involved in articulating gender-conscious planning in the past, present, and future. Looking at retrospective approaches, Gwendolyn Wright, of Columbia University, discusses how social values concerning home, family, and domestic life influenced nineteenth- and twentieth-century domestic architecture (Chapter 9).

Next, Dolores Hayden, of UCLA, outlines how some women, who she labels "material feminists," had visionary designs for homes, neighborhoods, and cities. She emphasizes their repeated efforts to employ cooperative and intergenerational organization to accomplish the domestic tasks of daily living (Chapter 10).

Two articles about the efforts of contemporary women to influence domestic architecture and community organization follow. Jacqueline Leavitt, of UCLA, discusses the lifestyle and concerns of modern, single parents, reviews selected European and American examples designed to meet their needs, and tells of her participation in a pioneering project of the Bergen County (New Jersey) League of Women Voters aimed at developing intergenerational housing through conversion of a suburban dwelling (Chapter 11). Complementing this work, National Congress of Neighborhood Women leaders Ronnie Feit and Jan Peterson tell about the poor and low-income residents of urban neighborhoods (Chapter 12). Firmly endorsing intergenerational housing, they include additional information about a broad range of exemplary housing activities being planned and executed across the country. Of particular interest is their discussion of a current program to develop a national women's agenda.

Turning to solutions for another population group, the low-income single person, architect Michael Mostoller provides a comprehensive survey of historical solutions for dwellings for this group (Chapter 13). He demonstrates the use of boarding houses, rooming houses, and apartment hotels, outlines their features, and calls for the incorporation of many of these into modern housing. Clara Fox then argues that shared housing of one form or another is the only way to provide affordable units in urban areas (Chapter 14). Of particular interest are Fox's and Mostoller's discussions of the Mini-Dwelling Unit (MDU), an arrangement recently devised by the Single-Room Occupancy Task Force of the Settlement

---

3. Included are single working women and elderly women with income ranges between $4,000 and $10,000.

Housing Fund. Both Mostoller and Fox claim that the MDU employs the benefits of multifamily living while retaining some attributes of the private dwelling. Characterized as a 105 square-foot room containing a small kitchen and a bed/sitting area, an MDU shares a bath and the building's corridor space for public uses. In some variations, it could feature a dining facility and full desk service for security purposes. The controversy surrounding this innovative plan concerns its treatment in the housing code, to which it does not conform.

A final contribution to the discussion about housing of the single person came from Lenox Hill Neighborhood Association's Celine Marcus (Chapter 15). Her presentation illustrates the work of the former settlement house and chronicles major changes in public-sector perspectives about acceptable senior-citizens housing.

In Chapter 16 Jane Margolies, a former seminar member, summarizes some plans for rehabilitating and renovating buildings. She observes that these projects designed by several seminar members are creative, yet surprisingly conservative. She also traces the influence of two architectural trends on the designs. One is a redefinition of the overall conception of the dwelling exemplified by the HMX-1 created by Santa Barbara architect Barry Berkus for *Housing* magazine. Its preeminent feature is its flexibility. Conceived as new construction, this 1,200 square-foot unit is designed for clustering on a site (7 to 20 units per acre). It contains two bedrooms separated by an open living/dining/kitchen space, an additional separate office-bedroom, three bathrooms, a loft, and three decks. A variety of family types could be satisfactorily housed with such a plan. Its costs, however, place it in reach of the middle and upper income consumer (Exhibit II.1a-b).

The other is the re-arrangement of specific functional rooms. Columbia University architect Susana Torre's kitchen project is one example. This kitchen enables more than one worker to prepare meals by employing open shelving displaying equipment and multiple work spaces to facilitate this process. Another is found in the East Midtown Plaza and Phipps Plaza West. There architect-developer Lynda Simmons took laundries out of the basement and placed them on an upper floor with a play and snack area adjacent, thereby making a dreary task more pleasant and promoting socialization potentially joined with child care (Exhibit II.2).

Following these studies, seminar members were divided into teams and asked to devise their own architectural plans. They were given access to multifamily units drawn from the city's stock of *in rem* (condemned) housing. They defined their clients and then drew up design and implementation plans for suitable dwellings. They were limited to rehabilitation and renovation of existing buildings and could not suggest new construction. These plans are summarized in Chapter 16.

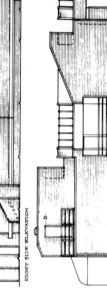

Elevations and floor plans HMX-1

FRONT ELEVATION

REAR ELEVATION

RIGHT SIDE ELEVATION

LEFT SIDE ELEVATION

SECTION

HOUSE ELEVATION

PATIO · CARPORT ELEVATION

UPPER LEVEL

LOWER LEVEL

Exhibit II.1a-b: Elevations and floor plans, HMX-1

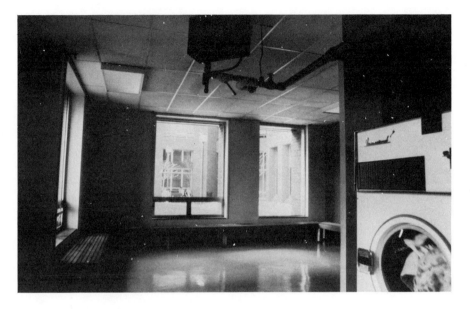

Exhibit II.2: Phipps Plaza West has the laundry on the first floor adjacent to other communal and play spaces.

# 9

# Women's Aspirations and the Home: Episodes in American Feminist Reform

## Gwendolyn Wright

When a Boston kindergarten association of the 1890s published a pamphlet to promote their school for young immigrant children, they included a parable about a large family of poor immigrants who lived in a crowded, filthy tenement apartment. The father was a shiftless drunkard and the mother was a listless poor soul. One day a settlement-house worker took two of the children to a kindergarten class, and at the end of the day, they were given a fresh flower to bring home. The mother was touched and placed the flower in a glass on the windowsill; then she realized that no light could penetrate the grime. Inspired by the beauty of the flower, she cleaned the window, which made her realize that the entire apartment was dirty and disheveled. Later that day, when her husband came home from the corner tavern, he was so startled by the sparkling cleanliness and order that he vowed to stop drinking and get a steady job. Which of course he did—and they all became successful, as well as healthy and honest, American citizens.[1]

This parable reflects the belief in the extraordinary power of domestic environments to bring about social change, a recurrent theme in countless American reform movements among not only kindergarten advocates, but also union organizers, anti-Communists, back-to-the-land health enthusiasts, New Deal planners, and feminists.[2] In fact, different generations and classes of American feminists have often defined the changes they envisioned in terms of housing. In these many and various roles, women have played an important part in the changing market for housing. Especially in the twentieth century, women have formed lobbying groups which influenced governmental policies at both local and national levels. Again and again, they seized upon certain kinds of housing as part of a problem that concerned them—and as part of the solution. This has been true of women who wanted work outside the home and of those who wanted better homes, even very traditional homes, for their families. (Some women, of course, wanted both.)

In so doing, these women were concerned with more than architecture. For instance, these concerns encompassed the role of government to provide certain social services or to direct the economy; the definition of a good family life; the possibilities for upward mobility; the benefits or dangers of mixing different classes, races, or ethnic groups; and the complex relationships of women and their homes, encompassing paying for the dwelling, cleaning, and beautifying it, making a pleasant place for family life, and being able to leave it for work or other activities outside the home.

Such women, in very different ways, were exploring their definitions of what kind of housing was best for women. I would like to present some particular occasions in the American past when different kinds of women took hold of housing, defining what they wanted, and sometimes redefining what their houses should look like. In doing so, I will tie these historical deliberations to some current issues about women and housing.

The awareness that housing often does not meet women's needs has become quite acute recently. This has led to several contemporary positions about what a "feminist architect" would pose as an alternative. One approach is to focus on the specific needs of single parents or women living alone—the groups that have been most neglected in the "traditional" view of home and family and whose numbers have been rising so dramatically that they can no longer be seen as marginal. Taking these women into account should be an imperative for developers, governmental agencies, and local planning boards. But the fact is that many of these women reject the idea of special buildings or projects designed specifically for their situation. Sometimes they see this situation as temporary, and sometimes they simply resent the idea of being segregated from what they still consider "normal life." And it is in that "normal life" of neighborhoods that women have, at least in the past, most effectively organized around housing issues.

This raises the question of whether a separatist feminist architecture can solve women's particular problems. Acknowledging these women's preferences, while trying to promote new solutions to the problems they encounter, represents a crucial dilemma for feminist thought and action. Yet there is great diversity within this group: some choosing to work; some wanting part-time work, perhaps at home, in order to be with their children; some choosing to remain single; others hoping to marry or remarry. A single new feminist ideal cannot meet all their needs. Nor should feminism try to impose a single model. The very idea of a stamp of approval for "feminist architecture" tends to overlook or rule out those who do not fit into clearcut modern categories, much as women who did not fit the mold of the young suburban mother were neglected in the past.

Another aspect of the feminist approach to architecture is the condemnation of the suburban single-family house as a trap. Who was behind this plot? Why are so many men (and women, too) so attached to their private havens? These questions are well worth asking, but the answers are not simple. Still, it has become routine to brand suburban houses as stifling places for women, places where they never had the means to express themselves, except through decoration and child-bearing. While the critique certainly has validity, it has led many women to resent feminism, believing that it rejects outright their value of home and family. In addition, this argument ignores the extent to which women have not been entirely passive in choosing these homes, the extent to which the stereotypes are simply too facile.

A third approach to the problem would be not to look for an architectural solution (or risk architectural moralism), but instead to focus on ways in which women can decide what they want, in the present and future, for their homes and families. This would, of course, raise the issues of consumer pressure, of class and neighborhood constraints, which inevitably influence these images. However, if we focus on the social and political goals which often underlie architectural taste, it is possible to circumvent the problem. One way to grasp the relationship between social goals and formal preferences is to understand how certain groups of women tried to take an active role in housing debates at times of major social and economic change, to analyze what kinds of housing style they endorsed. This focus on the past will hopefully suggest ways of responding to the present, and especially to the heated debates about home and family one hears so frequently from all sides.

Women's involvement with housing has, unquestionably, become politicized again of late, on the right and on the left. Both the "new progressives" involved in community organizing and feminist rights and the "New Right" who clamor for stabilizing the family and the neighborhood see the political potential of "family issues." But this stance is not entirely new. Nor is it simply concerned with different notions of the good family and the ideal home, both of which imply different roles for women. Women's efforts to organize around home and family issues inevitably raise larger social and political issues. When looking at earlier instances of such organizing, some crucial questions become clear: When did political forces motivate these domestic issues? How did advertising influence ideas about home and family? What biases and what strengths came from the orientation around home and family? And finally, how did these women's organizations try to influence both the housing market and governmental policies, and when did they succeed?

## THE CULT OF DOMESTICITY EXPRESSED IN
## NINETEENTH-CENTURY ARCHITECTURE AND DECORATION

My first example concerns the expression of style, taste, and personal identity in the home, supposedly the woman's domestic sphere but obviously also the realm of interior decorators and writers, many of whom were women. There are historical roots to the idea that one's home is the prime form of self-expression; it is a personalized statement about the family as a group of individuals, as members of a class, an especially emphatic declaration about the woman's personal taste and her abilities as a wife and mother. These connections began to be discussed in architectural treatises and builders' brochures in the decades after the Civil War. Before this time the individual house had been quite important, of course, but the individualized style of the dwelling had not received much special attention. Styles for houses followed rules—academic standards for particular revival styles or folk traditions for regional and national styles.

In the late Victorian period, the ornament for dwellings, even the simplest of workers' dwellings, became more and more elaborate; likewise, the layout of rooms broke away from earlier foursquare plans to look more like picture-puzzles. In theory, each house, and especially each suburban house, laid out on its own plot of land was unique: the irregular outlines revealed the occupants' search for individuality and their interest in functional design—or design to bolster certain "domestic functions." Each bay window, porch, and other protrusion was considered evidence of some particular activity taking place within: it made the space exactly right for playing the piano, sewing, reading, or tending a hot stove—whatever some member of that family did in a certain special place.[3] Closets and storage rooms provided for a larger number of possessions, while a music room, nursery, or library, even in quite unpretentious houses, suggested the period's growing obsession with children and culture.

The names of these many rooms—hall, sitting room, parlor, pantry, larder— were a further statement about family life and, quite often, about women's roles in the home. The overwhelming majority of these rooms and niches pertained to female activities, though some builders showed an interest in masculine spaces, including one who described an attic "growlery" where the husband could withdraw from the domesticity of the womenfolk.

According to the housing guides, often published by women decorators like Harriet Prescott Spofford, Mary Elizabeth Sherwood, or Ella Rodman Church, each detail of a dwelling, inside and out, revealed both the personality of a particular family and the virtues of family life as an institution. The architecture as well as the decor was anthropomorphized.[4] It supposedly represented particular people and also the particular cultural form of the very privatized nuclear family, which many Americans of the time considered God's chosen universal living arrangement.

Most of these female authors considered the family to be in danger, threatened by such social forces as urban crime, urban poverty, generational conflicts, a declining birth rate, and the unchristian avaricious values of market capitalism. They wanted the vivid, emphatic domestic symbolism of American houses to counteract these forces. In this hope they were naive and archaic, but they were also deeply worried about the quality of family life—and especially the quality of women's lives.

These sentiments and the structures used to embody them created a special world for middle-class women. With the expansion of the suburbs and the elaboration of the suburban home, familiar concepts of the cult of domesticity became popular: home as the man's refuge, the woman's protection, a place of peace and inspiration, a reward for diligence and thrift. This vision became more than abstract images. But neither the architecture nor even the suburban setting alone could insure the desired tranquility and moral uplift. It required the mother's presence. In the late-nineteenth century, middle-class children spent much of their time at home and few years at school. The mother was responsible for education, as well as character training and social skills; the home was the principal place for every aspect of this training.

And the mother, in turn, needed a parlor. Here the housewife and mother would show off the family's best possessions, striving to impress guests and teach her children about universal principles of beauty and refinement. She displayed her own handmade creations, or "household elegancies," which might include crocheted lambrequins, handpainted cabinets, shadow boxes, rustic furniture, or arrangements of dried flowers. Here too were the "artistic" pieces she had purchased: sculpture casts, vases, and bric-a-brac. However, the balance was rapidly shifting toward items purchased from a store or catalogue, for writers on interior decoration gave these the official stamp of art, which captured the refinement and culture that the middle-class woman and her home were supposed to encourage.

The irony is abundantly clear. In theory, these bucolic homes were retreats from commercialism and industry. Yet it was new technology—factories producing furniture and artwork and ornaments for façades, printing presses turning out books and magazines, all handsomely illustrated with model rooms and elevations—that made these dwellings look the way they did. This was the woman's realm, where she supposedly had the power to create an environment that looked the way she wanted and could raise her children with the values she admired; and yet, more and more, the belief that style could play a major role in home life left these women in awe of approved styles. Consumerism intensified the rhetoric of domestic values, while it undermined those values. Female interior designers were hired by department stores in the late 1880s to set up model rooms and advise clients. They favored an abundance of such rhetoric—and an abundance of household objects for the parlor. As one female decorator put it, "Provided there is space to move about, without knocking over the furniture, there is hardly likely to be too much in the room."[5]

In an effort to make her home an alternative to the commercial world, the housewife had become a diligent consumer. Perhaps hoping to spread beauty in American homes, and thereby to increase the respect given them, woman decorators became stylistic dictators, intimidating their readers and clients rather than encouraging their self-esteem. As authors and as readers, these women succumbed to the illusion of architecture as higher meaning, in and of itself—as per-

sonal triumph and social resolution—and lost, at least partially, the willingness
to accept variations, mistakes, or the changes taking place around them.

## WORKING WOMEN AND THEIR HOMES

There are a number of important precedents for something we are very aware
of today: women demanding better homes *and* better working conditions outside
the home. Rather than choosing between these two worlds, some women related
these two sets of needs.

One instance involved early twentieth-century industrial towns where employers were beginning to put into place what was just coming to be called
"welfare capitalism." The employer provided certain services—notably those
related to home and family—as well as better working conditions in an effort to
have a more stable, healthier, less rebellious work force. Programs for company-built and financed homes, as well as courses on home economics and industrial training, were organized by these companies and their "welfare departments" or "social secretaries" or "social engineers," who were usually trained
home economists or sociologists. They worked mostly with women—whether
these women were the wives and daughters of employees or workers themselves.

One well-known American experiment in welfare capitalism took place
through the National Cash Register Company in Dayton, Ohio. In 1892 the
president of the company hired Frederick Law Olmsted, Jr., together with a
group of sociologists and home economists, to build a combination clubhouse
and employee school, called the House of Usefulness. Here workers and their
families attended classes in hygiene and physical fitness, homemaking and child
care, and domestic and manual arts, all designed to counterbalance the exacting
demands of their jobs. The focus of the classes was on better homes and followed
the advice of social workers like Albion Fellows Bacon, who wrote, "Those who
are seeking the conditions of highest efficiency in the shop will find some of the
most important of them in the home."[6]

These benefits proved to be inadequate curbs against union activity, however,
and the NCR workers organized a strike. This is not just a simple story of the
workers seeing through the ploys of their employers. Many of the women workers' demands had to do with their homes, with the new ideas of home life they
had discussed in classes and read about in books. Their articles on housing, published in reform magazines like *Cosmopolitan* (it was a very different magazine
then), document this reaction.[7] In the course of learning ways to improve and
modernize their domestic interiors, these women began to insist that the company
help them have better, cheaper, healthier houses. In arbitration during the strike,
the president of the company agreed to provide to approximately half the work
force, company-built housing, available for sale or rent at a price well below the
market rate.

In due time, the employer benefited from this program, too. NCR advertisements showed pictures of this "Workers' Arcadia," as one commission on industrial conditions called the town. Moreover, the sociologists and managers used the housing program to enforce one of their beliefs: married women should not work outside the home. They provided housing for single female employees and for married women, as the wives of NCR employees. Management was able to enforce this preference through their choice of eligible households for company-built and financed housing. So housing itself, as architecture or even as financial assistance, did not in the end fully accommodate these women's needs; both the new homes and the program could be used to limit the opportunities available to working women.

## THE RISE OF MUNICIPAL HOUSEKEEPING
## AND THE "MODERN WOMAN"

During this same period, urban and suburban middle-class women were also becoming involved in defining grassroots housing policies, promoting reforms for their block, their neighborhood, and their city, in a diverse movement known as "municipal housekeeping." This was a time when increasing numbers of women entered the labor force, either as professionals or as clerks, saleswomen, typists, or service or factory workers. Middle-class women who did not hold regular jobs—and few of those who were married continued their employment—often spent a great deal of time working as volunteers in charity or civic organizations, campaigning for the National Consumers' League or their local women's clubs, lobbying for reform legislation, particularly for better working conditions for women and children, or securing neighborhood parks and municipal health services.

These women still considered domestic issues their primary concern—partially from a deep commitment to home and family, partially because this was defined as their appropriate sphere. But now, as Frances Willard explained the change, the mission of the new woman was "to make the whole world homelike."[8] Domestic problems were no longer the province of individual housewives; they required collective action. Every part of the city needed public services that supplemented the housewife's diligent work in her own home. These services ranged from garbage removal to construction inspection to public health nurses. Women demanded these public services through civic organizations, woman's clubs and home economics courses.

As today, there were fierce debates about whether participation in these public activities would destroy the family, or whether the rise in non-domestic activities for women was a positive response to changes taking place in American family life, a way of adapting the family and the individual to new conditions. Critics were irate and numerous.[9] Higher education for women came under attack, since college-educated women led these movements. Furthermore, they often did not marry (it being harder to continue a professional career), and when they did, they had one or two children at most. Women's clubs and volunteer social services, such as the Visiting Housekeepers and Visiting Nurses, also came under the gun, for they seemed too collective an approach to domesticity.

Even architecture seemed part of the conspiracy—or the key to the solution for those who favored women's right to work outside their homes. The modern, simplified bungalow and apartment, too, won praise from many "modern women" because they were easier to clean and therefore required less time. They also praised the new, more standardized façades, asserting that the trend would reduce competitive individualism. In rebuttal, critics of the "new woman" charged that the "labor-saving bungalow" and, especially, the apartment building—a "promiscuous [and] dangerous" institution where so many services were centralized and so much conventional suburban space reduced to the minimum—would encourage women to abandon private domestic life.[10]

Such criticism, although it may seem facetious today, was widespread, even in architectural circles. One architectural magazine declared in 1903 that "a woman who lives in an apartment-hotel has nothing to do. Her personal preferences and standards are completely swallowed up in the general public standards of the institution. . . . She cannot create that atmosphere of manner and things around her own personality, which is the chief source of her effectiveness and power."[11] Another zealous architect told a national housing conference that "it is a shortcut from the apartment house to the divorce court." Yet these same architects often designed apartment buildings, and the magazines published them. They were really criticizing social change, not architecture.

Despite such outcries, large numbers of women came together in clubs and lecture halls to discuss modern approaches to housing and their relationship to women's lives. The early home economics movement was the center of this popular feminist reaction, calling for better housing in the suburbs and inner cities: housing that was healthier, more practical, simpler, more economical, and more attractive. In courses at the University of Chicago, Marion Talbot, Sophonisba Breckinridge, and Edith Abbott advocated an approach to the new discipline of sociology. (Founded in 1892, this was the first university sociology department in the country, and home economists taught in this department for almost two decades.) Their approach was concerned as much with the real situation of women, families, and housing as with abstract theories of socialization. Linked with other reformers in the Chicago area and around the country, they opened their teaching to the community through night school classes, correspondence courses, and special lectures in technical schools, high schools, and even elementary schools. Their great emphasis was the need for improved housing: this meant more effective housekeeping, equal roles for women, and a new understanding of the many forces—commercial and political—influencing supposedly "private" home life.[12]

The key to civic progress, these women believed, was not simply the right housing, even if it was designed by women, but the collective action of an informed public. Women could not depend on experts or professionals to make all the decisions for them. Except in the case of women's suffrage, Talbot never believed wholeheartedly in progressive legislation, for instance. As she pointed out, legislation was too often written to benefit commercial rather than public interests, and written in a style that was too distant, too incomprehensible for the ordinary woman or man to realize this injustice. Participation, she contended, was the only way to have ongoing reform in housing and in women's lives.[13]

However, participation takes time and, even more, the ability to accept and incorporate varied opinions. This is often frustrating. And so the expansion of expertise, including feminist expertise, eventually overruled this commitment to participation. Experts like Christine Frederick, writing in 1910, claimed to be above fads and social biases and to speak for everyone when announcing standards for house design and social stability.[14] But she was not a lone charlatan. Everywhere scientific management triumphed over popular participation. Home economists began calling themselves "household efficiency experts" and "household administrators," imitating the experts who reorganized factory work. They set out to teach all American girls and women the "one best way," in the words of Ellen Richards, to clean a floor or vacuum a rug, which products to buy, and how to keep good accounts, rather than suggesting that there might be problems with the organization of the house and the household, ranging from commercialism to exaggerated sexual division of labor.[15] They now set out to perfect the way the house was run, rather than to encourage their students and readers to ask questions about housework and city management. Women were taught to follow the expert's advice and assured that this would liberate them, rather than to challenge assumptions about the home.

In an effort to rise above politics and political dissent, women's clubs, home economics departments, and other progressive women's groups interested in home and family actually turned away from their initial commitment to questioning and improving women's lives, inside and outside of their various homes. The appeal of expertise had dramatic, far-reaching effects—effects that are not, unfortunately, dissimilar to the current trend toward a disciplinary rigidity and isolation in today's women's movement. Expertise assured jobs for professionals; it depoliticized housing, especially median-income housing; but it took the wind out of a highly diversified, publicly oriented feminist reform movement.

## THE BETTER HOMES MOVEMENT

Later in the 1920s, there was another surge of interest in protecting home and family. Better Homes in America was founded in 1922, under the auspices of Mrs. William Brown Meloney, editor of *The Delineator*, a women's magazine of fashion. When her organization began setting up committees across the country to talk about housing issues, Herbert Hoover's staff in the Department of Commerce quickly called his attention to their success; it was agreed that Better Homes clubs would be the ideal means for spreading Hoover's theories about rationalism in home construction and traditionalism in home life, among the favorite ideas of the Department. Hoover sent over 1,000 copies of the *Zoning Primer* and agreed to serve on the advisory council of the Better Homes club. He soon became president of the organization and convinced Vice-President Calvin Coolidge to sit as chairman of the advisory council.

Within a year, Better Homes in America had branches in over 500 communities and headquarters in Washington, establishing even closer ties to the government and especially to Hoover's Department of Commerce. By 1926, there were more than 1,800 local committees; and in 1930, over 7,000.[16] They kept busy sponsoring builders' workshops, home-improvement contests, prizes for the most convenient kitchen in town, model house tours, and lectures on how good homes build character. Residents came together to discuss zoning, beauty, the Communist menace, adolescent problems, and racial strife—each of which could supposedly be helped through higher standards for the dwelling and the family life it sheltered.

The main force of the Better Homes movement was these local committees. Although the national headquarters and Hoover's Department of Commerce wanted to control this grassroots organization, there was actually a great deal of diversity among the local groups. Some, such as the one at Santa Barbara, advanced architectural controls through review boards, hoping to attract business and wealthy residents with soothing Spanish Colonial Revival. In one year, this committee sponsored 30 model homes, all in the same style. Other committees were equally interested in particular local reforms, and sometimes in groups outside their middle-class base. Home-remodeling campaigns were aimed at black families and white industrial workers, assuming that more attractive homes would encourage character development and upward mobility among the poor. The Hampton Institute, Tuskegee, and other black colleges offered special programs in home economics and remodeling in conjunction with their local, white, Better Homes committees. Even Indian reservations, mill villages, and Appalachian mountain settlements became the objects of improvement drives.

But it is worth noting that almost no attention was paid to multiple-family dwellings, and therefore to the larger cities, for the organization emphasized suburban, single-family homeownership. Architects of the 1920s helped define this ideal home with their suburban houses, ranging in price from expensive Tudor estates to the diminutive designs—stock plans available for $5 per room—of the Architect's Small House Service Bureau. (The Commerce Department also enthusiastically backed this program.)

Moreover, the social hierarchies of race, class, and ethnicity were rigorously supported in the Better Homes endorsement of the many residential building controls which proliferated during the 1920s. These included zoning ordinances preventing work places in residential communities and restrictive covenants preventing the sale of property to Jews, blacks, Mexicans, and Asians. Members of Better Homes clubs usually worked closely with real-estate brokers, pro-zoning urban planners, and business interests, as well as with other moralistic interests like the churches, the American Legion, and the Boy Scouts.

What does this quasi-ideological architectural movement of the 1920s tell us? Like the New Right today, members of Better Homes clubs used "family issues" as a key part of their moralistic and political campaigns to upgrade the country. They too recognized the political potential of a focus on home and family, rather than economic issues or foreign policy. They organized their strategies outside traditional party politics, but they worked with other similar organizations to force the political structure to address many of their goals. Thus not only does the private housing industry affect governmental decisions about residential construction and home financing, constantly intervening to streamline and rationalize, but so, too, do other private groups which have social and moralistic goals behind their campaigns for an ideal home, rather than purely economic aims.

While organizations like Better Homes in America were, for the most part, exclusionary, racist, and reactionary in terms of sex roles, this movement successfully defined and captured a political base *because* of its focus on issues—essentially those relating to protecting home and family—that are *not* inherently reactionary. After all, you can be concerned with what is happening to your neighborhood without being racist; and you can want to have a detached house without accepting a misogynist view of sexual differences. Many concerned Americans seem to have accepted this line of argument about the nature of housing and family issues, however, associating these concerns with reactionary politics. This has essentially been a matter of accepting Better Homes in America's definition of the ideal home, as formulated in the 1920s.

## THE POST-WAR SUBURBAN MOVEMENT

Finally, I would like to take up one more aspect of the history of women's roles in determining, or accepting, particular notions of the ideal home. This is a more familiar example: it involves the generation who moved to the suburbs after World War II, and also their children, many of whom cannot afford adequate housing today—even if they are having to change their definitions of what is adequate. In this case, government, builders, commercial interests, and social scientists put together a rather limited vision of what a good community was, as well as a very restrained and stereotyped image of the good home and good family. But it has come to seem as if this generation, especially its female component, chose the suburbs freely and completely, as if the houses really responded almost perfectly to their needs and desires at the time. We need to understand how and by whom the suburbs were defined.

In the postwar suburbs of the late 1940s and 1950s, the government took a definite stand, endorsing zoning to prevent multifamily dwellings *and* insisting that no single-family residence with an FHA mortgage could have facilities that would allow it to be used as a shop, office, preschool, or rental unit. This was obviously a strategy to prevent women from working—except for doing their own housework or "hobbies." That seemed a way to stabilize property values on this government investment, and to stabilize family life in the process. It is also important to note that "neighborhood character," in FHA terms, depended on overt policies of ethnic and racial segregation.[17] Thus, discrimination against minority groups went hand-in-hand with the effort to reinforce stereotypical housewife-and-mother roles for women. Until 1968 FHA officals still accepted unwritten agreements and existing "traditions" of segregation as part of their mortgage-guarantee investigations. There was, as yet, no statement regarding the officially endorsed zoning ordinances that kept out not only lower-income people, but also potential jobs for women and potential income for these families when they grew older and retired. (In fact, the American Association of Retired Persons, working with the Washington planner Patrick Hare, puts changes in these zoning ordinances at the top of their political agenda, for they recognize that the ability to rent out a unit or set up an office may be the only way for a retired household to stay in the same house.)

Nor was it only the government and the speculative developers who tried to strengthen the "traditional suburban family." Social scientists studied what they called the "average family" in the suburbs, and psychologists published "livability studies" that correlated the domestic environment with statistics on crime and family stability, constructing a pseudo-scientific defense of the belief that good family life was only possible in the suburbs. Here one could have what the Cornell sociologist Glenn H. Beyer, a specialist on housing, called the "family centered plan," a perfect fit for wholesome family living.[18] Architects like Richard Neutra and Eero Saarinen endorsed such "scientific analyses" of family activities and values, claiming that these studies formed the basis of their suburban home designs.

Popular magazines polled readers about what kinds of houses they wanted, though of course their sample was scarcely representative of the whole country; the results were used to buttress the idea that anyone who wanted an apartment, or even a "used house" was abnormal.[19] The house that received *all* the attention in magazines like *McCall's*, *Saturday Evening Post*, and *Parents* was an open-plan, suburban dwelling invariably inhabited by young children, their housewife mother, and their commuting father. The epitome of this "close-fit" approach to design and sociology was the family room (first called the "don't say no room") or the multi-purpose room) and the patio, which became the focal points of the ideal suburban home.

Some critics did notice the homogeneity of the suburbs, the uniformity of class, age, and dwelling type that seemed to undermine individuality—again reflecting a belief in the extraordinary power of the home environment to mold character. There was also a morbid attention to the danger of environments that were almost entirely female, at least in terms of the adult population most of the day, but only because this could lead to "domination by the little woman," as one psychologist put it in *Newsweek*.[20] So women were even criticized for the living conditions they had not themselves planned.

To try and involve women in helping builders and architects design houses, the Housing and Home Finance Administration held a Women's Housing Congress in 1956. The event lasted one day and brought together 103 white, middle-class suburban housewives to represent all American women. They *were not*, in fact, very satisfied with the housing choices available to them, contrary to what the builders and administrators expected. One woman, for instance, contended that the suburban house took its toll on women by giving them no place for privacy. "Fewer would go to our mental wards and divorce courts," she pleaded, "if they had one room, even a small one, just for themselves."[21] (Such women were not yet reading Virginia Woolf, yet they sensed a problem she had also evoked.) These women were talking about problems that were more complex than architecture, of course; these were problems about social expectations and the constraints of sex roles. But they posed these problems in *architectural* rather than social terms.

The reports of the Congress found the anger and frustration all very charming, reducing the women's criticism to female psychological characteristics and harping, rather than real expressions of dissatisfaction, even in such a uniform group. There is, in fact, a striking parallel with later Presidential attempts to set up a national congress on "the family" (Carter's was later changed to a more pluralistic "families") so as to create the impression of popular idealism and support for governmental policymaking. In both cases there was very little opportunity to have an effect, despite the disquieting evidence of a great deal more diversity and discontent than many had expected.

Although this example of a group of women trying to influence the design of suburban homes was clearly stillborn, it still has some implications. For the effort and its lack of effect perpetuates the belief, still quite widespread, that there is little opportunity for most of us to do anything about housing. By and large, we tend to accept the premise that most people are satisfied with what they have and how they live, that they certainly were satisfied in the past, and that change—when it does occur—comes only from the government or from the housing industry choosing to act and impose changes.

This sense of impasse relates directly to a limited image of the "ideal home" as either a fixed institution or, from time to time, a radical new prototype adapted to new circumstances, but not really very popular or appealing. The tyranny of our desire for a close, intimate *fit* between our houses, our neighborhoods, and our dominant cultural values leads to a romanticism about certain kinds of residential life. Often architects and the general public hold to a different formal vision, but hold the same professed goals, and curiously, the same belief in a fit. The forms seem perfect—because they seem to fit with, and therefore to reinforce, good families and harmonious communities. To question the architecture is to undermine the cherished values. To have a different kind of architecture than the one romanticized is to render the values inoperative or, at best, superficial.

This good or bad fit is one of the numerous myths about suburban life. The myth is connected to a widely held belief that in the past the ideal home was a shared concept and a comfortable "fit," involving little of today's frustration. I hope I have made the point that this was never true, not even for different groups of housewives. It is possible, as a final word, to look beyond artificial architectural solutions; to see and to embrace, in the present as in the past, varied efforts to take social problems in hand; and thus to recognize the power—and the limits—of domestic architecture.

## NOTES

1. Marvin Lazerson, *Origins of the Urban School: Public Education in Massachusetts, 1870-1915* (Cambridge, Mass.: Harvard University Press, 1971), p. 215.

2. For an expansion of this idea, see my *Building the Dream: A Social History of Housing in America* (Cambridge, Mass.: MIT Press, 1983).

3. One typical example of this approach is found in the works of the amateur architect Eugene C. Gardner of Springfield, Massachusetts, such as *Illustrated Homes* (Boston: James R. Osgood, 1875), *Home Interiors* (Boston: James R. Osgood, 1878), and *Homes, and All About Them* (Boston: James R. Osgood, 1885).

4. See, for example, Ella Rodman Church, "City Interiors," *Godey's Lady's Magazine*, vol. 108 (May 1884), 488, in which she likens the parlor to "the *face* of a house—the most notable part—and that from which visitors take their impression of the whole."

5. Harriet Prescott Spofford, *Art Decoration as Applied to Furniture* (New York: Harper & Bros., 1877), p. 222.

6. Albion Fellows Bacon, *What Bad Housing Means to a Community* (Boston: American Unitarian Association, 1910), p. 78.

7. "For Best Ideas on Organization of Home, $500 . . . By Fifty Young Women, Compiled by a Committee," *Cosmopolitan*, vol. 27 (June 1899), 167-71.

8. Frances Willard, *How to Win: A Book for Girls* (New York: Funk & Wagnalls, 1886), p. 54.

9. An example is Theodore Roosevelt's articles in the *Ladies Home Journal* and his book *Foes of Our Own Household* (New York: George H. Doran, 1917).

10. "Apartment Hotels in New York City," *Architectural Record*, vol. 13 (January 1903), 90.

11. See my *Moralism and the Model Home: Domestic Architecture and Cultural Conflict in Chicago, 1873-1913* (Chicago: University of Chicago Press, 1980) for a more extended discussion of these reformers.

12. See, among many other works, Alice Ravenhill and Catherine J. Schiff, ed., *Household Administration: Its Place in the Higher Education of Women* (New York: Henry Holt & Co., 1911); Marion Talbot and Sophonisba Breckinridge, *The Modern Household* (Boston: Whitcomb & Bar-

rows, 1912); and Isabel Bevier, *The House: Its Plan, Decor and Care* (Chicago: American School of Home Economics, 1904 and succeeding editions).

13. Marion Talbot, "Housekeeping in Relation to Social Progress: Influence of the Development of Science upon a Progressive Housewife," delivered before the Farmers' Institute in 1899, reprinted in *The House Beautiful*, vol. 14 (July 1903), 119-21.

14. Christine Frederick, *The New Housekeeping: Efficiency Studies in Home Management* (New York: Doubleday, 1912) and *Household Engineering: Scientific Management in the Home* (Chicago: New School of Home Economics, 1915).

15. Ellen H. Richards, *Euthenics, the Science of a Controllable Environment* (Boston: Whitcomb & Barrows, 1910) and *Sanitation in Daily Life* (Boston: Whitcomb & Barrows, 1910).

16. James Ford, "Better Homes in America," *Better Homes Manual*, ed. Blanche Halbert (Chicago: University of Chicago Press, 1931), p. 743.

17. *Planning Profitable Neighborhoods* (Washington, D.C.: U.S. Government Printing Office, 1957).

18. Glenn H. Beyer, *Housing: A Factual Analysis* (New York: MacMillan, 1958) republished as *Housing and Society* (New York: MacMillan, 1965).

19. *Urban Housing Survey* (Philadelphia: Curtis Publishing Company, 1945), p. 11; *The American Woman's House of Tomorrow* (New York: McCall Corporation, 1945).

20. Henry A. Davidson, cited in "Living Atop a Civic Mushroom," *Newsweek*, vol. 49 (April 1957), 40.

21. "These Women Are Talking About You," *House and Home*, vol. 9 (June 1956), 140.

*10*

# Designs from the Past for the Future

Dolores Hayden

Susan B. Anthony, the most tireless and practical of all American suffragists, was always challenged about her views on the future of the American family. Her critics asked if she believed the traditional Victorian family form would survive in the twentieth century; if she supported free love; if she worried that women who were feminists would have to live alone all their lives; and if she thought women with paying jobs would have to choose autonomy and career over family. To these queries, Anthony had a very strong answer: "Away with your man-visions! Women propose to reject them all, and begin to dream dreams for them-selves." This article is about women who dreamed dreams of their own about home, family, neighborhood, and city. Although it deals with the years between the Civil War and the Great Depression, the story holds significance for planners and policymakers dealing with the present and the future.

## THE MATERIAL FEMINISTS: THEIR THEORIES

The era between the Civil War and the Great Depression was a time of great debates about what was considered "women's work." This work included cooking, cleaning, shopping, child care, and nurturing—tasks essential to peo-ple's daily lives. This work was done by women without pay, and it was done in isolated homes.

Feminists of this era offered a critique of this work which involved spatial and economic analyses. First, they pointed to the problems of the traditional ar-rangement of women's work. A housewife worked alone at home, apart from public life. Even with model children and husband, a woman could have little impact on public life. Additionally, the traditional arrangement of domestic work made it extremely difficult for single men and women to have satisfying home lives; they were forced to live in residential hotels or in single rooms as boarders. Second, these feminists addressed the problems of women who were employed but still had to come home at the end of the day and do a second shift as housewives. They recognized that these were not only individual problems but also larger social and economic problems.

Finally, feminists in this era extended their critique to housing and urban planning issues. They pointed out that one cause of high housing costs was that each dwelling had to be a complete work place in which all domestic tasks could be accomplished. (The Victorian home was really a bakery, lodging house, laundry, and restaurant all in one.) In addition, they said that devoting so much space to private homes was done at the expense of public space. In this, they were echoing earlier transcendentalists like Henry David Thoreau, who had asked: "What's the use of a house if you don't have a decent planet to put it on?" and Ralph Waldo Emerson, who asked: "Does our housekeeping raise and inspire us or does it cripple us?"

Most of the women of this era who worked on these issues are still relatively unknown. In this article, they are called "material feminists," for they demanded a complete transformation of the economic basis of housework and of the spatial design and material culture of American society, a "grand domestic revolution." They called for the socialization of housework and child care under women's control. They recognized the economic and social value of their many skills as housekeepers and mothers, and they felt these skills should be the basis of their economic and political equity in society. They wanted men to recognize that these skills constituted half of society's productivity.

In their beliefs, the material feminists had much in common with labor unions of their era and communitarian socialists of the nineteenth century. The material feminists' demand for the socialization of housework and child care under women's control echoed labor's campaigns for workers' control in factories and offices. The material feminists believed, as did Uriah Stevens, founder of the Knights of Labor, or William Silvis, founder of the National Labor Union, that if workers could get together and reorganize the necessary work they did in a fair and humane way, the country would have better cities and a better national economy.

The material feminists also shared beliefs with American communitarian socialists who built more than 100 model towns between the late 1780s and the 1860s. The material feminists were interested in applying some of the ideas of the communitarian socialists, not to model towns on the frontier, but to the construction of American suburban and urban neighborhoods.

Despite similarities to both groups, the material feminists were unique as social reformers and made significant statements about the problems of a growing industrial nation. For this reason, their innovations deserve to be studied and understood, both as socialist and feminist theory, and as pragmatic proposals for housing and urban design.

## COOPERATIVE HOUSING SCHEMES:
## MELUSINA FAY PEIRCE, MARIE STEVENS HOWLAND,
## AND MARY LIVERMORE

Among the more striking proposals of the material feminists were schemes for cooperative housekeeping as advanced by Melusina Fay Peirce, Marie Stevens Howland, and Mary Livermore. They conceived and executed experiments to share household tasks. These programs aimed to reduce female isolation, to increase domestic efficiency, and to liberate women from routine, repetitious tasks.

In Cambridge, Massachusetts, in 1868, Melusina Fay Peirce organized 40 households to perform domestic work cooperatively. The groups rented a building in Harvard Square where the women installed the most advanced machinery for baking, cooking, laundry, sewing, and the sale of groceries. The idea was to have the women work together to produce cooked food and clean laundry, to deliver those products to their homes, and to charge their husbands for their services.

Peirce presented the philosophy behind "cooperative housekeeping" in a series of articles in the *Atlantic Monthly*. The articles described how the principles of producer and consumer cooperatives could be extended to women's work. Peirce took inspiration from some of the commercial developments of her day. She saw that the pre-Civil War tasks of the housewife which included baking, churning, sewing, caring for children, and washing clothes were being replaced by commercial enterprises, such as laundries and restaurants, where specialized equipment was used to serve large numbers of people. Peirce believed that if women could organize themselves to take control of this new machinery, they could gain economic independence for themselves.

Peirce took these arguments and turned them into a proposal for the reorganization of urban space. She proposed that families live in kitchenless houses, four to a block, and that every 36 households be united in a cooperative housekeeping district where all of the domestic work would be carried on with the latest machinery and according to the advances in the specialization of labor.

Peirce's experiment, which received tremendous opposition as well as tremendous theoretical acclaim, lasted only three years. Perhaps one of the most telling comments was made by a man whose wife tried to join the organization. He exclaimed: "What? My wife 'cooperate' to make other men comfortable? No indeed!"

Some of Peirce's ideas were taken up by Marie Stevens Howland. A contemporary of Peirce, Marie Stevens Howland had worked in the mills at Lowell, Massachusetts, from her early teens. She became involved with social reform movements in New York City and was associated with Stephen P. Andrews and other reformers who promoted ideas of free love, sexuality, and Fourierism. Howland soon became interested in issues of child care as they related to the transformation of home and family. She travelled in the early 1860s to France where she visited the *Familistère*, a housing complex for 350 iron workers and their families created by Jean-Baptiste-André Godin, Fourier's leading disciple in Europe. The *Familistère* included a restaurant and day-care facilities for the children of the community so that women as well as men could be employed outside the home.

Upon her return to the United States, Howland attempted to reproduce some of these reforms. Like Peirce, she was a critic of the isolated household: "Have the most perfect, isolated family possible," she argued, "it cannot supply the conditions for integral growth to the young, nor can it afford sufficient leisure and freedom from care to adults." Her solution was cooperative housekeeping and scientific child care. She developed a plan for an entire city of kitchenless houses with common housekeeping units and complete child-care facilities. Although she gained many supporters for her city of kitchenless houses, she never was able to build it.

Another material feminist, Mary Livermore, gained so many supporters for her ideas that a substantial number of experiments following her principles were executed. Like Peirce and Howland, Mary Livermore advocated cooperative housekeeping. However, Livermore offered a more rationalized version of the passionate enthusiasms of her predecessors. Not only did she synthesize their views within the structure of a capitalist society, but she also provided practical proposals, not utopian schemes.

A minister's wife, Mary Livermore helped set up battle kitchens and local aid societies to supply soldiers during the Civil War. After the war ended, she devoted herself to the cause of suffrage, travelling across the country and delivering lectures. In this work she urged sympathizers to use their energy in reorganizing their towns' housekeeping, a device which would free them for political work.

A woman of tremendous organizational talents, she wanted to apply the managerial and technical advances of her time to domestic work through housewives' cooperatives. She adopted this posture for defensive as well as political reasons. She believed that if women did not organize domestic work, men's businesses would do so by taking domestic tasks from the home in their effort to develop new products. This would result in further exclusion of women from paid work.

Sixteen families in Warren, Ohio, formed a community dining club which flourished between 1903 and 1923. They brought their dining furniture and dishes to a building in the center of town and drew lots to see where each family would place its dining table. Each family paid a fee per week for these meals. They hired female domestic economists to help run the organization and to do the cooking. Back in the abandoned private dining rooms many women set up offices for the national suffrage campaign.

## THE RISE OF SCIENTIFIC HOUSEKEEPING: ELLEN RICHARDS

Industrialization and urbanization shifted the focus of reformers away from promoting small-scale cooperative housekeeping efforts toward addressing broader economic and social issues. They became active in the slum reform efforts in industrial cities in the late nineteenth century. This work encompassed a range of activities including improving domestic food preparation by applying home economics techniques to menu planning, creating efficient public kitchens, and developing cooperative meal preparation schemes. While these efforts were focused on the poor, later middle- and upper-income groups adopted many of the methods under the rubric of "scientific housekeeping." Activists in this reform movement generally were highly trained professional women. They included Ellen Richards and Charlotte Perkins Gilman.

Ellen Richards, the first female graduate of MIT, was also the first of her gender to join the MIT faculty. As a scientist, she was interested in using the latest technology to improve the living and working conditions of the poor. She translated this interest into setting up public kitchens for workers' families. Her goal was to deliver the maximum amount of nutritious food at the lowest cost. She established six public kitchens. These kitchens, modeled after MIT laboratories, were exemplary for their spatial organization and use of sophisticated cooking and weighing equipment.

Richards believed that the principles involved in the public kitchen belonged not only in cities and were not only for the poor. For the 1893 Columbian Exposition, she showed how such an institution could fit into a suburban neighborhood. Her "Rumford Kitchen" was a scientific nutritional laboratory, disguised as a small, white clapboard house complete with an inviting front porch.

Richards's greatest influence was perhaps on the settlement house movement of her era. Jane Addams, founder of Chicago's Hull House, installed a public kitchen in the residence to serve women of the community as well as the settlement house workers. Others soon followed suit. In fact, Hull House and other settlements came to represent a prototype of the material feminists' ideals for community living. Over the years, the Chicago residence added to the public kitchen a common dining room, meeting rooms, and kitchenless apartments for the resident workers.

## BEYOND SCIENTIFIC HOUSEKEEPING AND COOPERATIVE HOUSEKEEPING: CHARLOTTE PERKINS GILMAN

A visitor to Hull House, Charlotte Perkins Gilman became the most successful and influential material feminist of this period. Synthesizing the ideas of previous reformers, she reached a broad audience by linking the then-popular ideas of evolution with theories about home and motherhood. At the base of her thinking was social Darwinist theory that held that evolution would help to free men and women. Turning this theory around, Gilman said that free women were essential to evolution. In her public speaking and writings, including *Women and Economics*, Gilman extended this thought to practical examples.

Gilman's most important convert was Ebenezer Howard, the founder of the British garden cities movement. She persuaded him to consider the "cooperative quadrangle" (an arrangement of garden apartments with tiny kitchenettes and a common tenants' dining room set in a landscaped setting) as the heart of any new residential scheme. Howard placed six of these projects in his garden cities and then boasted that he had freed women from unnecessary household labor. These plans, however, were never as widely adopted as Howard and Gilman envisioned; financiers of the garden cities insisted that the traditional household be the basis of at least 95 percent of the units.

An American architect, Alice Constance Austin, was also drawn to Gilman. In 1914, she created a design for a community in California which featured kitchenless houses and an underground network of electric trams to carry cooked food and laundry from a central facility in the city to the basement of each house. While quite utopian, her scheme reflected Gilman's belief that the home should be a place where a woman could rest; therefore all possible technologies were to be used to push the work activities away from the home.

Gilman influenced another American architect, Rudolf Schindler. In 1922, he and his wife, Pauline Schindler, a former Hull House resident, designed a cooperative dwelling for five adults in Hollywood, California. Since his clients were involved in professional work, Schindler devoted most of the interior space to large individual studios and placed little sleeping lofts on open porches on the second floor. The glaring fault in this plan lay in the organization of the first floor. As he assumed that only women would work in the unit's kitchen, the kitchen could be reached only through the women's workplaces.

## THE COORDINATION OF WOMEN'S INTERESTS:
## ETHEL PUFFER HOWES

The most sophisticated of these material feminists was Ethel Puffer Howes. A broadly trained, thoughtful scholar, Howes was educated in philosophy at Harvard and taught for several years at Simmons and Wellesley before she turned to developing feminist programs for the modern, educated woman. She believed that while suffrage had been won, basic questions of career and homemaking could not be resolved by the ballot. Consequently, she founded the Institute for the Coordination of Women's Interests at Smith College in 1926. Aiming to pursue practical solutions for gender-related issues, she brought the best intellectual talent to the Institute. Sociologists well versed in the changing shape of the family and its implications, housing experts familiar with innovative housing schemes in the United States and Europe, and historians conscious of the contributions of communitarian sociologists to community life contributed original studies, surveys, and data.

Drawing on their expertise she forged a broad and sophisticated program incorporating producer and consumer cooperatives, commercial activities, and cooperative services to meet the needs of contemporary working women. Among its components were a cooperative nursery school run by professional child-care specialists assisted by parents; a community kitchen which delivered dinners to families with working mothers; and a placement service for women wishing to return to the work force after raising their families. In addition, she taught a freshman course at Smith College dealing with the dilemmas faced by educated women blending careers and families.

She wrote extensively about these programs and ideas, arguing that housework as it was then conducted was a "sweated industry." Writing for popular women's magazines, such as the *Women's Home Companion*, and more scholarly journals, such as the *Atlantic Monthly* and the *Journal of the American Association of University Women*, she encouraged American housewives to form new kinds of organizations to deal with problems of domestic work.

In the few short years of the Institute's existence, Howes's accomplishments were substantial, especially in light of the powerful anti-feminism that emerged in the United States in the 1920s. At this time there was a severe backlash against feminism and its challenge to the traditional forms of work and homelife. In fact, some conservative groups inspired by that era's Red Scare began to associate feminism with Soviet communism. There were many women's anti-suffrage groups, such as the Women Patriots, whose journal, *Woman Patriot*, was dedicated to the "defense of the family and the state against feminism and socialism," who attacked the movement. Not only reformers, but many middle-of-the-road women belonging to such groups as the Young Women's Christian Association or the American Home Economics Association had to defend themselves against charges of being Bolsheviks and "taking their orders" from Alexandra Kollontai, former Commissar of Public Welfare in the Soviet Union.

After the late 1920s, many strains of material feminism were lost in the upheavals of the Depression and World War II. The massive suburban movement of the postwar period featuring the American dream house, which had for the woman a Bendix washer and a nice stove and for the man a huge grassy lot which he could landscape, is the subject matter of another article. Suffice it to note that disillusionment with the following years of suburban domesticity would rise as feminists such as Betty Friedan questioned the system that relegated women to lives dedicated to duplicative, routine chores in an isolated, single-family house.

## SUMMARY

It is important that the material feminists anticipated some of the problems which would crop up in the mid-twentieth century; their visions bear many lessons for today's reformers. These lessons include an appreciation of the limitations as well as the contributions of the material feminists.

Starting with the limitations, today's feminists should note that despite all their innovation, the material feminists did miss some important issues. First, they did not always try to get men to participate in their organizations on an equal basis. Although it may seem strange to contemporary audiences that the nineteenth-century activists did not want to involve men, these feminists felt women had very valuable skills which they should hold on to and which should be the basis of their economic equality. The same argument suggests why the nineteenth-century women's movement made family a feminist issue (and why the feminist movement in the last 10 or 15 years has had such a hard time making family a feminist issue). However, none of the cooperative groups and organizations spawned by the "grand domestic revolution" actually included examples of housewives using the strike as a logical weapon of labor organization.

Second, the material feminists underestimated the problem of competing with big business. Mary Livermore warned women about male-dominated business organizations which sought to expand into the areas of manufactured goods and services for the household, but she was not able to prepare feminists for the pressure from major corporations, such as members of the National Association of Manufacturers, to abandon their ideals. In addition, women found they could not compete with big business unless they organized women's labor in ways which were not egalitarian.

This led to the third problem. The material feminists often underestimated the problems of gender as they cut across race and class. Although the material feminists did not come from upper-class backgrounds themselves, they represented relatively well-educated and politically conscious elites. Women like Charlotte Perkins Gilman thought that housing could be run as a business by female entrepreneurs with feminist high-school graduates in domestic science washing the bathtubs and cooking the meals. What she forgot was that the women washing the bathtubs might have children and husbands too. Clearly, female elites cannot solve the problem of women's work unless they solve it for all the less-skilled and less-advantaged women as well. In the Soviet Union, China, Cuba, and Sweden, female elites have made the same mistakes; this issue is not so much a question of the overall economic structure of society as one of combining awareness of gender with awareness of race and class.

Women can do better than the grand domestic revolution in the next several decades. There are many developments on the side of reform that could lead to a more egalitarian family life and a more egalitarian society. In the last 10 or 15 years, for example, men have recognized their ability to nurture, a phenomenon which will play a significant part in any solution. More and better technologies have been developed that can be applied to the household. And people have a greater awareness of how to use and how not to use technology.

The point is not to replicate the past. Not only are there flaws in the approach of the material feminists, but today's world is different. Modern feminists have to look at the whole complex of activities that go on in the home and all the socially necessary work that women do. For example, women do more shopping and chauffeuring than in the past. They help with service agencies like boards of education and hospitals. In fact, they undertake a range of activities called "women's work" which is really the glue that holds life together. Food is not necessarily the enormous problem that the Victorian reformers thought it was; private industry with its provision of fast foods has alleviated some parts of this issue. However, daycare is still a significant problem. Since there are fewer children, there are fewer teenage daughters and unmarried sisters to take over the daycare if the mother is not doing it herself. These are but a few of the challenges that face today's feminists.

Many people think the problem can be solved by getting men to do half. However, this solution is questionable because there are too many households without men, and the record has really been rather poor in terms of men's actual participation.

I believe that the material feminists do have an important message that will assist in the forging of a new future for the modern woman. This lies in the material feminists' common appreciation of space as a key economic and social issue. They taught us that we must go beyond the architecture of gender inherited from the last century and embodied in the American dream house built for the patriarchal family. Their goal, and mine, is to move toward a dream of an American city which is perhaps close to the vision that Walt Whitman had in 1856 in his "Song of the Broad Axe": "Where women walk in public processions, in the streets the same as the men, where they enter the public assembly and take their places, the same as the men, where the city of the faithfulest of friends stands, there the great city stands."

In talking about the reorganization of home, neighborbood, and city, we are talking about Whitman's city of faithfulest friends—a new urban form. That conception recalls the words of a pragmatic reformer, founder of the Dining Club and many other political organizations in the 1890s. She really captured the spirit of the grand domestic revolution when talking about the transformation of the family. She said simply: "I know the thing can be done, and I ache to do it."

## NOTE

This article is drawn from Dolores Hayden, *The Grand Domestic Revolution; Feminist Designs for American Homes, Neighborhoods, and Cities* (MIT Press, 1981). All quotations are contained therein.

## *11*

# The Shelter-Service Crisis and Single Parents

Jacqueline Leavitt

"Mary Worth" is a nationally syndicated comic strip in which Aunt Mary, a white-haired older woman, gets into capers and offers advice and a strong shoulder when friends and relatives find themselves in trouble. The summer 1982 episodes featured Karen, an attractive, white, single parent in her late twenties or early thirties. Karen works in a publishing firm. She and her six-year-old son, Chad, live in a two-story, attached modern dwelling surrounded by trees and lush plants. When Aunt Mary comments on how nice the apartment is, Karen says "I try to do my best to provide a wholesome environment for Chad."

In the process of editing a book, Karen finds the illustrations of children are not accurate. When she suggests that her son serve as a model, the artist, Jeremy, invites them to his loft. Jeremy criticizes Karen for not taking Chad to the zoo, and she explains, "The lifestyle of a single parent doesn't leave much room for 'field trips'." In the last frame, Karen says, "Many times I'm forced to make a very difficult choice, between being a good parent . . . or a good provider."

The strip is noteworthy because single parents have not been a staple of the comics.[1] More typical subjects are nuclear families with children, such as in "Dennis the Menace" or "Blondie," or married adults, such as Andy Capp and his wife Flo. However, the single parent portrayed in the Mary Worth comic strip is not entirely representative of the single-parent population.

Nevertheless, Karen's professional status and race do not entirely shield her from problems that single parents face.[2] She is caught between work and parenting and has no spare time. Karen's occupation may be white collar, but it does not follow that she is well off. If she is like most single-parent women, it is likely that Karen will be a tenant for life and that her housing conditions will be more deficient than the average.

Inadequate housing is a major problem among single-parent households, par-

153

ticularly those headed by women. For the single parent, poorly serviced neighborhoods compound shelter problems. This chapter is concerned with the shelter-service crisis facing the average single-parent family. It argues for the need to view housing and services as a package. It describes the population of single parents and the problems they face and reviews some of the experiments taking place in Europe and America to alleviate shelter-service problems. Finally, it offers a proposal for a flexible housing unit that can be shared.

## SHELTER-SERVICE SUPPORT SYSTEM

To begin with, shelter is a necessity. Plumbing, electricity, heat, and ventilation are requirements of shelter; they are essential to health and human development. Housing is more than shelter; it provides space and an environment to meet a variety of human needs. It has room and facilities for basic activities like eating, cooking, washing, and sleeping; it satisfies psychological needs for privacy and quiet; finally, it accommodates activities like working, entertaining, playing music, and caring for children.

Most people operate their homes as self-service systems. Unlike the affluent who can pay for maids, housekeepers, hairdressers, valets, and babysitters, people generally do their own housework, maintenance, child care, and grooming. Each dwelling is a service container where all these necessary activities take place.

For single parents this service container presents severe problems. These problems stem from the fact that a single parent has a low income and is the sole adult in the household. Basic housing costs are high so that a home is expensive to maintain on one income. In addition, it is much harder as the sole adult to perform all the household tasks as well as the child rearing. The on-site services that single parents have to provide are time consuming and demanding. Because of her low income, the average single parent cannot purchase services on the marketplace.[3]

The predicament of single parents regarding housing and services is greatly affected by the neighborhood in which they live; hence, the importance of viewing housing and neighborhood as a package. A neighborhood that is a positive support system is rich in private and public services, including a variety of food, clothing, shoe repair, stores, cleaners, library, movie theatre, bakery, child-care center, senior-citizens center, and churches. In such a neighborhood, a single parent can carry out many tasks affecting the home. The neighborhood can provide even more support for a single parent if jobs are available locally. In the working-class community of Williamsburg in Brooklyn, New York, women who hold jobs in the local credit union (which they organized) are able to walk home in minutes, leaving enough time to prepare meals and supervise children.[4]

In contrast to the denser neighborhood in the city or at its fringes, where everything is accessible by foot, there is the suburban neighborhood with a shopping center located miles away, reached only by car. Furthermore, since the shopping center contains only those magnet stores that developers think will attract shoppers, several stops outside the center have to be made in order to complete errands. With all this travelling in the car, a woman has a more difficult time balancing multiple roles of housekeeper, mother, and worker in the paid labor force.

## VIEWS OF SINGLE PARENTS: A LEGITIMATE HOUSEHOLD TYPE

This article is based on the belief that the single-parent family is a legitimate household configuration. This is not by any means a universal belief. Information about single-parent families is often based on the assumption that this household type is somehow deviant. Studies have called such families "broken," "disorganized," or "disintegrated."[5] Even recent research confirms that despite gains made in thinking about women's marital status, feelings of unworthiness among female single parents persist. The single-parent family is yet to be accepted as a legitimate and permanent, rather than temporary, household type, despite the fact that about 30 percent of the single parents remain single.[6]

Not surprisingly, there is little data available about housing and single parents.[7] U.S. Department of Housing and Urban Development (HUD) reports provide some information, although the thrust of *Housing Our Families* is that single parenthood is a temporary condition.[8] The most extensive study on housing and single parents, sponsored by HUD, is *The Impact of Family Changes on Housing Careers* by Martin Rein and his colleagues.[9] This study is useful because it analyzes both men and women as singles and as "solo" parents, but it acknowledges that little is known about "solos."[10]

Within the group of single-parent families, there are differences not only of gender but of race, marital status, age, education, and income. Where possible, this paper recognizes these similarities and differences. This, however, is not always easy, because many studies treat single parents as a homogeneous group. Indeed, a problem in formulating a long-run strategy which would be responsive to the shelter-service needs of single parents is recognizing the differences within that group.[11]

### Some Similarities and Differences Among Single Parents

Despite differences, internal group identification might develop among single parents because of similar needs and constraints that appear to cross class lines. Some of these needs and constraints can be traced to the fact that the overwhelming number of single parents are women. This is not to argue that women are a class in themselves, but that becoming a single parent places most women in a singularly disadvantaged position with limited resources. Becoming a single parent through separation or divorce, the middle- and upper-income woman suffers a severe setback in finances and usually movement out of the family home. Most single parents move two or more times, especially in the years immediately after a breakup.[12]

However, regardless of the similarities among single parents, the reasons for not coalescing are also strong. Feelings of self-esteem may differ substantively among divorced, separated, widowed, and never-married women. These differences may be compounded by differences of race, and not offset enough by pervasive discrimination against women in general. Even though a woman may "fall" from a high income status, her race and education—"relative privileges"—may make her feel better or act as if she is better than other single parents.[13]

Policies of the state may further fragment single parents as a group. The state does not have a stake in fostering coalitions which in turn may lobby for expenditures for public services and assisted housing. Playing on differences, the state legitimizes some non-nuclear families, creating tiers of worthy single parents and unworthy ones. Given the history of public policy, this division may occur along racial lines and serves to further fragment this group.

Simultaneously, other parts of the state may act in ways that bring single parents together. In the past year, at least two cities, Baltimore and New York City, have held hearings on the needs of families with children. Most directly affected in this category are single parents who may face quadruple discrimination because of race, gender, income, and presence of children.[14] The hearings give visibility to the issues involved and serve to organize if not the actual constituency then the constituency's advocates.

There are also housing options under consideration by planners, designers, and builders which although not specifically oriented to the single parent may ultimately benefit them. California and New Jersey have sponsored affordable housing competitions to encourage creative designs and financial packages. Architects have sponsored competitions before, calling for "modest homes" at the turn of the century, and for "compact homes" more recently. In Europe, competitions in Sweden and the Netherlands have also been held. England has some examples of housing and child care exclusively for single parents, the results of advocacy work by a divorced parent, Nina West. This type of single-parent interest group politics around housing could develop in the United States.[15]

## WHO SINGLE PARENTS ARE

In 1980, 5.34 million of the nation's 30 million families with children under

18 were headed by women, 600,000 by single fathers. Single-parent families comprised 19.5 percent of these housholds. The decade of the 1970s saw a tremendous increase in single-parent formation, particularly among women. The number has nearly doubled since 1970. As of March 1980, 92 percent of the 12 million children living with one parent were with their mother.[16] It is that group of women which will be described further.

By 1979, there had been a 12 percent increase in family formation since 1970, a 51 percent increase in female-headed households, and an 81 percent increase in mothers with one or more children in the home (alternatively referred to as female householders). From 1970 to 1979 the change by race for these households with children under 18 at home increased as follows: 76 percent of all whites (26 million) from 8 to 14 percent; 85 percent for blacks (3.7 million) from 31 to 45 percent; and 92 percent for Spanish origin (1.9 million) from 15 to 22 percent.[17]

Single parenthood is more likely to be created through divorce, separation, and having children outside marriage than through widowhood. Of the possibilities, divorce is the primary reason for one-parent families, and divorce ratios are climbing among both blacks and whites, with a higher rate for black women. By 1979, one out of every two female householders had either never been married or had terminated the marriage by divorce.[18] As dramatic as that finding is, even more startling is the fourfold increase among both blacks and whites in never-married mothers from 1970 to 1979.

The median age of female-headed households with children still at home is younger than the overall population of women maintaining families. In 1982, 82 percent were under 45 years old; although white female households with children under 18 at home declined in median age, from 50.5 in 1970 to 43.7 years in 1979, they were somewhat older than black (38 years) or Spanish-origin (36 years) householders.[19]

Along with this change in median age has been a decrease in the proportion of female heads of households who did not finish high school. There was a high rate of growth for those with some college, but the difference by race is still evident. As of 1979, a majority, 55 percent, of the black women were *not* high school graduates compared to 37 percent for whites.[20] This has repercussions in terms of acquired skills that can be used in the paid labor force and is reflected in disposable income.

The 1978 median income for all female-headed families was $8,540, with white women having a median of $9,910 compared to $5,800 for black women and $5,580 for those of Spanish origin. The presence of children drops the median income for all races to $7,040, and the younger the children the lower the income. In 1979, of 9.8 million children under 18 living in families maintained by female householders, the total number of children under 6 years was about 2.4

million. Of families with children, the number of children under 6 years per family was higher for blacks (1.30) and Spanish origin (1.36) than for whites (1.20).[21]

The low income of single-parent families is a primary constraint in purchasing housing or other services. The census reports that "a woman with no husband contributing directly to the family income can expect to have only $1 for essential expenses to every $2 available to most families."[22] There is ample proof that lower income is a characteristic of women without a marriage partner or co-habitant.[23]

Very few women find their standard of living rising as a result of becoming a single parent. Rein's study of singles and "solos" found that even among those single parents who seem to be better off, and indeed are living in more decent conditions, problems persist. Existing housing does not always fit the new marital status. There may be too much space, particularly after children leave home, or, in trading down to reduce expenses, there may be a shortage of space and concomitantly a loss of privacy. The study found at all social-class levels that a divorced woman who stayed in the home she had shared with a husband "has committed herself to a higher housing standard than is normal at her income level." And, "her housing status may be superficially the same, but she sees things 'sliding downhill' and knows that the world will soon see this as well."[24]

Clearly, black and Spanish-origin women who have less income and fewer resources than white women suffer severe housing problems. Constrained by their lower level of education and the presence of more children under six, all factors which affect their child-care arrangements and ability to work full time, these minority single parents are more likely to be renters and to be living in public housing.[25]

Single parents experience more than average economic stress, and, as a result, their housing arrangements are often less than satisfactory. This can be said of low-income women with children who are forced to negotiate the publicly subsidized housing and service institutions, as well as newly divorced, middle-income women who cannot rely on ex-husbands and turn to service agencies or lower their housing status. However, given the differences among single parents, particularly around the relative degree of comfort experienced by white women, it is presumptuous to draw a conclusion about class identification. Much more would have to be known about the actual conditions in which single parents live, and more critically, about how they see themselves and their marital status (temporary or permanent, voluntary or involuntary), and their relationship to other single parents and to other female householders of a different color. This question transcends the subject of single parents; the significance of race, class, and gender in analyzing issues and predicting political and social outcomes is debated among scholars and activists and has only been touched upon here.

## THE HOUSEHOLD ECONOMY AND PARENTING

The needs of women who are single parents are similar to those of women in two-parent families; in both groups they are identified with certain tasks and they experience economic discrimination. However, the former face particular burdens and hardships. Of all the services in the household, the most time consuming is childrearing. For example, the well-known fact that the tasks of the housewife increase with the number and ages of her children has recently been documented in a study of about 1200 families in the Seattle area to show that a childless household requires 35 hours of work a week while a household with four or more children requires 62 hours.[26] The single parent who has no husband to share in some tasks and responsibilities of child care and household work must bear this load herself. Although child care is not the only need faced by single parents, it is the most serious because it impacts on virtually everything else, from finding a job, to keeping a job, to selecting transportation, to having a social life.[27]

### OTHER NEEDS

For the single parent, choosing where to live is weighted between being a good mother and having a social life. Some may select the same area as when they were married. Others may move because of varied reasons. They may be uncomfortable with their unmarried status and seek environments which make "fewer demands on their time and . . . have better supportive services, such as the socializing facilities . . . child care services . . . the lack of yard work and the reduced commuter time."[28]

The psychological effects of being a single parent include feelings of loss in making multiple moves or living insecurely.[29] Moving under any conditions can be nervewracking; it is much harder for single parents. The absence of another adult also means there may be limited opportunity for receiving emotional support. Many single parents feel extreme isolation.[30]

### THE SHELTER-SERVICE OPTION FOR SINGLE PARENTS: SOME EXAMPLES

There are ways to alleviate the problems facing single parents. A central problem is that single parents (as well as others) lack a supportive community housing environment. Leaving aside the question of whether this housing option should be conceived as permanent or temporary (an unanswerable question until the potential constituency works out the details in the planning, designing, and financing process), there is evidence that supports alternative housing predicated on sharing and including services other than shelter.

The concept of on-site services in buildings is not new. Planned unit developments have provided a variety of services, including the spa, tennis court, and golf course, usually on a fee basis. Sometimes the motivation for including services comes from an architect or developer; other times it is friends and individuals who come together and form an association. In Tappan, New York, an association of professional people with many children rejected the isolated subdivision house and designed and built an alternative.[31] After surveying the needs of each family, the group divided a 32-acre site into lots and reserved three acres for recreation facilities and meeting rooms. Each family had to volunteer at least one day a week for construction, working about 1,000 hours over a 30-month building period.

Shelter-service complexes are not new to Europe where there has been "more response to particular needs of population subgroups. Sweden has "service/ houses," or "collective houses" that provide child-care and cooked food service, and Denmark "refuses to build housing developments without communal facilities."[32]

However, even in this country some hope for a change can be found in housing and community development groups who have been responsive to the shelter-service crisis among female householders. In Hayward, California, for example, Eden Housing estimated a new market from a sizable turnout of single parents at general community planning meetings. Thus, in their project they included facilities such as a tot lot, laundry, and a communal building.[33] Some groups have adapted existing housing for sharing. A Philadelphia-based organization surveyed 21 group residences and discovered that "almost two-thirds of the households were located in single family houses rather than in apartment buildings."[34]

## THE SHELTER-SERVICE HOUSE:
## A CASE STUDY

In November 1981, the Bergen County (New Jersey) chapter of the League of Women Voters applied European and American precedents for shared housing to the design problem for a shelter-service house. The chapter embarked upon this project because it had become increasingly aware of the developing housing problems of two primarily female groups: single parents and the elderly. Its housing education and advocacy program, funded by the U.S. Department of Housing and Urban Development, was besieged with requests from them. Single parents were looking for affordable housing; the elderly needed a means of reducing their home maintenance and operating costs. The chapter convened a one-day workshop to review new ideas for housing the single parent. Seventy-two people participated, representing individual consumers and housing groups throughout Bergen County, housing providers from local, state, and federal government agencies, religious agencies such as the Catholic Community Services of Bergen County Foster Home Program for the Elderly, architects, and women's groups such as the Young Women's Christian Association, the National Organization of Women, domestic violence organizations, and women's studies programs.

The chapter commissioned architect Troy West and planner Jacqueline Leavitt to design a prototype unit to meet the needs of single parents as identified in the social science literature. In the process they prepared a bibliography for the chapter's use. West and Leavitt also prepared a package of materials, including plans of a house, which was sent to 12 participants in the housing-design workshop. This package included a letter requesting participants to use the enclosed framing plan to draw or write what activities they thought could take place in each part of the house. Although this task was not accomplished prior to the workshop, participants had had the opportunity to review the plans. At the workshop, there was a lively discussion as people evaluated the features of the prototype.

The original design premised that sharing arrangements would occur throughout the 2½-story house, that the lower level would not have its own kitchen, and that the house would be for three single parents and their children. Feedback from the workshop altered some premises, and the house is now planned to be intergenerational, including people whose children have already left home and singles without children. The premise is that sharing arrangements among generations serve several functions.

First, the age mix of four adults from their low twenties to mid-sixties, and six children from infancy through the teens, would enable socializing and development to take place in much the same way it does within a family. Workshop participants included older women with children no longer living at home, housed in structures too big for their needs. Based on their feedback, the design was changed to make the lower-level apartment autonomous with its own kitchen. One older person spoke of wanting to share her childraising experiences with single parents and be a surrogate grandparent, but also she wanted a place of her own.

Second, sharing arrangements among generations could make the house affordable. Assuming some form of subsidy would be required, the designers aimed to develop a scheme which would bear out the statement of Representative Edward R. Roybal (D-California), "that three units of shared housing could be subsidized for the same cost as one non-shared home."[35] The shelter-service house costs around $100,000. Given the low income of single parents, a deep subsidy would be required if only single parents are housed. The subsidy is less per house if the residents include an older single parent who has to sell her house and can bring equity into the venture, and a single who earns around $20,000.

The premise of sharing space throughout the house rests on each adult having "a place of one's own." This is accomplished by designing private bedrooms

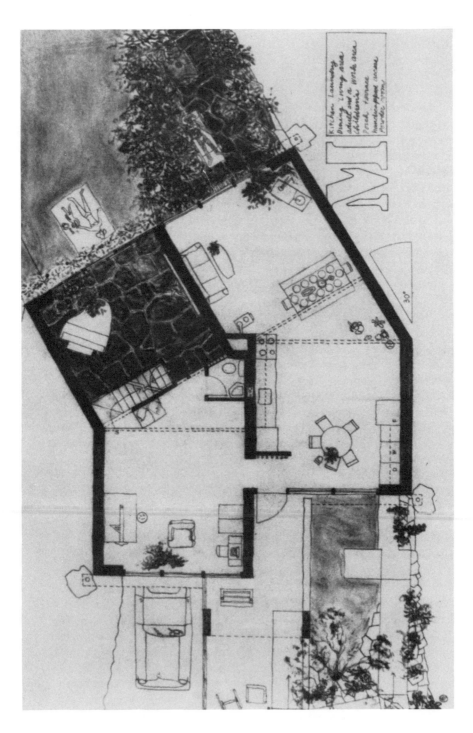

Exhibit 11.1a—M before input.

with a work area. In redesigning the lower-level unit into an accessory apartment, it also became clear that one set of stairs could be eliminated, thereby enabling the kitchen on the main level and two bedrooms for adults on the second level to be bigger. Subsequently, input from other presentations to single and two-parent families, including the New York City chapter of the Parents Without Partners, resulted in two work spaces on the main level being made more private. This is accomplished in one work space through the use of a sliding door, and in the other work space through provision of its own door immediately off the front entrance to the house (Exhibits 11.1a and 11.1b). The result is a plan that represents a merging of planning and architectural ideals with the articulated social and economic needs of selected women. In November 1983, the revised plan received the award for the most significant contribution to feminist design in the Feminist Architectural Design Exhibition at a conference on women and housing sponsored by California State University at Long Beach.

The design for the shelter-service house is based on consciously integrating housing for single parents into the neighborhood fabric through a system of infill units (Exhibit 11.2). From the outside the house resembles an ordinary house. It can be constructed as an individual unit or in clusters, and its simple framing structure allows it to be built completely or partially with self-help (Exhibit 11.3).

Four elements—solar, atrium, stair plumbing, and front porch—can be combined and angled in one of four positions to achieve maximum solar orientation (Exhibits 11.4a and 11.4b). The angled geometry gives privacy to the open plan. Instead of experiencing the entire layout at one glance, from front to back door, perception of additional space is more gradual, and private nooks can be created. Views of trees and flowers are an integral part of the design and help to establish visual boundaries beyond the glass doors and plywood or masonry walls (Exhibit 11.5). The atrium rises two stories, is topped with a skylight, and draws cool air through the entire structure and out glass-louvered ventilators in the skylight monitor. In winter, the louvers are closed, and the black wall of the skylight absorbs additional heat that circulates through the house.

If the outside of the house is ordinary, it is the flexible interior space, designed to accommodate a variety of household configurations and needs, that is less conventional (Exhibits 11.6a and 11.6b). There is about 2,600 square feet of unfinished space. The lower-level accessory apartment has 445 square feet and can be entered separately. It has its own kitchen, bath, and sleeping area. There is access to the outdoor patio. There are bathrooms with split facilities on each of the other floors in order to maximize individual use. On the second and loft levels are six additional sleeping areas. The loft could also be converted into a separate apartment with its own bathroom but no kitchen. The kitchen, dining, living, and work spaces are on the main level. It is anticipated that rooms on the main level can be used for more than one activity. The living room can function as a chil-

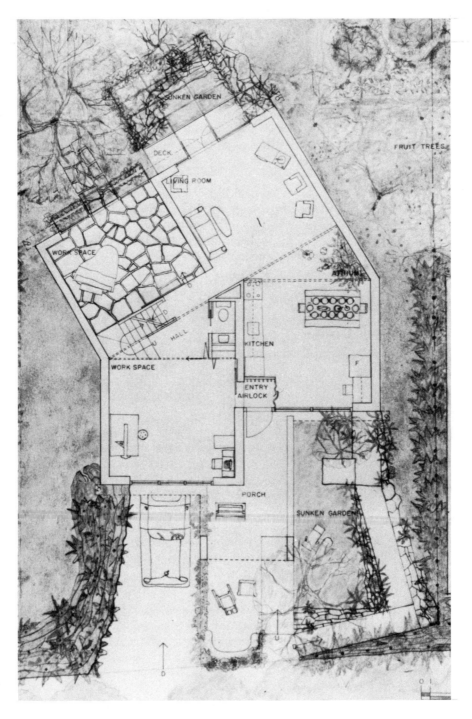

Exhibit 11.1b—First floor congregate plan after input.

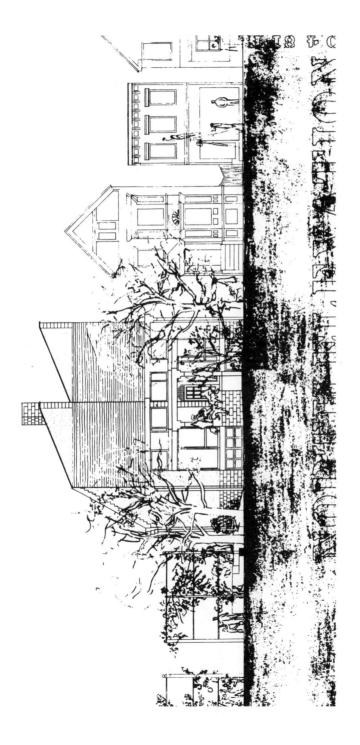

Exhibit 11.2—Infill.

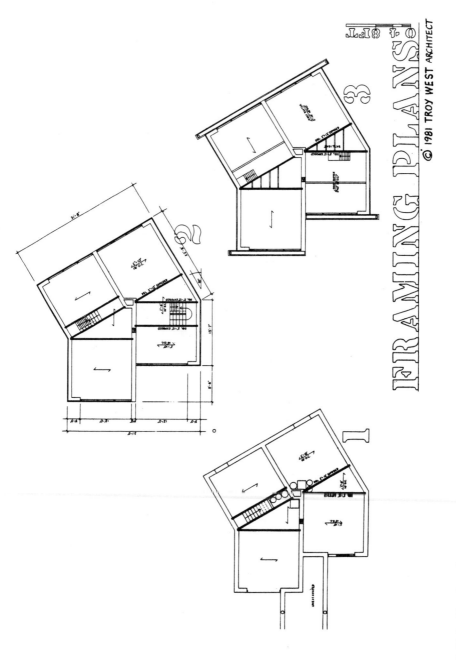

© 1981 TROY WEST ARCHITECT

Exhibit 11.3—Framing plans.

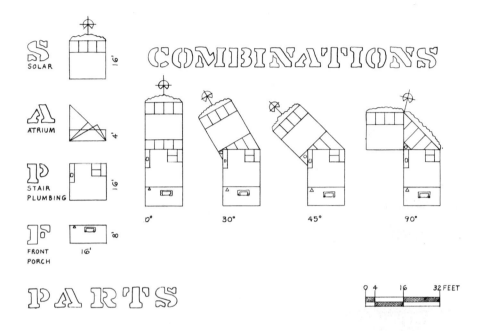

Exhibit 11.4a—Combinations and parts.

dren's playroom during the day, an area for relaxation in the evening. The two work areas, particularly the rear one with a sliding door, can be easily converted to a recreation room in the evening by keeping the door open. There is a front porch with storage underneath and a garden.

Imagine a typical day in this house. It is late afternoon. One single parent with a child under three years is employed as a word processor; she has been operating her machine in the front work area while her child plays in the rear work room. Upstairs, two teenagers home from school are occupied in their bedrooms. Another adult has been in her bedroom in the rear of the house, working at her desk, home because she has been sick. In the lower level, an older person is getting ready to come upstairs to help take care of the child and begin preparations for dinner. Although she has a separate kitchen and bathroom, she often shares in the meal preparation and babysitting. During the week, the older person might make a meal two or three times; the single parent would take her turn and also help with light housecleaning throughout the entire dwelling. During warmer weather, people spend time gardening; the children can play outdoors as well as inside. Residents act like a family although they are not related to each other. Support is provided for each other, and they are willing to work out conflicts that

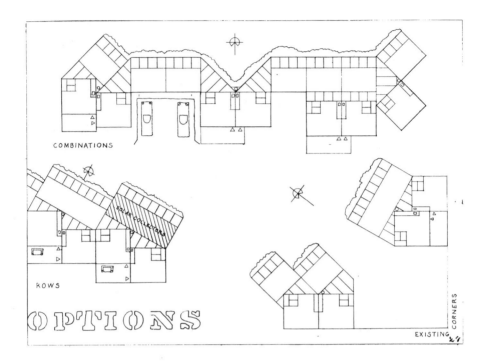

Exhibit 11.4b—Combinations and parts: options.

might arise. People can usually be found gathered around the kitchen table where they can hold informal meetings or just be social.

The shelter-service house provides the possibility of working at home, caring for children, and sharing expenses. This has the effect of providing an alternative child-care package and minimizing food and transportation expenses. In contrast to this supportive lifestyle is the life of a single parent with a part-time job and two children, living in a typical 20-unit tenement building in New York City. The mother has to be at work at 9:30, but she gets up at 5:30 each morning to prepare breakfast and bag lunches, get her two sons ready for school, dress herself, take one son to the bus stop and the other to a daycare center. At mid-afternoon, having picked up the younger child, she returns in time to greet the older child, prepare the evening meal, and get the children to bed. She has no spare time. It is impossible for her even to tidy her house.[36] She has no one with whom to share responsibilities. Her days are arranged with split-second timing.

## POSSIBILITIES FOR THE FUTURE

The public, seeing the changes in demographics and the increase in non-nuclear families, may begin to accept the single-parent family. However, it is

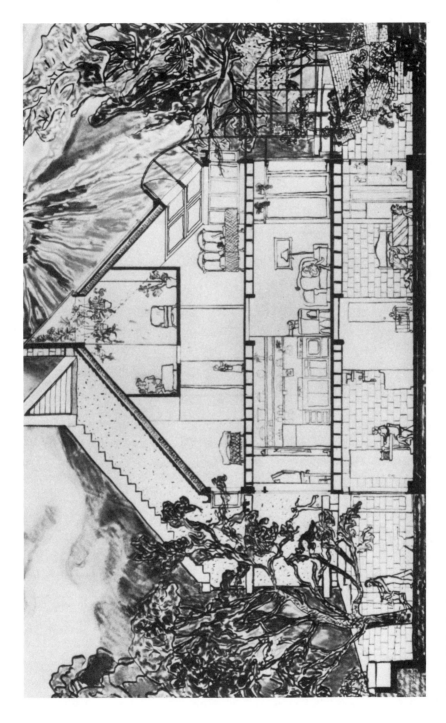

Exhibit 11.5—Section.

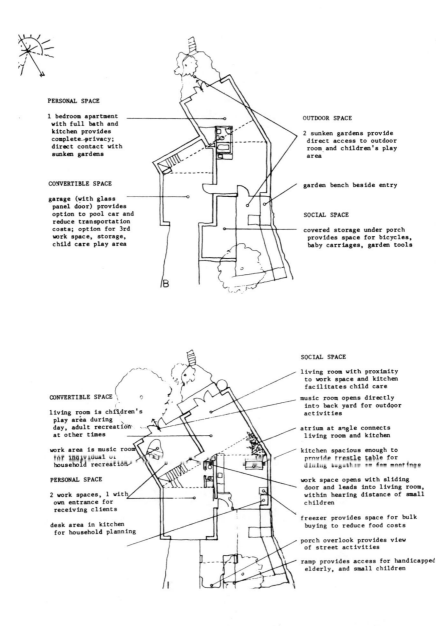

PERSONAL SPACE

1 bedroom apartment
with full bath and
kitchen provides
complete privacy;
direct contact with
sunken gardens

OUTDOOR SPACE

2 sunken gardens provide
direct access to outdoor
room and children's play
area

garden bench beside entry

CONVERTIBLE SPACE

garage (with glass
panel door) provides
option to pool car and
reduce transportation
costs; option for 3rd
work space, storage,
child care play area

SOCIAL SPACE

covered storage under porch
provides space for bicycles,
baby carriages, garden tools

SOCIAL SPACE

living room with proximity
to work space and kitchen
facilitates child care

music room opens directly
into back yard for outdoor
activities

atrium at angle connects
living room and kitchen

kitchen spacious enough to
provide trestle table for
dining together or for meetings

work space opens with sliding
door and leads into living room,
within hearing distance of small
children

freezer provides space for bulk
buying to reduce food costs

porch overlook provides view
of street activities

ramp provides access for handicapped
elderly, and small children

CONVERTIBLE SPACE

living room is children's
play area during
day, adult recreation
at other times

work area is music room
for individual or
household recreation

PERSONAL SPACE

2 work spaces, 1 with
own entrance for
receiving clients

desk area in kitchen
for household planning

Exhibit 11.6a—Annotated floor plans.

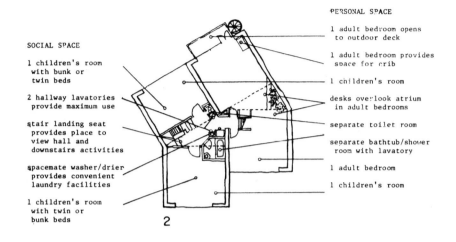

SOCIAL SPACE

1 children's room
with bunk or
twin beds

2 hallway lavatories
provide maximum use

stair landing seat
provides place to
view hall and
downstairs activities

spacemate washer/drier
provides convenient
laundry facilities

1 children's room
with twin or
bunk beds

2

PERSONAL SPACE

1 adult bedroom opens
to outdoor deck

1 adult bedroom provides
space for crib

1 children's room

desks overlook atrium
in adult bedrooms

separate toilet room

separate bathtub/shower
room with lavatory

1 adult bedroom

1 children's room

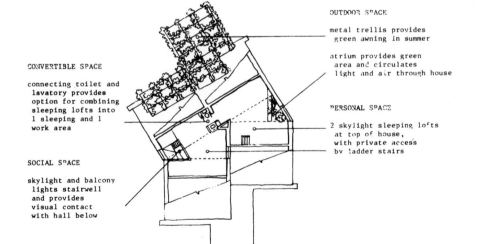

CONVERTIBLE SPACE

connecting toilet and
lavatory provides
option for combining
sleeping lofts into
1 sleeping and 1
work area

SOCIAL SPACE

skylight and balcony
lights stairwell
and provides
visual contact
with hall below

OUTDOOR SPACE

metal trellis provides
green awning in summer

atrium provides green
area and circulates
light and air through house

PERSONAL SPACE

2 skylight sleeping lofts
at top of house,
with private access
by ladder stairs

Exhibit 11.6b—Annotated floor plans.

doubtful that many will soon accept the single-parent household as permanent. Before this can happen, single parents themselves must feel some identification as a group.

Single parents, however, have been wary of calling attention to themselves, and therefore may resist living arrangements with other single parents. One study found that the notion of living with other single parents evoked negative images of living in public housing among low-income people. It is expected that middle and upper-middle income women would reject housing projects (exclusively for single-parent families), associating them with people of a different class and color.

Whether a flexible house like the one described above that is outwardly integrated into the community would be acceptable, and to whom, is unknown at this point. It may be that such a house would be chosen by the marginal few, who either share a particular vision or are prompted by economic and social need. There is a possibility that a constituency for shared housing can be organized among people with a common bond on the basis of religion, or working for the same employer, or being clients at the same facility. Alternatively, flexible housing that accommodates different household types may become an example for other groups. Something like this is happening in the private market for affluent non-traditional households where two "master" bedrooms are offered for "mingles," two or more unrelated individuals who live together.

Given the Reagan administration's attack on public expenditures for housing and services, it is useful to circulate new ideas that may lead to creating an environment potentially more supportive of each household's needs. The public sector can provide an example for the types of shelter-service options that can benefit more than single parents. For example, units of public housing can be combined to provide facilities for child care. In fact, the shared housing described in this paper can be implemented as a model within public housing in redesigned duplexes. The public sector also must make a commitment to organizing planning meetings that elicit people's feelings about sharing and about the permanent or temporary nature of their single-parent status. However, whether the public agenda moves in this direction depends to a large extent on single parents themselves developing into a powerful political force articulating their housing needs.

## NOTES

1. Jonathan Friendly, "Women's New Roles in Comics," *The New York Times*, February 28, 1983, Sec. 11, p. B5.
2. In 1979, "Although the incidence of one-parent families was much higher among blacks, two-thirds (68 percent) of all one-parent families were maintained by whites..." U.S. Department of Commerce, Bureau of the Census, Current Population Reports, No. 352, P-20, *Household and Family Characteristics: March 1979*, p. 3.
3. Susan Anderson-Khleif, "Housing Needs of Single-Parent Mothers," in Suzanne Keller (ed.), *Building for Women* (Lexington, Mass.: Lexington Books, 1981), p. 31.

4. See, for example, Fredelle Maynard, "Women Power," *Woman's Day*, November 16, 1982, pp. 62-65, 168-73.

5. Ruth A. Brandwein, Carol A. Brown, Elizabeth Maury Fox, "Women and Children Last: The Social Situation of Divorced Mothers and Their Families," *Journal of Marriage and the Family*, 36 (1974). Also see Alvin L. Schorr and Phyllis Moen, "The Single Parent and Public Policy," in Arlene Skolnick and Jerome H. Skolnick (eds.), *Family in Transition* (Boston: Little, Brown and Company, 1980), pp. 554-65.

6. U.S. Department of Housing and Urban Development, Office of Policy Development and Research, *Housing Our Families* (Washington, D.C.: U.S. Government Printing Office, August 1980), pp. 3-4.

7. The author, with the assistance of April Sponaugle, prepared a bibliography for the Bergen County, New Jersey, chapter of the League of Women Voters. A partial list with annotations is found in B. Judith Glassman and Mary Lou Petitt (eds.), *Housing for Single-Parent Families* (Trenton, N.J.: Department of Community Affairs, no date).

8. *Housing Our Families*.

9. Martin Rein et al., *The Impact of Family Change on Housing Careers* (Cambridge, Mass.: Joint Center for Urban Studies of MIT and Harvard University, 1980).

10. Ibid., pp. 2-11. Rein notes:

> We do not know a great deal about these solo mothers who never remarry. We *do* know that a fifth of young solo mothers and almost half of the older solo parents own their own homes. They are homeowners for two different social reasons. The older women whose marriages have dissolved are more likely to be living in their own homes to begin with and to keep their homes after they divorce. Younger women eventually acquire the resources necessary to purchase their own homes. We do not know how many of these young women there are, but we are sure there exists an active process of "settling in" and digging out among some of the permanent solo mothers. But not all solo mothers are so fortunate. Many continue to experience housing deprivation and financial stress throughout their careers as solo mothers.

11. Susan Anderson-Khleif, *Divorced But Not Disastrous: How to Improve the Ties Between Single-Parent Mothers, Divorced Fathers, and the Children* (Englewood-Cliffs, New Jersey: Prentice Hall, Inc., 1982), p. 5. Anderson-Khleif points out that differences in the divorce rate between different occupational and income groups is smaller, and cites Ross and Sawhill (footnote 17), that "Although single parents are overrepresented among the poor, non-poor single-parent families outnumber poor." On p. 8 she writes that, "There is no reason to believe that divorced mothers and fathers are all in the same situation or all act in the same ways. In may be that there are some very different situations, each with different implications for the socialization of children and the lives of women and men."

12. Robert S. Weiss, "Housing for Single Parents," in Roger Montgomery and Dale Rogers Marshall (eds.), *Housing Policy for the 1980s* (Lexington, Mass.: Lexington Books, 1980), pp. 67-76.

13. For a discussion of how a woman's class is often assumed to be that of her husband's, see Jackie West, "Women, Sex and Class," in Annette Kuhn and Ann Marie Wolpe (eds.), *Feminism and Materialism: Women and Modes of Production* (London: Routledge and Kegan Paul, no date), pp. 220-53.

14. A survey of 1,007 renters and 629 managers for HUD reveals policies and restrictions concerning children. This can occur through controlling the sharing of a bedroom by children of opposite sexes, a cultural norm mothers may feel without any assistance from management. The HUD study found there are more restrictions in apartment buildings and complexes than in single-family rental units. It was also found that such policies were more common in newer units which are of better quality. In all likelihood, the newer units are more expensive and one-parent families may self-select themselves out of that market. In *Housing Our Families*,

> There is evidence that no-children policies are increasing. Since 1974 the percentage of units in buildings and complexes with no-children policies increased from 17 percent to 26 percent. This increase reflects two trends. First, many more apartment complexes are being built as adult-only complexes. Second, buildings which used to accept children are adopting no-children policies.

In Atlanta, Georgia, Oakland, and Los Angeles, California, advocacy groups were formed to protect children's rights, and their families' to decent housing. To the extent that they are helpful, discrimination can be fought on a case-by-case basis. Given the other tasks the single parent has to do just to keep her or his head above water, and given the record of enforcing other human rights violations, it is doubtful that the complaint process will be effective except in scattered cases.

15. Andrée Brooks, "Divorce Suburban Style: Single at Midlife," *The New York Times Magazine*, May 24, 1981, pp. 31, 68-70, talks about SPAN, a coalition of 30 single-parent groups, comprising about 8,000 men and women members in Long Island, New York, who are building a constituency to lobby for increased child-care facilities, uniform child-custody laws, and improved public transportation.

16. New Jersey Department of Community Affairs, "Single-Parent Families: How Many?" (Trenton: Division of Planning, 1982); U.S. Department of Commerce, Bureau of the Census, Current Population Reports, *Marital Status and Living Arrangements: March 1980*, No. 365, pp. 4, 20.

17. U.S. Department of Commerce, Bureau of the Census, *Families Maintained by Female Householders 1970-79*, by Steve W. Rawlings, Current Population Reports, P-23, No. 107, p. 5. See Rawlings' "Introduction," for a discussion of the evolution of terminology referring to heads of households.

18. Ibid., p. 13.

19. Ibid.

20. Ibid., pp. 13-14.

21. Ibid., pp. 21, 24-25.

22. Ibid., p. 33. See George Sternlieb and James W. Hughes, *The Future of Rental Housing* (New Brunswick, New Jersey: Center for Urban Policy Research, 1981), p. 27, Exhibit 8. The median income by family type shows gaps between married couples, with and without a wife in the paid labor force, male households with no wife present, and female households with no husband present. The median incomes are as follows in 1979: $21,521 for married-couple families; $24,973 for married couples with wife in the paid labor force; $17,791 for married couples with wife not in the paid labor force; $16,888 for male households, no wife present; and $9,933 for female households, no husband present. The authors write that, "Both in terms of percentage growth as well as absolute scale, it is married couple families that showed the greatest level of increased affluence in the 1970s."

23. Janet A. Kohen, Carol A. Brown, and Roslyn Feldberg conducted a study in 1974 of 30 divorced mothers in the Boston area who had been divorced or separated from one to five years. The respondents varied in race and ethnicity: two were black; there were no Hispanics. The findings demonstrated that lowered income resulting from a divorce leaves the woman in an objectively lower class from the one based on the husband's income and occupation.

> The resources men bring to families are for the most part withdrawn following the divorce.... The woman's own paid work or welfare had to become immediate substitutes.... From an average pre-divorce family income of $12,500, the women in our sample fell to a post-divorce average of $6,100, a drop of just over half. This overall average obscures an important class difference—the higher they start, the farther they fall. The eight highest income families dropped 60 percent; the nine lowest families dropped only 19 percent. The less the husband had contributed, the less he could take away.

Janet A. Kohen, Carol A. Brown and Roslyn Feldberg, "Divorced Mothers: The Costs and Benefits of Female Family Control," in Peter J. Stein (ed.), *Single Life: Unmarried Adults in Social Context* (New York: St. Martin's Press, 1981), pp. 288-395.

Not all researchers have found this result. In fact, Ruth A. Brandwein presents findings that show that divorced mothers were *not* poor before the divorce. She writes:

> Much of the downward economic mobility among divorced mothers can be viewed in terms of economic discrimination against women. A mother at every class and income level is expected to depend for the major part of her and her children's support on the income of her husband, and economic opportunities for a woman without a husband are limited as a result. Women are given less job training, and are concentrated in low income, insecure occupations.

Ruth A. Brandwein, Carol A. Brown, and Elizabeth Maury Fox, "Women and Children Last: The Social Situation of Divorced Mothers and Their Families," *Journal of Marriage and the Family*, 36, (1974).

24. Rein et al., pp. 5-10, especially Chapter 5, "Single-Parent Mothers Who Stay."

25. Rawlings, p. 22; The National Low Income Housing Coalition notes:

> Although not generally thought of as such, both the Section 8 program [where the government pays the difference between 30 percent of the recipient's income and the fair market rent] and public housing are predominantly women's programs. Female headed households make up over three-fourths of the participants in the Section 8 program for existing housing. Fifty-three percent (53%) of the participants are female headed households under 62 years of age and 25% are elderly female headed households. Likewise, about 75% of those households who have been approved for the program but have been unable to find a suitable unit are female headed households. The mean annual income for the female headed household recipients was $3,263 compared to $4,588 for the male recipients.
>
> Public housing also has a majority of female headed households in residence, although precise figures are not known.

National Low Income Housing Coalition, "Triple Jeopardy: A Report on Low Income Women and Their Housing Problems," October 1980, p. 8.

26. Scott Burns, *The Household Economy: Its Shape, Origins, and Future* (Boston: Beacon Press, 1975), p. 17.

27. See, for example, Sheila B. Kamerman, *Parenting in an Unresponsive Society: Managing Work and Family* (New York: The Free Press, 1980).

28. See Gwendolyn Wright, *Building the Dream, A Social History of Housing in America* (New York: Pantheon, 1981), p. 274. For the entire study referred to, see Donald N. Rothblatt, Daniel J. Garr, and Jo Sprague, *The Suburban Environment and Women* (New York: Praeger, 1979).

29. Susan Anderson-Khleif found the following for working-class families at the lower economic range:

> The ex-husbands often have meager incomes and sporadic work histories. When the marriages break up, there are practically no resources and not many household possessions. Many women from such marriages move from one poor apartment to the next and live in poor neighborhoods. Perhaps the apartment is dark and dreary and needs repair, or maybe the apartment is all right but up three or four flights of stairs in a rickety old building. Sometimes the housing conditions were poor during the marriage too; but this subsequent housing is truly poor.

Among others, she finds the following:

> They suffer financial strain and a good deal of worry, plus the social embarrassment of untidy property in well-kept neighborhoods. Middle-income and working-class women who manage to keep their houses on a shoe-string after divorce find home maintenance an especially severe problem. They are apologetic about the looks of their homes and are distressed, wondering whether they will be able to keep their homes after all.

Susan Anderson-Khleif, "Housing Needs," in Suzanne Keller (ed.), *Building for Women* (Lexington, Mass.: Lexington Books, 1981), pp. 27, 28.

In discussing moves forced by insufficient funds, the Rein et al. study says that it affects all status levels and both renters and owners.

> In the case of owners, much of the problem is due to the fact that the costs of staying in the house go far beyond meeting the mortgage payments.... Upper-middle-class women sometimes find themselves solving the problem by trading their $100,000 houses in for $60,000 ones. Lower down the ladder, trading in larger, more expensive houses for smaller, less expensive ones also occurs, but more lower-middle women move over to rental status in order to transfer the financial and physical burdens of housing unit maintenance over to a landlord.

Rein et al., pp. 4-8.

30. Enid Gamer, Coordinator, Child and Adolescent Services, South Norfolk, Massachusetts Area Office, Department of Mental Health, in correspondence with the author, in the author's file. Gamer and her colleagues proposed housing for single parents, using self-help in the planning and construction stages as one positive way of overcoming isolation.

31. National Organization of Women, Legal Defense and Educational Fund, "New Environments for New Family Needs," from a conference report held November 19, 1979, pp. 19-20.

32. Alfred J. Kahn and Sheila B. Kamerman, *Not for the Poor Alone: European Social Services* (Philadelphia: Temple University, 1975), p. 58.

33. Correspondence with Carol Galante, Project Developer, Eden Housing, Inc., Hayward, California.

34. *Shared Housing Quarterly*, July 1982, Vol. 1, No. 1, p. 3. Contact SHRC, 6344 Greene Street, Philadelphia, Pennsylvania 19144.

35. June Regoznica, "Families: The Shared Solution," *Working Woman*, October 1982, pp. 130-32.

36. Brandwein, p. 595.

# 12

# Neighborhood Women Look at Housing

Ronnie Feit and Jan Peterson

The National Congress of Neighborhood Women (NCNW) is an umbrella organization of local women's community groups and women leaders. It forms a grassroots women's network around the country. This network is multi-ethnic, multi-racial, and multi-class, and comprised predominantly of poor and working-class women who are black, Hispanic, Italian, Irish, Polish, German, Scandinavian, native American, and Asian-American. These women are active in their neighborhoods in a variety of local programs encompassing housing, education, economic development, employment, and leadership support.

NCNW's mission is to provide a voice, an organizational structure, technical assistance, training, and support to neighborhood women in their efforts to improve their lives and neighborhoods. The women we represent and serve have mostly felt ignored by, or uninterested in, both the mainstream women's movement and the neighborhood movement. Despite some changes in their attitudes about the women's movement, most still feel that neither movement has been sensitive to their needs and values—the first because it is too middle class; the second because it is male-dominated. Above all, these women want respect for who they are, and this has been in short supply, even in their own neighborhoods.

As part of its mission NCNW has promoted better housing for poor and low-income women and their families. The focus, however, has not been on housing issues, but on the empowerment of neighborhood women in every area of concern to them. In 1982, frustration with the limited results of fragmented efforts led to the conclusion that empowerment must include a comprehensive action strategy. The strategy adopted, after over a year of analysis and planning, elevates housing issues to a key position.

## THE RATIONALE OF THE STRATEGY: THE OBSTACLE COURSE

The more NCNW reflected on our experiences with some of the most dynamic grassroots women leaders in the country, the more we had to admit that their prodigious accomplishments had been at almost unbelievable personal cost. It was the executive-mother, "I-can-do-it-all," superwoman syndrome, grassroots version. The leadership support we gave these women had helped stave off burnout (they had told us so), but it had not changed the demands made on them. Theoretically, leadership support, as we taught it, should have led to shared burdens and less of a need for extraordinary sacrifice. It seemed our strongest leaders moved too fast for that, and our weakest ones moved too slowly.

As we focused on the obstacle course neighborhood women negotiated each day just to survive, we decided that the obstacle course itself had to change comprehensively. It was clear to us that the design and operation of poor and low-income neighborhoods and communities, both their "hard" physical structures and their "soft" organizational aspects, worked against the efforts of poor women to attain self-sufficiency and decent lives for themselves and their families. Though we had seen some studies which had taken note of the irrational and exhausting burdens communities place on neighborhood women—such as the lack of affordable, decent housing, the shortage of housing for large families, the dearth of child-care services, the gaps, inconsistencies, and fragmentation of social-service programs, the distance of jobs from where women live, and unsafe, inadequate public transportation—there had been little public effort really to come to grips with the problem in all its dimensions.

We realized that no one had adequately analyzed how the combined impact of many features of poor and low-income neighborhoods, and the communities in which they exist, kept women and their families from leading more productive lives. Welfare poor, working poor, and working-class women live side-by-side in these neighborhoods. No one, to our knowledge, had taken a serious, holistic approach to changing the conditions, policies, and practices that together oppress them all. Rather, the approach has been to offer single-shot programs in isolation from each other at inconvenient times and locations, and to offer them to target groups crudely defined on the basis of income.

The work of many thinkers and professionals, including Dolores Hayden, Elise Boulding, Hazel Henderson, Jacqueline Leavitt, Susan Saegert, Betty Friedan, and the women of the American Society of Planning Officials, deepened our understanding of the clash between the realities of the current day and communities designed for nuclear families with breadwinner fathers, stay-at-home mothers, docile, supervised children, and homogeneous populations. We felt there was an additional clash between social-welfare policies and social-welfare realities at work in poor and low-income neighborhoods. This has been a divisive force in neighborhoods, splitting the working class from the poor and serving no one adequately. Our thinking and our experience led to several conclusions on which we based our new strategy:

1. Basic redesign of many features of the neighborhoods in which poor and low-income women live is essential to enable them to live decent lives.
2. Community development efforts which do not include the perspective of neighborhood women in all their phases (policy making, planning, research, and implementation) are likely to yield results which fail to meet the needs of these women and their families.
3. For such women, in order to have sensitive community redevelopment occur, a systematic and detailed analysis of the combined impact of community structures, systems, policies, and practices on the lives of neighborhood women must be made. The public must be made aware of this impact; and, there must be an organized effort with a strong political base to change insensitive community development processes and their legacy.
4. The intelligence, organizing ability, and commitment of neighborhood women leaders who hold poor and low-income neighborhoods together are the greatest resources the effort to create women-supportive communities can have.
5. No attempt to build on these strengths of neighborhood women can succeed unless it helps the women overcome many problems of diversity and female socialization. These women must learn how to do comprehensive critical thinking about the impact of their communities on their lives.
6. Neighborhood women cannot accomplish basic change alone. Others with power and information must understand their problems and work with them. To build a political base, they must work through existing or new community organizations. In addition, they need to work with the many influential women outside the neighborhood in the public and private sectors who are willing to help. A new working alliance of these two kinds of women has great practical and political potential, but poses its own problems of diversity and consciousness. It will often require careful structuring to be effective.

Before outlining the current shape of the strategy and the practical moves we have already made to implement it, some background is important. Our conclusions and strategy have grown out of the organizational and programmatic development of the National Congress of Neighborhood Women. Some history helps to put our ideas into context and throws light on their validity.

NCNW began partly as a defense of the values of neighborhood women, particularly white, working-class, ethnic women, who in the 1970s were feeling misunderstood and unheard. Sporadic protests in white ethnic neighborhoods against school busing, racial integration of housing, or the bulldozing of white ethnic homes in the name of urban renewal and planning had sometimes been ugly. The media and the country seemed to have labeled white ethnics racist, reactionary, violent, or ignorant. The women were convinced that this was not a fair picture of their families and friends. No one was looking behind these out-breaks to the long, patient, non-racist efforts most white ethnics had made to pre-serve deeply held values of home, family, and work and the way of life that ex-pressed them. Few understood the pressures that way of life was under. And few appreciated the religious values that opposed both racism and violence.

In 1974, Barbara Mikulski, now a congresswoman from Maryland, Nancy Seifer, who later wrote "Nobody Speaks for Me," and Ronnie Feit and Jan Peterson prevailed on Monsignor Geno Baroni, then head of the National Center for Urban Ethnic Affairs, to call a conference of neighborhood women leaders and community organizers in Washington. Their agenda was to consider the role of neighborhood women in the neighborhood movement. This small conference of 30 led to a larger assembly of 150, mostly, but not exclusively, white, ethnic women. The women at the second meeting voted to form an organization of their own that would affirm their values and roles, help them improve their lives and neighborhoods, and represent neigborhood women accurately to the world at large. Peterson, a few months later, found a way to finance a national staff for the new organization in the Greenpoint/Williamsburg section of Brooklyn, New York, by using CETA public-service job funds. She raised rent for a storefront office from bake sales. Monsignor Baroni gave his blessing, and the National Congress of Neighborhood Women was born.

Given this beginning, it was not surprising that the central themes of NCNW were respect and recognition for the strengths of neighborhood women and a focus on dealing with diversity in a sensitive and constructive way. Issues of class, race, and ethnicity were at the forefront of attention. Unlike the leaders of many women's organizations, no one at NCNW pretended such differences did not exist. The challenge was to find commonalities, dispel myths and fears, and work together to create neighborhoods in which people could live decently.

The first major NCNW program was a neighborhood-based accredited college program originally funded in 1975 by the Rockefeller Brothers Fund. It was de-signed for mature women in the Greenpoint/Williamsburg area of New York City. Neighborhood women, many of whom had never finished high school, worked with visionary administrators and faculty of the LaGuardia Community College of the City University of New York to plan the college. They partici-pated in the design of the curriculum, the choice of texts, and the selection of fa-culty. They scrutinized every idea, word, and attitude for anything which might be offensive to the students. They also sought a program that would enhance women's understanding of how to improve their community. They instituted peer counseling, a student government association, and family nights to reduce hus-bands' fears of what education might do to their marriages. The program was a magnificent success. Since 1977 it has graduated hundreds of neighborhood women (and a few men who asked to attend) and continues today. It confirmed that programs designed with the participation of those whom they are meant to assist and with true respect for their input work well. The student retention rate of our college program has been, from the beginning, far higher than the student retention rate of standard programs at nearby, on-campus colleges.

The success of the college program bolstered our belief that grassroots women were a major neighborhood resource whose potential for building strong neighborhoods was enormous but largely unrecognized. It was obvious to us that it was mainly women's volunteer work that supported the civic and service activities in the neighborhood. Yet, women seemed invisible, held few of the recognized leadership positions, and did not make policy.

This was an observation that was dramatically reinforced in our next big funded program. In 1977, Monsignor Baroni became assistant secretary of the U.S. Department of Housing and Urban Development (HUD). He brought with him a long appreciation of the important roles local women played in neighborhood stability and preservation. He also believed that government planning and programs were often unresponsive to the needs of neighborhood residents. Therefore, in 1978, his Office of Neighborhood Self-Help Development awarded a grant to NCNW to research the role and needs of poor and low-income women in neighborhood housing and improvement programs. The grant allowed us to 1) conduct a survey to determine the nature of female participation in community groups, particularly housing organizations; 2) convene a national assembly of women from neighborhood groups to articulate their leadership and community development needs; and 3) publicize community development programs which were supportive of women's concerns as models for others to follow.

In the first stage of the project, NCNW surveyed a representative sample of 30 neighborhood organizations to analyze the role of women within these groups. In particular, we studied levels of participation by women and their effectiveness in articulating their needs. The results substantiated many widely held assumptions. Most importantly, they revealed that most movements for better housing were initiated by women, but when funding came to local communities from either public or private sources, their leadership usually diminished. Thus, in many cases, while women had initially attracted the funding, they were excluded from the planning, design, and implementation of the very programs they had successfully advocated. The result was a massive divergence of female and organizational priorities.

In order to outline the lost priorities and address the exclusion of women from power, NCNW embarked on a second stage of the project, the formal articulation of poor and working-class women's neighborhood and leadership needs. In October 1979, we assembled in Washington, D.C., diverse representatives of 40 urban and rural neighborhood groups from every region of the country. The conference was entitled "Neighborhood Women Putting It Together."

Among the topics the women dealt with was housing. The design and operation of public housing was one of their targets. The conference participants charged that public housing lacked flexible space to meet the needs of a variety of family types. They called for larger kitchens, more closets and storage space, easier access to outdoor areas, laundry rooms, public areas designed to facilitate social interaction, daycare facilities, and recreation, social service, and shopping facilities in the housing complexes.

They recommended that HUD take steps to insure that women, who constitute the majority of the public housing tenants, be included in the planning, design, construction, and management of public housing. To make this inclusion meaningful, they recommended that HUD train women in management, architecture, engineering, urban planning, finance, and construction. They suggested that government agencies coordinate the planning of public housing so that the housing could also include programs to meet the needs of entire families. As examples, they suggested that community centers and health clinics be incorporated in high-density or isolated housing developments.

The women made it clear that they did not want to be viewed simply as recipients of services and subsidies. They felt they had valuable experience and skills to offer. Having provided services informally and managed a variety of community. activities with little funding or support, they had useful perspectives and knowledge to bring to the planning and management of housing and related services.

They were also concerned with private housing in their neighborhoods. They noted the shortage of rental housing which could accommodate extended families, single parents and children, and unrelated individuals. They recommended that these needs be addressed. They complained of the unwillingness of banks to lend money for the purchase or rehabilitation of private homes in poor neighborhoods. They were concerned about the ability of single women, especially the elderly, to repair and maintain their dwellings. They wanted training for women in household repairs and maintenance.

They felt that planners did not understand the relationship of housing to neighborhoods. They emphasized that housing for poor and working-class families should not be planned without investigating their neighborhood environment, behavior patterns, and cultural traditions. They called for planners to find out what informal helping network existed in the neighborhood, where the people congregated and why, how they amused themselves, where and how often they went to church, and what their celebrations and ceremonies were like. They knew that these patterns give neighborhood life its flavor and evolve out of different ethnic, religious, and class needs and tastes. They pointed out that planners who develop new housing for poor and working-class groups on middle-class models, without taking cultural patterns into account, create sterile neighborhoods and destroy vital connections.

Many women spoke of the problems created by the lack of affordable housing near to jobs or children's schools, relatives, and needed services. As family caretakers, they felt they had to be near those who depend on them. They must be able to get home from work quickly to pick up children from school, to shorten the time children are left unsupervised, or to care for sick or disabled family members. Often, they reported, they had had to turn down jobs or training opportunities because this employment was too far from home. They noted that the jobs, if any, near where they lived were usually dead-end, menial, low-paying, and unstable.

The women were pessimistic about the likelihood of better channels of communication developing between government and themselves. They feared that if government bureaucrats consulted with them, these officials would use bureaucratic language, "pull rank" in subtle ways, intimidate them and be unable to hear what they had to say. Noting their own lack of confidence in dealing with professionals, they called on government agencies to be aware of this problem and help women deal with it. They also acknowledged that many of their organizations had weak administrative capacities which were easily overwhelmed by government regulations and procedures. To make a real partnership possible, they requested management training to develop skills in preparing budgets, keeping records, writing proposals, and raising funds. Finally, they called for funding to stabilize and strengthen their organizations.

One of their recommendations for developing the capacity to influence government officials was the formation and funding of a low-income women's network based in Washington. This office would disseminate information about federal policies and programs, and collect input from neighborhood women and pass it on as necessary, direct local women leaders to the right offices and contacts when they came to Washington, and generally serve as a clearinghouse and resource center. They also wanted this network to develop a women's impact statement for national neighborhood policy. NCNW was ultimately funded to establish such a network and did so for one year. When the Reagan administration came into office, the project was not refunded, and the potential of the arrangement was never fully realized. The impact statement they wanted remains to be written. NCNW has continued relations with many of the women involved, however, and several now sit on our National Steering Committee.

The third stage of the HUD project involved identifying and publicizing community development programs which were supportive of women's concerns. Not surprisingly, women played strong leadership roles in all of these programs. To find these groups, we surveyed and evaluated several projects encompassing many types of community activities. Later, we developed case studies of the more significant efforts to serve as guides for other groups. Among the programs were several concerned with housing. These included Project Green Hope in New York City, a unique support center for female ex-offenders, which among other things, taught women to restore housing in which they eventually lived; the Evanston (Illinois) Community Development Corporation, a traditional development corporation whose women-dominated staff created a housing rehabilitation program geared to female heads of household; and Operation Life in Las Vegas, Nevada, which a welfare mother, Ruby Duncan, started as a welfare advocacy program and developed into a multifaceted development corporation that has created a medical center, a public library, and turn-key housing, while training women for the new jobs created in the process. In each program, women planned and created organizations to meet their own needs; and, in so doing, they empowered themselves and created programs that worked for women.

## LEADERSHIP SUPPORT AND DEALING WITH DIVERSITY

By 1980, as we worked with the network of low-income women we had met through the HUD project, we used our newly developed methods for giving leadership support and dealing with diversity with growing confidence. These techniques had evolved from our peer-counseling training in our college program, personal experiences with consciousness-raising, methods used by self-help and coping groups, and the re-evaluation counseling movement. They were inspired by our commitment to staff relationships that were participative and to creating feelings of openness and trust among neighborhood women.

Our methods involved the use of small groups in which women could express some of the exhaustion, fear, confusion, hurt, pride, and hope they felt as leaders in the community. The groups also provided a safe, structured, and helpful setting for deepening women's self-awareness. They began to see themselves in terms of gender, class, ethnic, and racial identity groups and as people with opinions.

We had learned early in our work that many neighborhood women of all backgrounds, if asked in standard discussion settings how they felt about being a woman, or poor, or black, or Italian would respond, "I never thought about it," or "fine." Similarly, if asked in such settings what they thought about issues such as what kind of housing would meet their needs, they often fell silent or echoed the stereotypes pictured in women's magazines or on television. To get beyond these responses, our support group leaders use developmental questions that bring out what people feel, know, and want, but do not easily articulate. Working up to the present through evoking past experiences is one approach we used. If we asked women, for instance, to talk about what they liked or did not like about the housing they grew up in, we began to tap the stream of feelings and ideas about housing that lies beneath the surface. Our "dream sessions" which focus on what women would like to have if money were no object are particularly effective in getting to new visions—some of the most imaginative ideas we have heard anywhere about housing design and community development have come in such sessions.

We introduced these ''leadership support'' methods to our network members in workshops around the country, and we trained them in forming and leading such groups. The immediate effects of these methods were so energizing to the participants and so conducive to communication breakthroughs among women initially quite wary of each other that we introduced them into our conferences. In combination with issue and skill work, the support groups proved unifying and liberating. They led over and over again to something we had not initially expected. They inspired women to express deeply held feelings about their faith in God, their hope for a loving community, and their joy in finding others who shared their feelings. This has been very moving to all of us.

We have experimented continually with these methods, applying them in different combinations and learning their strengths and weaknesses. While they are not a solution to all our interpersonal and inter-group problems, we feel (and participants regularly confirm) that they help to bring diverse people together. We feel they are indispensable to finding out what women have really experienced and what they really want. They are essential to our new strategy for making communities work for women.

## LESSONS FROM ST. LOUIS

The usual housing lessons from St. Louis are those of the Pruitt-Igoe project. They relate how it was blown up by the city ten years after it opened because it had become a pit of crime, deterioration, vandalism, and filth. When NCNW held a meeting of our national steering committee and corporate board in St. Louis in 1983, we visited the Pruitt-Igoe site and marveled at the vast acres of empty, level grass that remained where it had been.

We were in St. Louis, however, not to bemoan the shortsighted concepts of public housing design and management as exemplified by Pruitt-Igoe, but to see and learn from an entirely different public housing experience—the work of Bertha Gilkey's tenant-management corporation active just a short distance away from Pruitt-Igoe. We had met Bertha Gilkey in 1980 through contacts made at the HUD conference. A vibrant, charismatic black woman in her thirties, she had led a successful fight against deterioration of St. Louis's Cochran Houses, where she had been born and still lived. She had begun her fight in 1969 when she was a teenager, and in 1976, she led a successful rent strike that ultimately resulted in Cochran's renaissance and the development of additional public housing in downtown St. Louis.

Bertha demonstrated that public housing could be well-managed by trained residents organized to enforce community-developed standards. She has shown that concern for individual civil rights must not be used as an excuse for failing to react to behavior which is destructive to the community and to public housing. She proved that tenants would make and accept difficult screening, eviction, and other tough management actions if they had found new strength in their communities. She has also shown that multifamily dwellings inhabited mainly by poor women and children can be the incubators of economic self-sufficiency. She and her tenant-management corporation have developed a tenant-owned and managed health clinic, food service company, and janitorial firm which have created jobs and revenues for the community while improving the quality of life. We saw the clinic, ate the food, and observed the immaculate condition of the buildings. It seemed like a miracle to us and to the women with us who lived in public housing in other cities.

Bertha stressed to us the importance of mastering the art of matching federal programs with local resources, of making friends with the powerful, of using all the leverage the law provides, and of getting technical assistance from people who share your values. She also taught us, by example, the power of vision, persistence, and patience. Because Bertha and her tenant and technical assistance allies had carefully thought through their needs, she was never tempted in negotiations with the city to accept offers that would have given them less than they needed. The tenants had developed a comprehensive plan for Cochran that included fundamental and innovative changes in its design as well as its rehabilitation and modernization. The design changes were essential to reduce their management problems and allow Cochran to function as a community. Had they not done this homework, they might have squandered the leverage their organizing had gained.

Bertha emphasized that constant organizing, so called "soft management" programs (e.g., social service, recreational, employment, youth, and cultural programs), and unflagging maintenance of community norms were essential to the restoration and maintenance of community. The latter not only required persistence, but also took "guts" and a willingness to break the code of silence about neighbors who violated the rules. Bertha stressed that such willingness was only possible when the community was united in support of the standards. It also took what she called "stroking," the constant encouragement of residents' efforts to build decent lives.

Much of what Bertha Gilkey said in St. Louis and in other NCNW meetings was not new information. What she said was powerful because she had put it all together and made it work on a grand scale. Together with other female public housing tenants, "socially the lowest of the low" as she described herself and them, she turned a community around, and they are still moving.

Other women like Bertha are in NCNW's network. The accomplishments of Esther Cota and her Guadalupe (Arizona) Association have also been remarkable. Like Bertha, Esther and her associates looked for a holistic approach to community development, one that combined housing with other life-support programs. Among other creative moves, her association built senior-citizen housing next to a school and then built a greenhouse next to these. (The greenhouse supplies the vegetables which are the staples of the Hispanic and Yaki Indian diet.) The seniors tutor the children and together they grow vegetables for their food. Like Bertha and her group, the Guadalupe women stress community values, discipline, and self-help and use the political system to their advantage. Many other stories of neighborhood women's leadership show a similar pattern.

## NCNW's NEW COMMUNITY DEVELOPMENT STRATEGY

Our new comprehensive community development strategy also stresses neighborhood women's leadership and values, group discipline, self-help and the use of the political system to advantage. It is based on our network experience as well as on what we have learned from testing our concepts in our "laboratory," the Greenpoint/Williamsburg neighborhood. Since early in 1983, with grants from the Campaign for Human Development and others, we have brought together 30 women leaders from diverse identity groups and neighborhood organizations. In regular quarterly meetings, they meet as a body and monthly they meet in separate issue task forces to judge the impact of the local community on women's lives, to develop a comprehensive community development agenda based on this "women's analysis," and to plan how to move elements of that agenda in their organizations.

There are six issue task forces, which focus on housing, employment and economic development, health, child care, education, and community planning. NCNW staff members back up their efforts, and the Pratt Institute Center for Community and Environmental Development provides technical assistance, helps research efforts, and instructs in the planning process. (We have also incorporated some of the participatory planning methods used by the Institute for Cultural Affairs, and their trainers have worked with us.)

In the area of housing, for example, Pratt Institute students, guided by questions raised by the task force, collected housing and demographic data for the district and placed the information on planning maps. This is aiding the task force in visualizing the interconnections between housing, services, and city infrastructure for populations of women (such as working mothers, single parents, and single women over 50) who have many housing problems. They are using the maps to illustrate the obstacle course these women face each day. The housing task force has held its meetings in the various public housing complexes in the neighborhood. At each site, it has assessed how well these institutions are serving women.

The work of the task forces, while still preliminary, has already had an impact on the community. The housing task force, for instance, has become involved in community plans to take over and reuse the city-owned but abandoned Greenpoint Hospital. It has pressed the community to use several of the smaller buildings in the complex for permanent intergenerational housing for those vulnerable to homelessness, particularly single female parents and single women over 50 years old. Additionally NCNW has become a member of a new community development corporation formed to bid on the redevelopment of the site. With feminist architects Katrin Adam and Barbara Marks, we have developed intergenerational housing plans designed to foster cooperation and mutual support between the two types of women residents.

The housing task force has also taken up the issue of security in one complex of nearby public housing. There, 90 percent of the tenants are women, many of whom live behind triple-locked doors and fear using their hallways or elevators or letting their children leave their apartments. The task force is supporting residents' efforts to get tenant management as a means of controlling their environment. The housing task force has helped tenants draw up "report card" forms to score the Housing Authority on areas of concern to them. They expect these report cards to be a useful organizing tool and to have some impact on policy. They have also organized meetings of the tenants with Brooklyn District Attorney Elizabeth Holtzman on security and crime issues.

Simply bringing neighborhood women leaders together has had unexpected results. For example, once they were in the same room, the women realized that a large number were members of the Community Planning Board yet they had never met together to influence board decisions. This has now changed. They have formed a Women's Caucus of the Board and have already played an important role in recent board elections and decisions about housing and parks.

Our long-term strategy resembles our approach in Greenpoint/Williamsburg but adds other elements. It is designed to empower neighborhood women leaders, neighborhood by neighborhood, state by state. They will analyze the impact of their neighborhoods on their lives and formulate their own community development agendas. Then, using their neighborhood organizations, educating policy makers, making alliances with women in power, and employing the media, they will organize their communities for action around these agendas.

Poor and low-income women will come together across class, race, and ethnic lines into women-leaders groups within their neighborhoods. The groups will form new women's partnerships in the larger power structures of society. The process will begin in each state with an intensive dialogue between a core of neighborhood-based grassroots women and a small group of politically influential women. At the dialogue, they will develop a preliminary neighborhood women's agenda for community development for each state, agree to the terms of the working partnership between the two groups of women, and design preliminary action strategies for the neighborhoods represented. At the end of one year, representatives of the women-leaders groups will evaluate results, make plans for the future, and draft a neighborhood women's agenda for community development that is based on that year's work. Throughout the organizing, they will brief policy makers and the media about the effort.

We have already begun to implement this strategy in New York State. With initial funding from the New York Department of State headed by Gail Shaffer, we have planned our first dialogue to occur in September 1984. It will focus on housing and economic development. Grassroots women from Buffalo, Syracuse, Albany, Mount Vernon (a suburb of New York City), Brooklyn, and NCNW's national network will meet with public and private sector leaders from the state and across the country.

We believe the success of our strategy will depend upon three factors in addition to adequate funding: (1) in every neighborhood, we must have a strong leadership core of good organizers who are sympathetic to our goals, able to offer practical managerial support centered in one strong neighborhood organization, and willing to work with the NCNW and recruit a representative local women-leaders group; (2) we have to train the local women in our leadership support methods and our techniques for making a "women's analysis" of community development; and (3) we have to identify and recruit a core of influential non-neighborhood women and facilitate a realistic working relationship between them and the women leaders groups. Because barriers of time, place, style, and situation interfere with communication and cooperation, this will require careful planning and brokering. To overcome diversity problems, both groups will need to understand NCNW's leadership support concepts and agree to their standards. Based on our experience thus far, we are optimistic that we can do all of this in New York State. We will count heavily on our affiliate groups to do the same once they feel able to launch similar efforts in their states. We expect to learn as we go.

## CONCLUSION

Neighborhood women tend to live physically circumscribed lives. They are likely to spend most of their lives in one neighborhood and not to travel frequently or far. Most do not drive cars. Those who do travel are clear about where they belong. They have always seen their housing and their neighborhoods as inseparable parts of home. We believe that this view of housing and neighborhood is not simply one that has been forced upon them by circumstance and history. It is true that the financial and emotional costs of moving are higher for them than for most other groups in society, and that their options are limited by their low incomes, their sense of family responsibility, their socialization, and the real and perceived dangers of sexual and physical assault they face in public spaces. It is also true that the cost and scarcity of appropriate housing is reducing their options even further. But something positive is at work here as well.

Neighborhood women of all backgrounds understand and value people's need for stability and community, for face-to-face nurturing, for personal recognition, acceptance, approval, and for time to be together. The American message of "up and out" has never appealed to them, even when it was possible for them to act upon it. They wish to move up but not out. They wish to know more and grow more but not on terms that cut them off from their life-support systems, that leave their families and roots behind.

This is a viewpoint that others in American society are beginning to appreciate. We have begun to see people moving into ethnic neighborhoods because of their "warmth" and sense of community. We have seen the third generation which moved to the suburbs coming back—when they can—to the old neighborhood. We see people moving out of big cities to smaller towns in search of more personal living conditions.

Something important is happening. A new vision of how to live is struggling to be born, and it is coming more sharply into focus as it becomes more difficult to realize. The absence of nurturing communities is fostering a new demand for nurturing communities. In a world of changing women's roles, women can no longer provide so much of the nurturing as they provided before. They need nurturing themselves. It begins to look as if we will have to redesign the "American dream," as Dolores Hayden has suggested. The need for communities that support the lives of neighborhood women is only a more extreme vision of the need that exists for everyone. The empowerment, analysis, organizing, and partnership efforts we advocate for neighborhood women are, we believe, examples of what the rest of society needs as well. We get the feeling that the next American frontier, the place where the important and exciting challenges and opportunities are, is not international markets, outer space, or high-technology laboratories. It is in America's homes and neighborhoods. On that frontier, the neighborhood women's perspective will be critical.

# 13

# A Single Room: Housing for the Low-Income Single Person

Michael Mostoller

An inspection of our cities today lays bare a housing crisis of unforeseen dimensions—a crisis in accommodations for the single adult, particularly those having low incomes. Across the country, approximately one-quarter of the population now is headed by a single person. In New York City, almost half of all households consist of one person. A large proportion of those living alone are single women over 65.

It is the low-income single adult who fares the worst in the housing market. Additionally, many low-income single adults are further hampered by old age, the loss of a spouse, physical handicaps, chronic histories of institutionalization, and unemployment.

These single people traditionally have found shelter in boarding houses and other minimal accommodations that meet their needs for cheap, simple dwellings. A housing type in New York City has provided for this population, the single-room occupancy hotel—commonly known as the SRO hotel. These SRO hotels rent individual rooms, generally between 60 and 120 square feet, by the week or month. These rooms are furnished but do not have kitchens or bathrooms. Common facilities are shared by eight to ten occupants.

Previous studies have shown that for many years, low-cost hotels have served a useful and respected purpose in New York City by providing a convenient living arrangement for those unable or not desiring to assume housekeeping responsibilities. Serving as a resource mainly for single individuals, they offered both an independence of lifestyle and a minimal requirement for furniture and household accoutrements. Single workers, transients, temporary residents, and individuals with modest incomes could benefit from a plentiful supply of inexpensive single-room occupancy hotels. However, over the past 20 years, such hotels have lost their essence of respectability, and their resident population has been stigmatized.

Exhibit 13.1—Homeless man, 14th Street, New York City (Michael Mostoller).

Exhibit 13.2—Boarding house room, Philadelphia, c. 1850 (unknown artist, Philadelphia Museum of Fine Arts).

These hotels have declined in several respects. First, due to advanced age and physical deterioration, most SRO housing quality has declined. Second, the unique aspect of hotel living is the housekeeping services provided. Because these services are labor intensive, costs have been escalating faster than inflation. This cost squeeze has led to a general decline in the amount and quality of housekeeping services offered to tenants. A recent study by the Metropolitan Hotel Industry Stabilization Association, Inc., has documented the rapid cost escalation for this industry from 1968 to 1979. Third, a tax abatement called "J-51" has made it profitable to convert these buildings to luxury housing. This and other real-estate trends and building abandonments have caused the number of legal SRO's in New York to decline from 298 buildings (50,000 rooms) with a 26 percent vacancy rate in 1975 to 189 buildings (19,000 rooms) with a 9 percent vacancy rate in 1983.

In New York City a severe struggle for control of the urban territory is taking place. This struggle is occurring between rich and poor, families and single people, mannered society and outcasts. A continuum of housing types for the extremes of income and housing need is required to address this crisis. At one end of the continuum are the upwardly mobile, affluent singles whose incomes may give them a wide range of housing types and choices. At the other end are the homeless (Exhibit 13.1). In between are the people who live in one room, the single-room occupants. They are the focus of this work.

A historical survey of singles' housing is useful in illuminating how the housing market has accommodated this group. This history is colored by conflicting themes. For example, Victorian morality held that living outside the family was somehow deviant; yet, the marketplace provided a variety of units for those living alone.

## THE BOARDING HOUSE

During the nineteenth century the boarding house was the main source of housing for singles. While its roots go back to the beginnings of American cities—Thomas Jefferson is said to have stayed in his Washington boarding house on the day of his inauguration and to have taken his customary evening meal there as well—the boarding house greatly expanded to fulfill the vast new requirements for accommodations born of the rapid industrialization after 1850. The late nineteenth century could truly be called the age of the "boarding" house.

The boarding-house phenomenon is described by Gunther Barth in his book, *City People*:

> Many members of the middle class took over houses at the edge of the central business district, vacated by owners who had moved their families to the periphery of town or into the suburbs to get away from encroaching warehouses, office buildings, and small factories. They subdivided the old residence and rented single rooms or entire floors to lodgers, or ran boarding houses outright [Exhibit 13.2]. By 1856, the custom was so widespread in New York that Walt Whitman accepted the estimate of judicious and extensively informed observers who assumed that seven out of ten dwellings were used that way. Counting permanent hotel boarders in this group, Whitman thought that almost three-quarters of the middle and upperclass inhabitants of New York did what the little girl so aptly described when asked where her parents lived: "They don't live, they BOARD."[1]

Quoting a chronicle of the nineteenth century, Barth's account continues:

> Like death, no class is exempt from . . . this universal Barrack system. [The author's] lurid accounts of the many varieties of the institution drove home again and again the point that the boarding house did not and could not substitute for a home. However, he also considered it useless to rail against the inherently mischievous features of our anomalous Social State as long as it was next to impossible to find a suitable dwelling in the big city for those who wanted to live at once privately, decently, and economically.[2]

It is important to emphasize the last point: in actuality, the boarding house was usually a respectable middle- and lower-middle-class housing type. It provided a

Exhibit 13.3—Rooming house, New York City, c. 1910 (Charles Lockwood, *Bricks and Brownstones*, Abbeville Press, NY, 1972).

social space, or house parlor, for socializing and entertaining, a dining room with meal service, and private furnished rooms—in sum, private accommodations for the individual.

Cities all over the country were the same, as travelers, writers, and foreign visitors document. From Dreiser's *Sister Carrie*[3] in which Carrie initially boards with her sister and brother-in-law, the most intimate boarding situation, to accounts of entire houses let out to boarders with meals served, the invisible underside of nineteenth-century life is chronicled.

## THE ROOMING HOUSE

The boarding house was gradually replaced in the twentieth century by the "rooming" house (Exhibit 13.3). The rooming house provided a degraded form of boarding; no social services, meals, or facilities were provided. It was, however, the most important housing for for singles until World War II.

A 1940 study by the Community Service Society, *Life in One Room*, considered the rooming-house problem in Manhattan:

> In the main, the people who live in rooming houses are among the lowest paid workers and the housing accommodation obtainable within their income must be cheap. Low cost is the basic necessity. They frequently cannot afford to buy furniture, and their income is often not sufficiently assured to make it possible for them to contract long-term leases for apartments. Their economic status makes it necessary, therefore, for them to obtain housing accommodation which includes needed furniture, and which can be rented for a short period of time without contracting any obligations.
>
> The hotel might have been the answer to this demand, but the hotel was usually too expensive and cheaper hotels were far too few in number to meet the demand for cheap, furnished, short-term accommodation.[4]

The buildings used for rooming houses were originally built for other uses. The study discusses three types. The first type was the converted single-family house such as the brownstone. The housekeeper and/or landlord generally lived in the basement and rented all the rooms on the upper floors. Twelve to 20 rooms would typically be provided, housing 20 to 40 people. Generally there was one bath per floor and no kitchen for residents.

The second type of rooming "house," much less prevalent than the first, was a converted apartment in an apartment building. Apartments with large bedrooms would be rented by an operator who normally would retain the living room for her own quarters and lease individual bedrooms to others. The "operators" were almost always women who subdivided the apartment, probably upon widowhood.

The third type was a converted old law or new law tenement. As the housing

Exhibit 13.4—Room, National Conservatory of Music (Joseph Byron, *Interiors, New York*, Dover, NY).

squeeze intensified during the 1930s, more and more conversions of this type occurred. Clearly more than a rooming house and less than a hotel, these 80- to 100-room buildings struggled for an identity, briefly calling themselves "residential clubs." The mode of operation of these hotel/rooming houses was different from the first two owner-occupied structures: sub-landlording and ownership of several hotels by an absentee landlord returned in this tenement revival. These buildings featured shared bathrooms and sometimes shared kitchens. No "hotel services" existed generally, or if they did, they were minimal in scope.

The study estimated that at least 300,000 people lived in 25,000 to 35,000 buildings in New York of this type. Other studies, including one of Harlem in the prosperous 1920s, indicate that, at least in certain sections, Whitman's nineteenth-century estimate that 75 percent of family accommodations included boarders still prevailed.

## HOUSING FOR SINGLE WOMEN

It is important to note that in both the boarding house and the rooming house males predominated. The housing opportunities for women were extremely different. Institutions such as the National Conservatory of Music and Barnard

College had rooms for women (Exhibit 13.4). These accommodations were designed to be temporary and served only a special purpose. James Ford, in *Slums
and Housing*, showed that the problem of women's housing was complicated by
two issues which made it both vulnerable and unique: low wages for women and
their special need for protection.

> The number of accommodations for unemployed women and the lowest wage
> group is smaller, and for the middle, or shop and office worker group, rather larger
> than in the case of men. Commercial enterprise finds it economically impossible to
> provide adequately for the lower-income groups of women, since their small wages
> make it impossible for them to pay rentals that will bring an adequate return of in-
> vestments.[5]

Therefore Ford notes that these accommodations are privately endowed. He continues, addressing the issue of women and the single state:

> For the problem of the single employed woman is complicated by her relatively low
> income, by the recognition of her need for social protection, as well as by her need
> for amenities of life which the rooming house does not afford. Such amenities cover
> not only decent wholesome rooms, but also wholesome food and adequate diet at
> reasonable prices, common rooms for recreational life and provision for entertain-
> ment of the opposite sex.[6]

Ford's list of residences for women takes the form of a complex chart, noting
places, locations, quantities, and inhabitants. This chart is especially evocative
both for its formal qualities and for the information it contains. Its complex non-
linear structure indicates the intricacy of a society coming to grips with a delicate
and complicated problem—the housing of its single women. It makes clear the
complexity of the response of that now-vanished society. This society was diverse religiously, economically, and ethnically (the hallmark of American urban
life) and mustered its forces to answer a unique need born of the urban life. The
wide range of accommodations and groups involved is especially striking if we
consider that while the lodging for men has decreased by half from 1909 to 1981,
the accommodations for women have all but disappeared.

The mid-twentieth-century transfer of responsibility for housing accommodations to either the private sector—which produces tiny, luxury studio apartments
and gigantic condominiums—or to government "public" housing reveals the
two-dimensional quality of contemporary culture. Either you are "in" or "down
and out." Recent political developments indicate the extent to which this view of
society has become endemic and indeed has become national policy. The horrors
faced at the outset of the philanthropic reform movement may soon return when
government abandons the charge given it by the conscious shift in the 1930s from
a privately organized economy to a civic one.

Ford assesses the residences for women in detail. His recommendations for the individual room include the upgrading of furniture standards, as well as upgrading of lodging "hotels," and the addition of recreational and social rooms. Concerning housekeeping, his conclusion is that "without exception . . . the officers of these houses . . . recommended that there should be no housekeeping suites within the lodge houses. It was universally felt that the provision of such suites would bring a different kind of tenant who would not assimilate properly in the type of social life which these houses cultivate." Simultaneously however, recommendations were made to construct separate housekeeping buildings for unmarried women and for working mothers and children. Age mixing was considered undesirable at that time. Certain other categories were considered problematic, such as professional entertainers and residents who were mentally or nervously upset.[7]

Ford ends with more recommendations:

> Conclusions general among the managers are that dormitories are undesirable, that demand for double rooms is declining, and that the best plan is to provide solely for single private rooms . . . rooms for entertainment and the reception of guests are essential . . . rooms that are not equipped with wash basins should be abandoned for those that are; that furniture should include more than the customary bed, bureau, and chair, to the extent at least of including a desk and a bookcase and one or two comfortable chairs in addition to the desk chair; that day beds with attractive covering should be provided for single rooms rather than bedspreads; that attractive pictures should be available for the walls, but that guests may properly be encouraged to substitute their own; that wall and floor surfaces should be clean but not forbidding.[8]

## THE LODGING HOUSE

All of these institutions were designed for the middle- and lower-middle-class person. Housing for the poor single was entirely different. In the 1860s, Gordon Atkins reported that 18,000 people lived in cellar lodgings—"the dens of death"—and in 1869, 300 cellars were still in use as lodging houses. Even the police were involved in lodgings, providing shelters for a total of 147,427 in the police stations in 1873.[9] These accommodations were so vile that reformer Jacob Riis led a decade-long effort to close them, accomplishing this mission in the 1890s. These were the "dives," the dens of iniquity where one could stay overnight for ten cents and obtain a glass of beer for five cents.

These invisible lodgers lived in the midst of the families of the tenements. They were in cellars, back yards, and inner rooms. An 1856 description of these conditions vividly describes these dwellings on New York's Lower East Side:

> At No. 17 Baxter Street the committee penetrated through an alley passage, where the black mud was two inches deep, to a rear entrance under the building; the base-

ment rooms, with floors five-and-a-half feet below street level were occupied as a
dance-house and barroom . . . two beds for lodgers were in the dance room. The
class of basement or cellar lodgers accommodated in such places pay from sixpence
to a shilling per night; average number of lodgers to one bed is three and no distinction is made between male and female.[10]

These lodgers were hidden around and about the tenement; they were also part
and parcel of its operation.[11] Contemporary accounts document this phenomenon: "Here is a family—father, mother, and four children—taking in fourteen
boarders and living in three rooms."[12] In another tenement: "There are fifteen
people of all sexes and ages in two little rooms, a great portion of which is taken
up with old rags and refuse."[13] This example indicates that not only were tenant
and lodger one interlocking system but that "work" had also become part of the
housing. "All kinds of occupations are carried out in the bedrooms themselves:
rag-picking, feather-plucking, tailoring, shoemaking, slaughtering, and what not
else. . . . Many are the rooms which are let out in the daytime by the miserable
occupants to a dozen male and female tailors, who work, hollow chested and
consumptive, fourteen to sixteen hours a day on their garments or sewing
machines, filling the room with a stifling atomsphere and influencing the children with their ribald jokes."[14] And, of course, at night the lodgers return. The
actors in this human drama formed a series of necessary linkages: dayworker and
lodger to tenant, tenant to sub-landlord, sub-landlord to owner.

The lodgers are an inextricable part of nineteenth-century housing ecology; yet
when reform occurred, they were disenfranchised. By 1895, the Tenement
House Act of 1891 and its successors had outlawed the use of tenements as
lodging houses.[15] Housing activists such as Lawrence Veiller stimulated this
phenomenon. His views were articulated in the basic reformers' text, *Housing
Reform*. This book expressed a popular belief: "Especially should it be made il-
legal to carry on a common lodging house in a tenement house. The mingling of
the ordinary lodging house pattern with the tenement house dweller is not a good
thing for the community."[16] This nineteenth-century attitude linking the private
lodging house to crime, disease, and social degeneracy would continue well into
the twentieth century.

While lodgers were being displaced from tenements, some reformers focused
on providing some relief through the creation of municipal lodging houses. This
brand of New York housing reform originally grew out of "charity" work. One
philanthropic group set up the first reform housing in the city—the establishment
of the Old Bowery Mission in the heart of the tenement house district—the
notorious "Five Points" area. Five Points was so named because Little Water,
Cross, Anthony, Orange, and Mulberry Streets converged into an open area surrounded by, as a contemporary account informs us, "miserable-looking buildings, liquor stores, innumerable, neglected children by the scores playing in rags
and dirt, squalid-looking women, brutal men with black eyes and disfigured

faces, proclaiming drunken brawls and fearful violence."[17] In the midst of this slum, the New York Ladies Home Missionary Society of the Methodist Episcopal Church set up work programs, established religious activities, and founded a lodging home for the destitute as early as 1853.

Similar efforts began to occur around the newly industrialized world in the latter half of the nineteenth century. For example, the eighth special report of the United States Commissioner of Labor, *The Housing of the Working People*, published in Washington in 1895, gave special attention to model lodging houses, observing that "model lodging houses fill an important sphere in the housing of working people." The report then described model lodging house reform in Glasgow and London. It noted that in 1871, 23 percent of the families in Glasgow took in lodgers to meet this need. Model lodging houses were built in Glasgow; there were six houses for men with 1,967 beds and one for women with 125 beds. "The arrangements are such that each lodger has a private compartment with 400 cubic feet of air space. The cubical system has been chosen. . . . There are such conveniences as reading rooms, dining rooms, baths, and facilities for cooking and washing. It is customary for lodgers to cook their own meals."[18] At the same time Glasgow philanthropist Robert Burns profited from four other homes, having 512, 670, 118 and 593 beds.

The report also recorded other experiences. In London, a municipal lodging house was opened in 1892 for 326 men. Its design reflected great concern for health measures, particularly fresh air. Dormitories were arranged in two halls, each 70 feet by 32 feet, with three tiers of galleries ranging around a central wall. Although these efforts were admirable in their provision of shelter, both the municipal and private efforts were highly charged with Victorian morality. The chapter on lodging houses of the eighth report concludes:

> such institutions (model lodging houses) have a profound sociological value, dealing as they do as a rule with the lower strata of working people, or indeed, with those who have lost social caste. The strict discipline and regulation to which inmates are subjected are of great importance. Social workers also have a good chance to come in contact with the inmates, and an excellent opportunity is created, by providing sound recreation, to overcome the baleful saloon habit and the philosophy of the streets.[19]

The report ends with the statement that "Bad housing is terribly expensive to any community. Moreover, it accounts for much that is mysterious in relation to drunkenness, poverty, crime, and all forms of social decline."[20] The lodging house was charged with the task of the moral reform of the lowest of the working class: "the incorrigible, the drunkard, the criminal, the immoral, the lazy and shiftless."[21] Reformers held this view in spite of the fact that in the majority of cases, the male residents of the Glasgow homes actually did work. Public officials such as the lord provost of Edinburgh disclosed, "These classes . . . should

Exhibit 13.6—Municipal Lodging House
(Ford, *Slums and Housing*, see footnotes).

Exhibit 13.5—Mills Hotel
(Michael Mostoller).

be driven from their hiding places into municipal lodging houses where they could be under police control, and sexes separated, and the children placed in institutions where they might grow up to be useful members of our society.''[22]

In keeping with European reform traditions, New Yorkers also made efforts to blend work with housing for the single, poor individual. One such experiment was described in a contemporary account, *Health, Housing and Poverty*. It notes that:

> To test the sincere desire to work of those who applied to it for assistance, the Charity Organization Society had maintained a woodyard since 1888. This later developed into a Wayfarer's Lodge in 1893. Here, about a hundred men were accommodated nightly and fed a dinner and breakfast, provided they put in about three hours of labor, chopping wood. No one could stay more than three days in a week or six days in a month without special permission. Each wayfarer had to take a bath and have his clothing fumigated before going to bed. No drinking or smoking was permitted.[23]

Other groups engaged in similar activities. One established a laundry to provide a labor test for women seeking aid. Later, it developed a workroom for unskilled women to serve a similar function for women as the Wayfarer's Lodge did for men. In the early 1880s, the Society for Improving the Homes of American Mechanics established lodging houses at 89 and 93 Centre Street and 74 Park Place.[24] Finally, in the early 1900s, the City and Suburban Homes Corporation, a developer of low-cost family dwellings, also built a ''working-girl's'' hotel with a capacity of 325 women.[25]

The most important examples of this type of housing were the Mills Hotels built by Darius Ogden Mills, a bank president, and the Municipal Lodging House. The first Mills Hotel, built in 1897 on Bleecker Street, occupied the entire block between Sullivan and Thompson Streets. It was a remarkable building and housed 1,000 men, charging them ten cents a night (Exhibit 11.5). Designed by Ernest Flagg, an innovative pioneer in housing architecture and the designer of the Singer Building skyscraper (now destroyed) and the Singer factory loft on Broadway in lower Manhattan, it featured a double series of rooms surrounding two great nine-story, glass-covered courtyards. This model was similar to European utopian schemes. Mills opened two other hotels in subsequent years. (Symptomatic of our contemporary ''utopia,'' the first hotel recently has been converted to luxury condominiums and is called ''The Atrium,'' that ubiquitous sign of modernity.)

The Municipal Lodging House, built by New York City at 432-438 East 25th Street in Manhattan, opened in 1909 (Exhibit 11.6). It contained six dormitories and could house 912 men. In conjunction with other facilities, the city sheltered about 7,000 men a night in dormitories with double-decker beds. Showers, fumigation, a dining room, laundry, and health-care facilities were included. A Woman's Building was provided in 1935 at 309 West 14th Street.

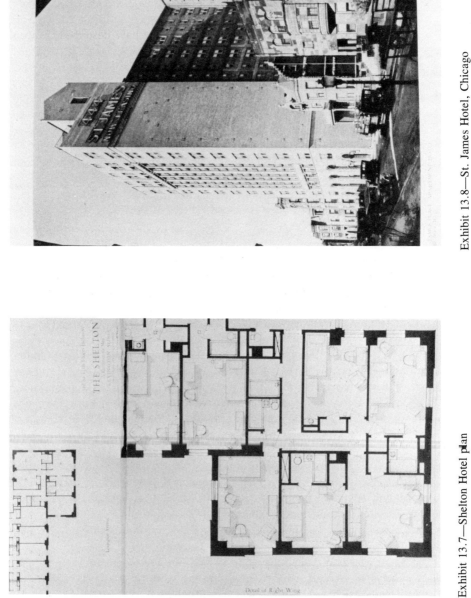

Exhibit 13.8—St. James Hotel, Chicago (Sexton, see footnotes).

Exhibit 13.7—Shelton Hotel plan (*Shelton Prospectus*, New York 1923).

## THE APARTMENT HOTEL

While boarding and lodging houses would be transformed in the twentieth century to the rooming house, a new housing type emerged for single individuals, the apartment hotel. As Barth, Handlin and Plunz have described,[26] urban middle-class families had moved from detached homes, row houses, and brownstones to apartment hotels by the end of the century. With continued urbanization, an increased standard of living, and the greatly increased density of the city, apartment houses also accommodated singles. This variation essentially was a smaller version of the family apartment. Reduced in size, it had no separate dining room (its separate sleeping room was diminished or eliminated) and a greatly reduced kitchen. At street level, a wide variety of communal services were offered, as in the hotel. This fusion of hotel services and permanent, but minimal (often furnished) rooms, of course, became known as the "apartment hotel." This seems merely an upper-class variation of the boarding house, but the initial developments, which were more like apartments, were the visible tip of an emerging iceberg—the need for small efficient dwellings for single people, i.e., "bachelor" apartments and a consequent need for common services and social and recreational facilities within the building.

The initial hotels contained units for couples and singles. Soon, however, the latter type dominated the market. In a 1924 issue of *The Architectural Forum* dedicated to apartment hotels, an article entitled "Efficiency Planning and Equipment" not only begins to establish minimum room standards and efficient layouts, but also posits a multipurpose one-room home that was a "living room by day" and a "bedroom by night." This transformation was accomplished by an ingenious fold-down bed/dressing room arrangement that surpassed European efforts of the same era (Exhibit 13.7). Other essays in the journal reported how widespread the form was. Apartment hotels were shown in New York, Chicago, San Francisco, Cleveland, Washington, St. Louis, Pittsburgh, Rochester, Boston, and Kansas City (Exhibit 13.8).[27]

The ongoing breakup of the family that had been disguised in the growth of lodging and boarding houses finally was acknowledged by the development of this new dwelling type. This truly twentieth-century form, the highrise apartment hotel, acknowledged the increased status, wealth, and independence of the single person. The single individual, without family and servants, needed an "efficient, private, economical" dwelling and an organized household in a building which could provide recreation, society, and sustenance.

The apartment hotel phenomenon continued throughout the 1920s. In 1928, the *Architectural Record*, in a summary of the work of the decade, featured "studio" and "bachelor" apartments as well as the now standard hotel apartment. Once again, cities all over the entire country were mentioned. A year later R.W. Sexton published a book on the new residential buildings of the century entitled *American Apartment Houses, Hotels, and Apartment Hotels of Today*.[28]

Realtor H. Douglas Ives of the Fred F. French Company defined the social and

Exhibit 13.9—Typical New York SRO. Broadway (Michael Mostoller).

economic conditions behind the new housing type. Writing in *The Architectural Forum* of September 1930, he observed:

> The increasing difficulties of transportation, the overcrowded subways and the traffic jams that occur on the streets during the night hours are rapidly causing workers of moderate means who are employed either in the Grand Central zone or Wall Street to live farther and farther from their places of employment for the sake of living in one of the traditional type of apartments, or whether they might not be much better off living in one of the newer type of efficiency apartments of two or possibly only one room, whose aim is to relieve the burden of the housewife or businesswomen, most of whose daylight hours might be spent in acquiring the means necessary to live.[29]

Here for the first time in the professional literature women are mentioned among the consumers of the units. Note, however, that all observers conceived the dwelling type as a miniature but "complete" house. They seem to indicate that while the new demand is valid, it represents either a miniature "family" of one or a transitory period in the life of young workers on their way from one family type to another.

Ives also paid great attention to new topics. He emphasized the technical improvements, kitchen design, heating, and lighting that must go hand-in-hand with miniaturization. Similarly, each building included a great range of amenities for the common social life that the new non-family life style required.

## THE SINGLE-ROOM OCCUPANCY (SRO)

World War II brought a new development in housing, the single-room occupancy unit (SRO). Designed to accommodate the influx of single, low-income workers into the city, it developed from the fusion of the two single-person housing types—lodging/boarding/rooming house and the apartment hotel. Centered on the Upper West Side of Manhattan, the SRO resulted from the conversion of either large apartment buildings or small tenement houses into "rooming house" hotels. These units featured furnished rooms but no common rooms. By the end of the war, a vastly increased single, low-income working population occupied three housing forms: the inexpensive apartment-hotel type, the rooming house, and the SROs (Exhibit 13.9).

The SRO is the current predominant urban type of housing for the single, low-income person. A glimpse at some units and how their residents occupy them is a useful demonstration of their functioning. This information assists in constructing proposals for improved housing for this group. One example, a room in the Parkview Hotel in Harlem, is occupied by Mrs. H. who came to New York City from the South and is very independent (Exhibit 13.10). She has an adopted son and nephew whom she visits occasionally but with whom she desires not to live. She rarely leaves her room, going to the market once every two

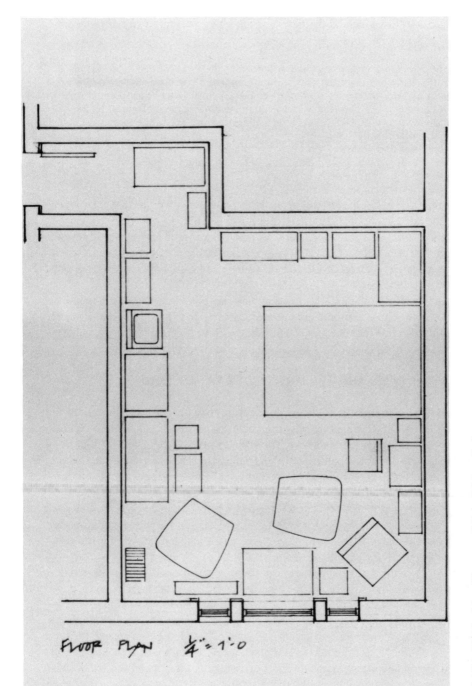

FLOOR PLAN  $\frac{1}{4}" = 1'-0$

Exhibit 13.10—Mrs. H's room (Michael Mostoller).

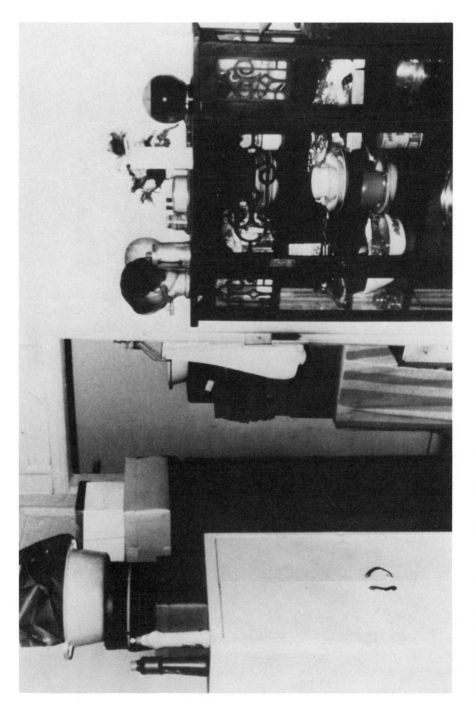

Exhibit 13.11—Mrs. H's room (Michael Mostoller).

Exhibit 13.12—Mrs. H's room (Michael Mostoller).

weeks. She takes a great deal of pride in her room. Even though it is small, she has thoughtfully arranged things so that space is used efficiently. Entering through a small vestibule, one encounters the bed and a set of chairs arranged near a window. There are differences here; in a typical house, the family buffet would not hold a wig stand, and cleaning utensils would not be next to storage (Exhibit 13.11). Nonetheless, there is order. The television, the religious objects, family picture, broom, fly swatter, and wisk broom are arranged with much care (Exhibit 13.12).

While people such as Mrs. H. use hotels as homes, other SRO residents use the hotels as hotels. This second group tends not to accumulate possessions. For them, the provided furnishings and conveniences are more important. The standard items such as the bed, table, and wardrobe or dresser are seldom suitable to life in a single room and are both oversized and underused as a result. I am currently working on a new series of furniture for such conditions.

Regardless of how they use their individual rooms, every resident depends on the network of corridors and public rooms, the kitchen, and bathrooms. In most cases, these common rooms and facilities are in poor condition. Nonetheless, the tenants attempt to do the best they can. They post rules for using facilities; they decorate bathrooms and even individual bathroom stalls (Exhibit 13.13).

Clearly, bathrooms and kitchens in these hotels need to be remodeled and improved. Among housing specialists, there is a question about whether to keep the kitchens as common rooms or to provide kitchen facilities in individual rooms. Some have recommended that kitchens be moved to the rooms when buildings are renovated. As a participant in the work to develop a new room prototype with the Settlement Housing Fund—the Mini Dwelling Unit—I can conclude that in all cases except where a social services agency is active in managing the facility, the kitchen unit should be moved to the room because of vandalism.

Besides the kitchens and bathrooms, corridors are important common spaces with possibilities for greater use by residents in new ways. Where corridors are empty and unused, residents could be given the opportunity to take control of the spaces. Areas could be created at the elevator, for example, to provide for the gathering and socializing that is a feature of the single-room hotel, well documented by Joan Shapiro in her study *Community of the Alone*.[30]

There are numerous other ideas for improving the SRO hotels. Schemes for renovating hotels could include a variety of room sizes and types to meet the housing needs of a diverse group of residents. A proposed 1982 renovation of the Whitehall Hotel on Broadway and 101st Street by the Columbia University Community Services Organization included single hotel rooms, double rooms, and triple-room studio apartments. However, the building subsequently was converted to luxury apartments (Exhibit 13.14).

This concept would reintroduce into the "single-room" hotel a wide range of accommodations. This was attempted in 1983 by the Washington Heights Community Group model shelter, but the idea was rejected by city agencies. Propos-

Exhibit 13.13—Tenant-renovated bath, Park-view Hotel, Harlem, 1982 (Michael Mostoller).

Exhibit 13.14—Displaced tenant, Whitehall Hotel (*Columbia Magazine*, February 1982).

als under development by the Vera Institute of Justice in Harlem and Chelsea maintain the common kitchen to promote socialization and attempt to provide both single and double rooms (Exhibit 13.15).

## SUMMARY

Housing for the single adult in cities today is complicated by two factors, one demographic and one economic. The demographic factor is critical to the housing problem, and it is simple. Our society is aging. The impact of this fact on housing types can be seen in a proliferation of elderly housing forms. "Elderly housing," "nursing" homes, "independent-group residences," and enriched housing for the frail elderly all testify to the new demands being made on the residential stock by older people. And of course, the SRO is the last refuge of many poor elderly, for they most often live alone.

In fact, the SRO is an important form of shelter for women. In 1970, in New York, aged women outnumbered aged men by a ratio of 143 to 100. In 1980, 50 percent of all the city's housing units were occupied by single people. One-third of them were elderly, and three-quarters were women living alone. They totalled 203,000—the population of Des Moines, Iowa.

The other factor that complicates the city housing picture is high real-estate costs. The housing prices are so extreme that the minimum apartment is seen by developers as the wave of the future. With such slogans as "the 300-sq. ft. home and other ideas for the 1980s," "small will be smart," and "the boarding house will be back,"[31] it is clear that the lodging type is being co-opted by the professional and upper-middle class. In New York this is currently reflected in the tax-exempt J-51 conversions to luxury apartments that have cut the stock of SROs to a quarter in five years. This economic struggle between classes for the housing stock will probably intensify in coming years, in what Christopher Lasch calls "the war of all against all."

We face a set of serious conditions. Lodging and rooming houses have vanished in all but one or two limited areas. The residential hotels for women are almost gone. Cheap hotels vanish at an increasing rate. The SRO is an "endangered species." The city shelters housed many more homeless men seventy years ago than now. This debilitated stock has just had to absorb the individuals "of the asylum" due to deinstitutionalization. The economic crush is forcing middle- and upper-income renters into the lodger market. An enlarged need for single units for the elderly has developed. Clearly, the housing type most in need of study and development in the 1980s is the "house" for the single person.

## NOTES

1. Gunther Barth, *City People: The Rise of Modern City Culture in Nineteenth Century America* (New York: Oxford University Press, 1980).

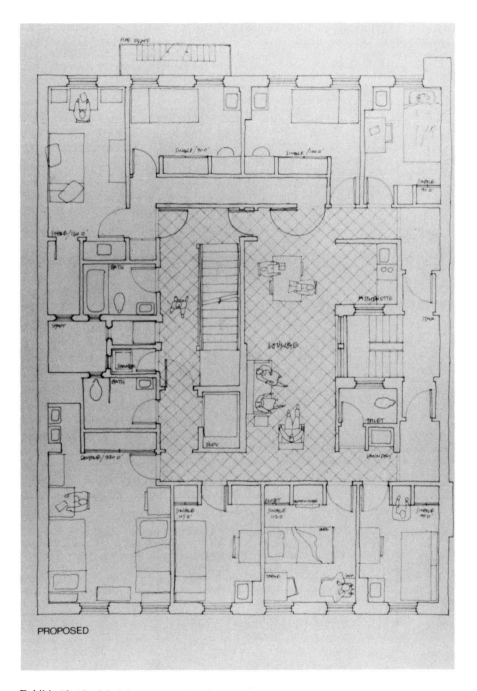

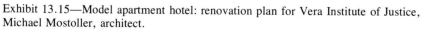

Exhibit 13.15—Model apartment hotel: renovation plan for Vera Institute of Justice, Michael Mostoller, architect.

2. Ibid.

3. Interestingly and perversely, the novel begins with boarding and ends in the Bowery shelters and streets that her paramour, Hurstwood, seeks out after his fall from "social caste."

4. Community Services Society on Housing, *Life in One Room: A Study of the Rooming House Problem in the Borough of Manhattan 1940* (p.a.).

5. James Ford, *Slums and Housing, With Special Reference to New York City: History, Condition, Policy.* 2 Vols. (Cambridge, MA: Harvard, 1936), p. 755.

6. Ibid., p. 759.

7. Ibid., p. 759-60.

8. Ibid., p. 764-65.

9. Gordon Atkins, *Health Housing, and Poverty in New York City 1865-1889* (Ann Arbor: Edwards Brothers, Inc., 1947), pp. 57 and 64.

10. *Report of the Special Committee on Tenant Houses, 1856-1857, Documents of the Assembly of the State of New York, Eighteenth Session, 1957,* quoted in Ford, op. cit., p. 134.

11. Indeed the tenement receives its name from the system of tenant-age: of tenant, sub-landlord, owner, and short-term rental periods. See Atkins, op. cit., p. 18.

12. "Report of Sanitary Aid Society 1887" quoted in Atkins, op. cit., p. 222.

13. Ibid., p. 222.

14. Ibid., p. 223.

15. Robert W. Deforest and Lawrence Veiller (eds.), *The Tenement House Problem* I, II (New York: Macmillan Co., 1903), p. 106.

16. Lawrence Veiller, *Housing Reform, A Handbook for Practical Use in American Cities* (New York: Charities Publication Committee, 1911), p. 120.

17. Ladies of the Mission, *The Old Brewery and the New Mission House at the Five Points,* quoted in Ford, op. cit., pp. 114-16.

18. U.S. Bureau of Labor, *The Housing of the Working People,* prepared under the direction of Caroll D. Wright, Commissioner of Labor, by E.R.L. Gould (Washington, D.C.: Government Printing Office, 1895).

19. Ibid., p. 405.

20. Ibid., p. 436.

21. Ibid., p. 440.

22. Ibid., p. 441.

23. Atkins, *Health, Housing and Poverty.*

24. Ibid., pp. 225-26.

25. Ibid., pp. 288-89.

26. Gunther Barth, op. cit.; Richard Plunz, "Institutionalization of Housing Form in New York City 1920-1950," *Housing Form and Public Policy in the United States,* Richard Plunz (ed.), (New York: Praeger, 1980); David Handlin, *The American Home: Architecture and Society 1815-1915* (Boston, Toronto: Little Brown, 1979).

27. *Architectural Forum,* "Apartment Hotel Reference Number," Vol. XLI, No. 5 (New York: Rogers and Manson, 1924):

> In Europe at that time, avant-garde architects, either in individual designs or in model designs in building expositions or in model settlements, stressed the existent minimum dwelling; efficient layout, maximization of use through careful design and "bachelor" apartment prototypes. LeCorbusier, Breuer, Gropius and Ernest May, among others, contributed to the development of a small efficient dwelling. Their efforts confirm the American bachelor apartment hotel.

28. R.W. Sexton, *American Apartment Houses, Hotels and Apartment Hotels of Today* (New York, 1930), p. 309.

29. H. Douglas Ives, "The Moderate Priced Apartment Hotel," *The Architectural Forum Apartment House Reference Number* (New York, 1930), p. 309.

30. Joan Hatch Shapiro, *Community of the Alone* (New York: Association Press, 1971), p. 150.

31. "The 300 Sq. Ft. Home and Other Ideas for the 80's," *Housing,* Vol. 59, No. 1 (January 1981), p. 72 ff.

*14*

# Shared Housing:
# Its Rationale, Forms, and Challenges

### Clara Fox

One way to expand housing opportunities for low- and-moderate-income persons is shared housing. What is shared housing? Shared housing occurs when two or more unrelated persons or households, each having their own private space, share common areas in an underutilized one-family home, a large apartment, or another type of building. Cuts in the federal housing budget, high health costs, particularly long-term care for the physically and mentally disabled, and the growing number of homeless individuals have significantly increased the need for the development of shared housing facilities. Although sharing is appropriate for anyone who needs housing, this paper looks to shared housing as an effective means for sheltering specific low- and moderate-income groups, such as single persons, one-parent families, the elderly, and disabled or homeless individuals.

In recent years, many cities, particularly New York, have become the loci of severe shelter crises faced by a low-income population, predominantly female, of single persons, single parents, and elderly individuals. These groups are illustrated by the following statistics. In New York City in 1981 it was reported that: single persons accounted for 39 percent of all renters; 60 percent of all renters over 65 years old live alone; and 47 percent of female-headed households are renters.[1] Two factors have made finding shelter a difficult task: (1) the short supply of affordable rental units, and (2) restrictive zoning practices which prevent the creation of accessory apartments and other suitable forms of housing in single-family homes.

In response to the unequal balance of the supply of affordable rental units and the demand of the low-income population, many have created ad hoc housing forms. For example, the New York City Housing Authority estimates that about 15,000 families in the city are living doubled up.[2] Some working, single-parent families share housing or have developed informal support systems (e.g. child care) within the buildings where they lived for many years. Single individuals have been doubling, tripling, and even quadrupling their resources to rent studio, one-, and two-bedroom apartments, particularly in the higher rent areas of the city. For a long time, there did not seem to be a problem for single, working individuals; however, rents have become so high that even when apartments are shared, the rent is unaffordable. Finally, elderly individuals are sharing their homes and apartments with increasing frequency. It is the creation of these ad hoc housing forms which indicates both the shortage of housing for low- and moderate-income persons and the need for more supportive communities. It is for this reason that the shared housing approach should be formalized and promoted.

## URBAN COOPERATIVE FOR THE SINGLE-PARENT FAMILY

One type of shared housing for low- or moderate-income, single-parent families is the urban cooperative. Very often this single parent is a female with one or two children who is working or is a recipient of public assistance. In the latter situation, the parent who wants to work or needs training to enter the job market often cannot get either because she has no place to leave her children. In the case where the parent is working, child care is also a major obstacle in the ability of that parent to cope economically and emotionally with problems at work and at home.

Much research and even some demonstrations have taken place in trying to develop shared housing prototypes. To meet the need of both single-parent families and elderly individuals, inter-generational living illustrates one kind of urban cooperative. Obviously, a housing match where a parent could share a home with an older, agile person who could look after the children, prepare their meals, and perhaps give them some "tender loving care" while the mother worked would be highly desirable. The older person would receive payment for services—payment which would enable him/her to meet economic needs as well as fulfill some emotional need. In turn, the parent would feel secure in the fact that her children would be protected and cared for during the day and sometimes at night, leaving her time for some socializing. In short, we would have an extended family situation—if the match is good.

A more ambitious urban cooperative program would enable several single-parent families (10 or more) to join together, acquire a building at low cost, create a multifamily cooperative, and share in its upkeep financially and through in-kind services, such as informal day care, physical maintenance, shared purchasing, and cooperative meal preparation. Such a setting would allow some parents to work, others to get job training, still others to use their household and child-rearing skills.

New York City's in-rem stock offers opportunities to experiment with urban cooperatives for single-parent families or for intergenerational, cooperative living. The city currently sells buildings to tenants for cooperative conversion at $250 per apartment. To assure the success of the cooperative, the buildings used for urban cooperative purposes should be rehabilitated at minimal costs, and taxes should be abated for several years so that even public-assistance residents can meet the maintenance costs.

If this kind of housing would be actively encouraged, the single head-of-household parents would be helped out of dependency and poverty.

## THE MINI DWELLING UNIT FOR THE SINGLE INDIVIDUAL

For many single persons, special services and protective support systems are needed. Here I refer to broad groups including lower-income working persons, students, divorced women going back to school for retraining, and the SSI and home relief population. For the latter, many of whom are permanently disabled or in rehabilitation treatment programs, special programs are needed. However, for the independent, mature, lone individual, shared housing is a viable alternative. Economically affordable rents are absolutely essential for them. To try to meet the need of the single, working, lower-income individual, the Settlement Housing Fund has been working for the past three years on a program to re-legitimize the old single-room occupant hotels by developing standards for a new type of housing unit in New York City, to be called the Mini Dwelling Unit (MDU) (Exhibit 14.1).

Essentially, the MDU would provide a decent-sized room, with a Dwyer kitchen unit consisting of a small, compact stove, refrigerator, and sink. To save costs, bathroom facilities would be shared—one toilet and one separate shower/bath for every four rooms. Community space, such as a laundry room and meeting places, would be included. Each building with 50 or more units would have 24-hour desk service and security. Buildings under 50 units would have an intercom system and some form of internal tenant security (e.g. tenant patrols).

We have conducted numerous interviews with current single-room occupancy residents, managers, and service providers, and we have received support from all the public agencies involved in this type of housing. We have convinced them that at this time of diminished housing resources, very high housing costs, and a rapidly growing low-income, single-household population, it is essential to codify a new form of permanent housing which does have shared facilities and opportunities for congregate living.

To demonstrate the potential of the MDU and the viability of housing for low-income, single individuals, the Settlement Housing Fund working with HUD and the city Human Resources Administrator obtained a commitment of 300 units of Section 8 moderate rehabilitation housing for single-room occupant units. The city has increased the number, and currently four non-profit groups,

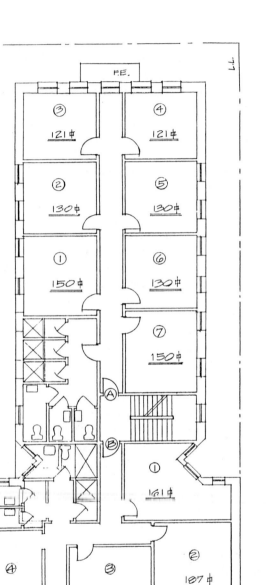

Exhibit 14.1—The Single Room Occupancy Task Force of the Settlement Housing Fund, chaired by Lynda Simmons, commissioned this plan to renovate a New York City tenement to accommodate several Mini Dwelling Units.

including the Settlement Housing Fund, are renovating over 500 units of housing, located in Brooklyn, Manhattan, and the Bronx, for single individuals. We have succeeded in attracting private capital investment to these projects and, with the inclusion of shared housing in the 1981 Housing Act, more development will undoubtedly follow. Unfortunately, the MDU has not yet been codified; however, the Community Service Society, Phipps Houses, and the Settlement Housing Fund are working together to obtain legal code changes administratively and through legislation.

## IMPLEMENTING SHARED HOUSING PROGRAMS: ROLE OF NON-PROFIT SPONSORS

This discussion, and other research and written materials describing shared housing, have laid out the opportunities, purposes, and desired goals in shared-housing programs. However, after all these are presented and actively promoted as desirable housing alternatives to serve a variety of lifestyles, some basic questions remain. Who will undertake the numerous tasks and responsibilities for sponsoring and operating these programs? Who will monitor and evaluate them when they are undertaken and become operational? What kind of funds and human resources are needed?

I raise these questions because I am quite concerned about the abuses that can easily develop if we just throw open the whole field of shared housing to any sponsoring group that wants to become involved. I maintain that shared housing sponsors need extensive training, adequate funding, and careful supervision. This applies to well-meaning not-for-profits as well as to for-profit developers, and individuals coming together informally.

In my opinion, non-profit sponsors have a special role to play, but it must be understood that they are not miracle workers. They need expertise, funding, and accountability. I am emphasizing this because we have a strong tendency in these days of shrinking federal resources to do exactly what President Reagan has urged—namely, to depend more and more on volunteerism in order to make up for the lack of public funds. Although I believe strongly in the mutual support systems that shared housing can create, I want to caution non-profit groups not to undertake a shared housing program unless they are certain they have the supports needed to function effectively and productively.

Non-profit housing groups and service agencies should join together to plan, sponsor, develop, and operate shared housing for the populations I have discussed. Obviously, careful matching and early and ongoing counselling are essential to the success of these programs, but the economic and social rewards to individuals and society can be really significant.

Among the problems that sponsors will find are the following:

1. Finding suitable buildings;

2. Obtaining seed money for startup costs;
3. Community resistance;
4. Finding institutional lenders (banks) who will give mortgages to shared housing facilities;
5. Identifying or developing special management skills;
6. Identifying and obtaining needed services for special groups living in shared housing; and
7. Obtaining necessary governmental commitments and involvement.

## ROLE OF GOVERNMENT

As indicated previously, informal shared housing arrangements are quite common and serve various needs, particularly for single individuals and the elderly. Furthermore, taking in "boarders" or "roomers" has long been a practice among lower-income families who have an extra room and need additional income. However, attempts to formalize shared housing in today's limited housing market are new phenomena which require the active intervention of government in order to legitimize and finance such housing for lower-income individuals.

In fact, some legislation has been enacted nationally, and some programs have been initiated locally, which can and should be used by government and private sponsors to stimulate the development of shared housing. I have already mentioned the national Housing Acts of 1981 and 1983 which allow the use of Section 8 existing and moderate rehabilitation programs for single-room occupancy units and for shared housing facilities. The problem lies in obtaining adequate funding for these programs at a time when the federal government is providing very minimal funds for any subsidized housing program. It is essential, therefore, for shared housing advocates to continue the pressures that have led to the recognition and inclusion of this form of alternative housing into the spectrum of federally financed housing programs.

In New York, the city is using some of its Community Development Block Grant funds, combined with its Section 8 moderate rehabilitation allocations, to expand the single-room occupancy stock. Much more of this type of funding is required. A low-cost city loan program should be established for single-parent families who want to acquire a building and form urban-type cooperatives, as described earlier. Non-profit organizations should be identified and funded to assist in such projects.

New York State has allocated $50 million for the development of special purpose housing. While the emphasis is also on single-room occupancy, single-parent families should be targeted for assistance. The low-income elderly who have homes or apartments with extra space should also be encouraged and assisted financially and emotionally to share their homes with compatible individuals or families. Government-funded counselling programs are necessary for all these programs. Low-interest mortgages, grants, and rehabilitation financing are also essential.

Finally, but most important and relevant, the Department of Health and Human Services in Washington (and state and city Departments of Social Services) must not reduce the shelter or basic grant allowances (a flat grant prevails in the majority of states that do not separate shelter and the basic needs allocation) for the SSI population (elderly and disabled) or any public-assistance recipients who decide to live together and share rent and living expenses. Since the total grant in New York State, for example, is below the basic living standard, cutting back on allowances when individuals or families (usually single heads of household) try to survive by sharing their housing is punitive and self-defeating.

In summation, shared housing is an idea whose time is now; it requires government and individual commitment as well as public and private financing. Most important, it is a workable program which offers many creative opportunities for lower-income individuals and single heads of households to live independently and productively.

## NOTES

1. Michael Stegman, *The Dynamics of Rental Housing in New York City* (Piscataway, NJ: Center for Urban Policy Research, 1982), pp. 79-82.

2. Telephone interview with Ray Hensen of the New York City Housing Authority, April 23, 1984. No written survey has been conducted.

# 15

# The Elderly and Their Housing Needs: The Lenox Hill Neighborhood Association

The Upper East Side, extending from 59th to 96th Streets between Fifth Avenue and the East River, is known as Manhattan's "golden ghetto." The neighborhood has the highest per capita income of any part of the city and of most of the nation.

The wealth on the Upper East Side exists now beyond Fifth and Park Avenues. With the demolition of lowrise tenements, the assembly of sites by developers on the side streets and the building of luxury apartments, affluence has spread from Central Park to the East River on many streets. During the last decade alone, the population of the area nearly doubled to over 200,000. However, at least one in 14 residents live below the poverty level; and more than 80,000 low- and moderate-income people have been displaced by newcomers moving into expensive highrise apartment buildings.

Despite the proliferation of luxury buildings, some old tenements remain on almost every block, particularly east of Third Avenue. Apartments in these tenements are largely occupied by the elderly, who constitute about one-fifth of the area's population. Most of the units are railroad flats; many are still not centrally heated, and some lack private bathrooms. Tenants use a common toilet in the hall, and washtubs in their kitchens serve as bathtubs.

The needs of the elderly population in the Upper East Side are, in part, met by social service agencies and private organizations. The Lenox Hill Neighborhood Association, a settlement house founded by alumnae of Hunter College, provides many of the needed services. LHNA sponsors a senior citizens center with about 1,800 members who receive hot lunch and participate in special interest groups. It offers an outreach program to the homebound elderly, which provides ongoing personal assistance to about 900 older adults, thereby making it possible for them to remain in their own apartments in a familiar neighborhood. In addition to these programs, LHNA has endeavored to address the housing needs of the elderly.

LHNA works with city officials to provide decent, low-cost shelter on the

Upper East Side for the low-income elderly. Its aim is to avoid the trauma of up-
rooting lifelong residents who rely on their churches, medical services, and na-
tionality stores in the area. Many of the residents are older women who originally
came to America 40 or 50 years ago from central and western Europe. Their lives
have been bounded by this community, and thus, even moving them 30 blocks
may pose severe psychological problems. LHNA has been instrumental in the
construction of two senior citizens housing projects in the area. The history of
each project illustrates some of the special housing needs of this group and il-
luminates more general concerns of elderly women.

In 1959, LHNA began working with the New York City Housing Authority to
develop over 400 dwelling units in the Stanley M. Isaacs Houses and 555 units in
the John Haynes Holmes Towers on 93rd Street and First Avenue. At that time,
planners believed that housing should not be built exclusively for the elderly, and
they set a limit of 45 percent for the elderly in the Isaacs project and 55 percent in
Holmes. The units for the elderly were one-bedroom apartments with special
amenities, such as grab bars in the bathrooms, lower cupboards in the kitchens to
avoid precipitous reaching, special door buzzers, and other kinds of security devices. Incorporated into the original program were services for the aged. For
example, New York's first Meals-on-Wheels program was started here, funded
partially with state funds matched by private support. A concierge or resident ad-
visor was provided with an apartment in the housing project and was on call for
emergencies 24 hours a day.

Ten years later when the Ira Robbins Houses, a vest pocket project of 150
units, was built on the corner of 70th Street and First Avenue, the situation was
completely different. Real-estate values in the area were now so high and the site
was surrounded by so many highrise luxury apartment buildings, it took nine
years of concerted community effort to persuade the Housing Authority that the
site was feasible. There also had been changes in the philosophy of what kind of
housing should be provided for the elderly. Building housing projects exclusively
for the elderly had become acceptable. In addition, the size of the apartment units
had been reduced to studio or efficiency apartments, eliminating the separate
bedroom. It was claimed this was done to spread the dollars further.

The reaction of the elderly tenants demonstrates what design elements they
consider desirable, in fact, essential in their housing. The case of one 78-year-old
woman reveals the resistance of the elderly to living in one-room apartments.
This woman, who had lived in the neighborhood since she was 14 years old,
qualified for an apartment in the new building because she was not only elderly
but also disabled. In fact, the only way she could leave her apartment in a three-
story walkup was to descend the stairway backwards. Nonetheless, she turned
down the offer to live in the new housing, an elevator building, because she
could not face moving to a studio apartment. Another design feature important to
elderly tenants is a kitchen that has a door. Finally, a major concern was to pro-

vide security without isolating the tenants. The elderly were frightened of teenagers; however, they wanted to be part of the mainstream and liked to watch children at play and other street activities. Thus, it was important to include protected public space for them.

# 16

# Four Rehabilitation Projects for Urban Households

Jane Margolies

The high cost of construction combined with bouncing interest rates have triggered a plunge in new-home building in recent years. At the same time, there has been a surge in housing rehabilitation as a way to meet housing demand. In New York City, tax abatements and other subsidies have fueled housing rehabilitation. Landlords taking advantage of a tax abatement program, J-51, rehabilitated 387,275 units between 1964 and 1982.[1] Two other subsidies, Article 8-A and the Participation Loan Program, assisted the rehabilitation of 47,000 units between 1977 and 1984.[2]

Most of this rehabilitation has produced units traditional in design. Perhaps adequate for "traditional" families in which women are fulltime homemakers, these units can cause problems for female-headed and dual-career families, single women, and elderly women.

Students in the Women and Housing Seminar considered a number of recommendations in formulating proposals for the rehabilitation of four sites. Working in four teams, they first defined non-traditional household forms as target groups with particular housing needs. Each team then picked a building, drafted plans for redesigning it to meet the needs of the target group, and then sought ways to finance the project.[3] The teams tried to be creative but realistic in their projects, a goal they found difficult to achieve.

Most difficulties were because of the assignment's constraints. The first constraint was that students only propose rehabilitation—not new construction. Thus, there were limitations as to how much existing buildings could be altered. A second constraint concerned limited financial resources. The low incomes of female-headed families and elderly women, coupled with dwindling housing subsidies, forced students to keep rehabilitation costs low. Finally, students could only propose changes to buildings that would be acceptable to women in their target groups.

Because of these limitations, students gave up some of their original plans for

229

the buildings. In the end they either had to scale down their proposals, or rely on dubious financing schemes. However, despite shortcomings, the projects differed from conventional housing in some significant ways. Furthermore, the proposals demonstrate some barriers to innovation in a development system based on values rooted in an earlier period. The very modesty of the proposals is testimony to the need to examine current public and private financing practices.

## PROJECT I:
## OBSTACLES TO INNOVATION

For their project, Denise Boyce and Irene Fanos had three objectives. First, they wanted to provide housing to serve all ages and household forms: traditional, female-headed and dual-career families, couples without children, and single women. Second, through redesigning their building they hoped to foster some communal activity among these different groups. "We entered the project with grand notions of communal spaces, especially communal kitchens,"[4] they wrote. Finally, the team, stating that "the importance of a community in which supportive services are available and accessible should be understood as an essential part of any lifestyle setting,"[5] wanted to provide housing near stores, support services, and cheap public transportation.

To translate these objectives into practice, Boyce and Fanos proposed rehabilitating a "dumbbell" tenement in the Kingsbridge section of the Bronx. The five-story building, 3422 Bailey Place, was an *in rem* (condemned) property which had been gutted but was structurally sound. The team chose this building because of its good condition and the vitality of the surrounding neighborhood. Health-care clinics and social-service centers were within walking distance of Bailey Place. A major commercial spine, Broadway, lay one block away. There was ample park and recreation space, public and parochial schools, and a small manufacturing area. Subway and bus lines crisscrossed Kingsbridge. Boyce and Fanos observed that "the more than adequate public transportation system eliminated the financial burden of car ownership."[6]

Although the team found a neighborhood that met their objective of a supportive community, they were not as successful in redesigning the building. For instance, they were able to incorporate only a few of their original ideas for communal spaces. Three reasons caused them to abandon the other ideas. The first two were economic: given the low incomes of their potential tenants, they wanted to keep rents down. To create a communal kitchen, they would have had to eliminate at least one apartment, and to compensate for the loss of rental income, they would have had to hike rents commensurably for the remaining apartments. Second, recognizing that current appraisal and mortgaging practices frown on unusual arrangements, Boyce and Fanos worried that nonconventional communal spaces would have made it difficult to sell the building. The third rea-

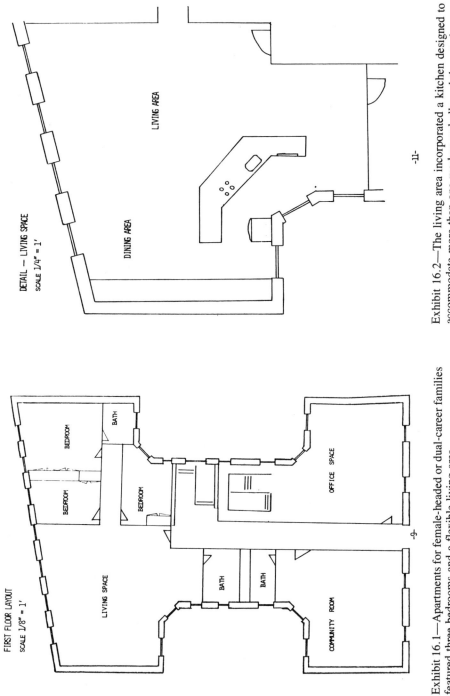

DETAIL — LIVING SPACE
SCALE 1/4" = 1'

LIVING AREA

DINING AREA

-11-

Exhibit 16.2—The living area incorporated a kitchen designed to accommodate more than one worker and allowed them to be involved in others' activities in the remainder of the living area.

FIRST FLOOR LAYOUT
SCALE 1/8" = 1'

BEDROOM

BEDROOM

BATH

BEDROOM

LIVING SPACE

BATH

BATH

COMMUNITY ROOM

OFFICE SPACE

-9-

Exhibit 16.1—Apartments for female-headed or dual-career families featured three bedrooms and a flexible living area.

son was social; when interviewing potential tenants, the team found extreme resistance to the idea of communal spaces, particularly kitchens. The women interviewed insisted on traditional arrangements. Facing these obstacles, Boyce and Fanos confined their communal spaces to a community room, laundry room, and a workshop.

Like the common spaces, the individual apartments did not radically depart from traditional ones. However, they did vary in layout, reflecting the team's desire to create units suitable to different households. For female-headed and dual-career households, Boyce and Fanos designed three-bedroom apartments (Exhibit 16.1). By removing some interior walls, they devoted about half of the total floor space to an "active living area." This space included kitchen facilities on one side, allowing whoever was working in the kitchen to interact with others or to supervise children in the living area (Exhibit 16.2). To accommodate more than one person preparing meals, the team adopted New York architect Susana Torre's concepts of an "island work center" and open storage cabinets.

Boyce and Fanos also tried to provide privacy for the adult(s) in these three-bedroom apartments. They used three measures to do this: clustering the bedrooms so they were separate from common areas; accoustically insulating the master bedroom with a wall of closets; and providing two bathrooms—one opening only to the master bedroom. In some apartments, however, this solution created other problems. In addition to the fact that parents may not want their bedroom sandwiched between the children's bedrooms, children had to walk from their bedrooms to the other end of the apartment to use a bathroom.

Using the same base unit, Boyce and Fanos designed apartments for couples with a single child or without children (Exhibit 16.3). These apartments had two bathrooms and two bedrooms (the second bedroom could be a work space). Otherwise, they were similar in layout to the three-bedroom apartments.

Loft apartments, designed for single women, differed in layout. Most lofts consisted of a bath and an enormous "living area" which included the kitchen facilities. The open layout of loft apartments allowed occupants to use the space as they wished. Some loft units were paired and connected by a common kitchen (Exhibit 16.4). Probably the most innovative feature of their proposal, this common kitchen was all Boyce and Fanos were able to salvage from their dream of a large, communal kitchen. The common kitchen, which could be closed off from the individual loft units, provided an opportunity for some companionship for the singles while allowing them their privacy and independence.

## PROJECT II:
## THE DAYCARE DILEMMA

Linda Bucciarelli, Margaret Elwert, and Janet Galanor proposed to renovate a multifamily building to serve a mix of households: traditional, dual-career and female-headed families, and single individuals. "Rather than limit ourselves to a

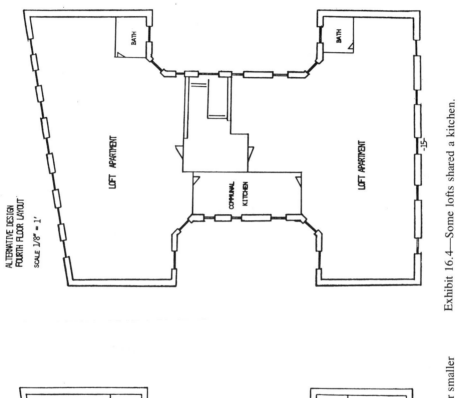

ALTERNATIVE DESIGN
FOURTH FLOOR LAYOUT
SCALE 1/8" = 1'

LOFT APARTMENT

COMMUNAL KITCHEN

LOFT APARTMENT

BATH

BATH

-15-

Exhibit 16.4—Some lofts shared a kitchen.

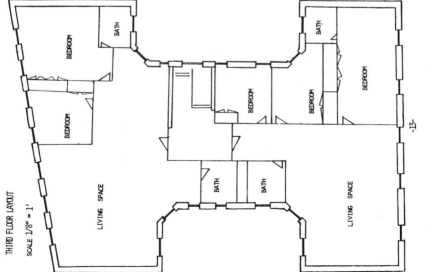

THIRD FLOOR LAYOUT
SCALE 1/8" = 1'

BEDROOM

BEDROOM

BATH

LIVING SPACE

BATH

BATH

BEDROOM

BEDROOM

BEDROOM

BATH

LIVING SPACE

-13-

Exhibit 16.3—The two-bedroom unit would be suitable for smaller families.

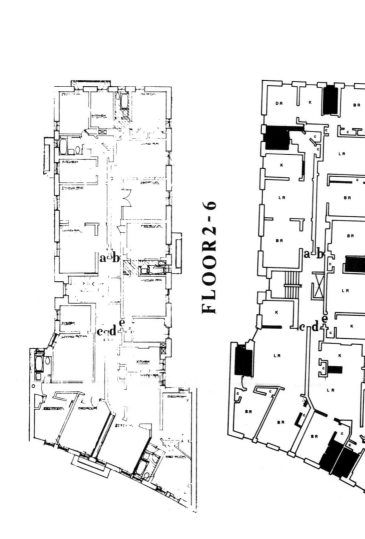

**FLOOR 2 - 6**

**FLOOR 2 - 6**

Exhibit 16.5/6—(Above) The original floor plan of 845 Riverside Drive. (Below) Students changed the layouts to provide for more flexibility.

single type of female population," the trio wrote, "we decided to plan our project around the women found in the area in which our building is located."[7]

The building, 834 Riverside Drive, was located in a working- and middle-class neighborhood near Riverside Park in Manhattan. It was an elevator building with 31 apartments. Owned by New York City, it was structurally sound, but needed a new boiler, extensive repair to the plumbing and electrical systems, and new bathrooms and kitchens.

The team, however, wanted to do more than basic rehabilitation. They aimed to create apartments that freed women to pursue careers or other interests. To this end, they redesigned the kitchens. Where practical, they proposed knocking down walls between kitchens and living rooms. In addition, since the kitchens were too small to eat in, they tried to create an area near the kitchens for dining. For example, they took a room from an A-line apartment and added the space to a B-line apartment next to the kitchen (Exhibits 16.5 and 16.6). The trio also proposed changes to the building's common areas. They added a laundry room in the basement, recognizing that while "not particularly innovative," it would be a convenience that "should make life easier."[8] A more innovative but ill-fated recommendation was for a daycare center.

Interest in including a daycare center in the building was in keeping with the aim to free women for careers or other interests. They designed a daycare center for 30 children, proposing to convert three rear apartments on the first floor (Exhibits 16.7 and 16.8). However, after calculating the cost of renovating and operating the center, they realized that without some form of subsidy, it would be too expensive for the households in the building and the neighborhood. The estimated renovation cost for the center was $10,529, and the annual operating cost, including salaries and rent, was $107,600. After subtracting projected private donations of supplies and furnishings worth $5,440, the annual price of daycare per child was $3,500. This price was too high for most households in the building, especially for black and Hispanic female-headed households who had the lowest incomes. Reluctantly, the daycare center idea was given up.

Instead, a plan for home child care was adopted. New York City regulations permit an adult to care for up to five children in a private home. This arrangement, then, could benefit participating working parents and their children, as well as provide a job for a childcare worker who lived in the building in an apartment designed to accommodate both family and childcare activities. A C-line apartment was enlarged by adding space from an adjacent hallway (Exhibit 16.5 and 16.6), and the kitchen and living area were opened so that the childcare worker could supervise children at all times.

## PROJECT III:
## HOUSING THE ELDERLY

Lisa Boyd and Douglass Roby converted a nineteenth-century convent to con-

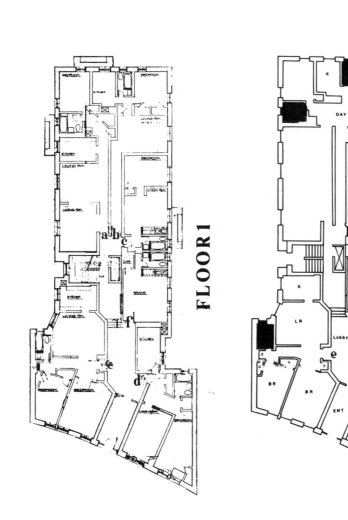

**FLOOR 1**

**FLOOR 1**

Exhibit 16.7/8—(Above) The original first floor plan. (Below) The first floor plan could accommodate a day care   center.

gregate housing for 13 elderly people. They presented an economic and social rationale for this approach to housing the elderly. Noting that the elderly often live alone on fixed incomes, Boyd and Roby argued that when designed as the reuse of an existing building, congregate housing could be less expensive for an elderly person than private accommodations. They also pointed out that while the elderly cherish their independence and loathe institutionalization, they also desire contact with others, especially if their families live elsewhere and friends are deceased. Congregate housing could offer a "nice balance of individual privacy and community participation so difficult to find in either private dwellings or institutions."[9]

However, Boyd and Roby emphasized that congregate housing is not for everyone. Residents have to be physically able to care for themselves with some help, but without constant medical attention. Residents also must work cooperatively to accomplish the cooking, cleaning, and other tasks. Congregate housing was viewed as an extension of the neighborhood in which it would be located and from which it would draw the elderly residents. "The atmosphere most strongly to be guarded against is the sense that members of the house are being 'sent away' to an old people's home. Rather, they must be made to feel that they are joining a society in their own neighborhood."[10]

The nineteenth-century convent proposed for congregate housing was located in "Southside"—South Williamsburg, Brooklyn. Southside is a working-class community possessing adequate public transportation, schools, and services as well as some light industry. Roman Catholic and Orthodox churches unite the community's various ethnic groups. Participation and support from the Southside community, especially the churches, was an important component of the project, as discussed later.

Built in 1892, the convent is a heavy, brick Romanesque revival structure in good condition in spite of having become an *in rem* (tax delinquent) property in 1980. The convent's size and interior layout were characteristic of the building's age and type. The ground floor contained public reception rooms, a small chapel, a common room and large kitchen and refectory. The two upper floors contained bed-sitting rooms, ranging in size from modest to tiny, and two bathrooms.

Since the building was originally designed as a group home, it could be easily converted to congregate housing. The only major reconstruction would be the replacement of the outdated 1892 plumbing. On the ground floor, the kitchen and refectory only needed refurbishment. Here, common meals could be prepared and served. Three other rooms on the ground floor could be converted to a television room and a manager's flat with a small office to be occupied by someone hired from the community. The chapel and parlor could become a work space that might be used for a small business, such as a telephone answering service or daycare center. A small business would provide supplemental income, engage residents in an activity, and create a link between the congregate home and the Southside community.

For the second and third floors, Boyd and Roby planned apartments of various sizes—studios, one and two bedrooms. They added bathrooms to each apartment. Both floors also had a kitchen and dining area so that residents occasionally could cook individually for themselves or a guest.

However, the success of congregate housing is premised on the philosophy of cooperative living. Cooking meals cooperatively and doing routine cleaning keeps maintenance cost down and "involves members with each other in a natural and non-compulsory way."[11] Residents contract for the meals and housekeeping services they desire and the amount of work (e.g. serving meals, working the daycare center) they wish to offer. Their meals and housekeeping costs are deducted from their "work income." Naturally, such a cooperative arrangement functions only if residents are able-bodied and willing to work together.

To finance their project, Boyd and Roby relied on two sources of funding besides the residents themselves: (1) New York City, through its Division of Alternative Management Programs (DAMP), could contribute $5,000 per unit to overhaul the plumbing and electrical systems; and (2) they wanted the city to sell the convent at nominal cost to a non-profit management corporation. The corporation, organized in the Southside community—perhaps by the local churches—would supply volunteer labor for rehabilitating the convent, manage the congregate home, and provide ongoing financial support. The estimated rents (including meals) would range from $158 to $196 per month.

While this congregate housing project is creative, the financing arrangement was extremely precarious. Although Boyd and Roby's expectations of the city's contribution seemed fair, their estimated costs of site development and operation were much too low. In addition, the plan hinged on the willingness of the community to organize a management corporation that would contribute labor and funds. There was no consideration of the possibility of community opposition.

## PROJECT IV:
## HELPING THE DUAL-CAREER FAMILY

Linda Goodman and Camille Sprio addressed the housing needs of the dual-career family with children. They believed that despite the predominance of this group, little attention has been paid to its housing needs. This oversight was due to two misperceptions: first, these families can always afford to buy their own homes; and second, their housing needs are satisfied by conventional housing.

In fact, with the rising costs of building and financing new homes, the dual-career family cannot always afford to buy. Although these families have two incomes, the women probably contribute far less than their husbands since women generally earn less than men. In addition, the amount of money devoted to housing would be reduced by the cost of replacing (through daycare, babysitters, and cleaning help) the unpaid labor of the mother as fulltime homemaker.

Exhibit 16.9—Façade of the main building on the Stamford site.

Even if affordability is not a problem, dual-career families cannot always find the housing they want. The typical suburban, single-family home creates enormous problems for such a family, especially for the woman. Kitchens, for example, are designed to accommodate only one worker: suburban locations result in time commuting to work and driving to and from errands. Since a woman usually shops, chauffeurs children, and cleans the home—in addition to her fulltime job—the unsuitability or inadequacy of a dwelling and its location fall heavily on her.

From their analysis of the housing problems of the dual-career family, Goodman and Sprio summarized this group's housing needs: access to work, shopping and daycare; flexible layouts to allow parents to work at home if they desire; and affordable purchase and maintenance prices. Noting the increasing number of dual-career families in the suburbs, this team decided to tackle a non-central-city housing problem. To meet these objectives, they proposed converting a factory to a commercial and residential complex.

Goodman and Sprio chose a factory in Stamford, Connecticut. They based their choice on the assumption that the site would provide access to jobs. Stamford is the job center of southwest Connecticut, and it is rated third, behind New York City and Chicago, as the headquarters of Fortune 500 companies. The eight-acre site, less than a ten-minute commute to the central business district, was located in a mixed commercial/residential neighborhood. It was situated on

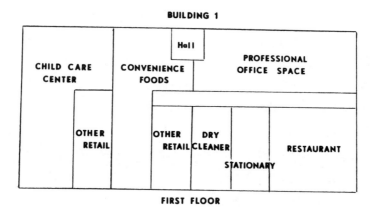

PLANNED COMMERCIAL USES

Exhibit 16.10—They incorporated services for convenience and income.

Southfield Avenue on an inlet of Stamford Harbor. This site was selected because of its location and because the factory buildings were eligible for historic
certification; therefore, they would receive tax credits under the Economic Recovery Tax Act (ERTA).

There were two main buildings on the site. One building, a rectangular box
structure, sitting parallel to Southfield Avenue, had two full floors and a partial
third floor (Exhibit 16.9). Because of its street-front location, the building lent itself to commercial use. "Just as housing can be brought closer to services, services can be brought closer to housing," the team stated.[12] Therefore, they
planned to include in this commercial portion of the complex services dual-career
families frequently use, such as a food store, dry cleaners, takeout restaurant,
and a daycare center (Exhibit 16.10). They also included professional office
space to increase the income-generating potential of the property. Ideally, residents of the complex could rent the professional and commercial spaces, taking
advantage of the opportunity to work close to home.

The second floor of this building was designed as rental apartments. One of the
apartments would be reserved for a resident staff person, whom the residents' association would hire and pay from a dues charge. In return, the staff person

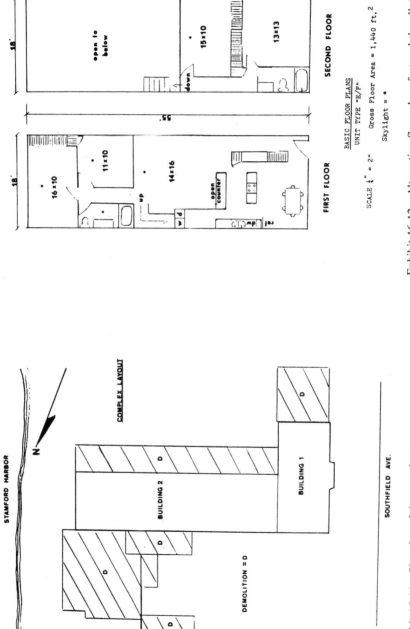

Exhibit 16.12—Alternative floor plans featured the allotment of rooms to different uses.

Exhibit 16.11—Site plan of the complex.

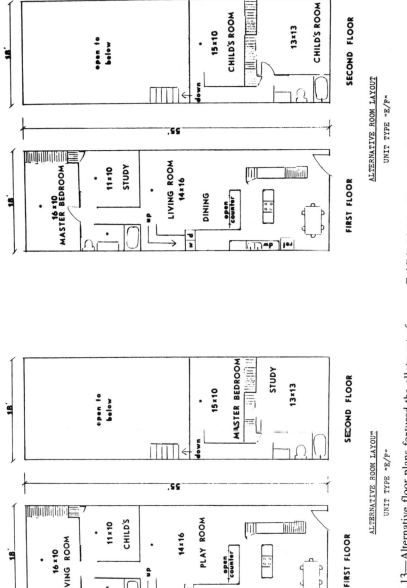

ALTERNATIVE ROOM LAYOUT
UNIT TYPE "E/F"

Exhibit 16.14—Alternative floor plans featured the allotment of rooms to different uses.

ALTERNATIVE ROOM LAYOUT
UNIT TYPE "E/F"

Exhibit 16.13—Alternative floor plans featured the allotment of rooms to different uses.

would provide at reasonable cost a variety of services, such as apartment cleaning and errand running.

The other building, perpendicular to the front building, extended back to the inlet (Exhibit 16.11). It was converted to 46 condominium units. The size and shape of the building created difficulties in designing individual units, however. For example, since there were windows only along one side, Goodman and Sprio were forced to design long, narrow units and to install skylights in rear rooms.

The basic unit was designed to give occupants a maximum amount of flexibility in their use. The team suggested three alternative use plans for the units (Exhibits 16.12, 16.13, and 16.14). Only the kitchens and bathrooms had set functions. All units had large eat-in kitchens. Half the kitchen could be used either as a dining area or a children's play area. A counter, mounted on rolling wheels, could be moved where needed. Its exposed corners were rounded to reduce danger to children (Exhibit 16.15).

Goodman and Sprio also showed sensitivity toward children in their layout of the grounds. They set aside extensive large common play areas while preserving the natural landscape. The play areas were visible from the front windows of all units so adults could supervise children from inside their homes.

This plan was expensive. The team, truly creative in designing the project, also tried to be inventive in financing it. As mentioned earlier, they chose the factory because they could take advantage of tax credits. But this was just a tiny savings. Since the target group was not eligible for any direct governmental assistance, Goodman and Sprio turned to the private sector for help. They proposed forming a consortium of corporations to assist in providing housing for their employees. The team felt that in addition to enhancing their corporate images, the consortium members also would benefit from the promise of housing when recruiting qualified workers. "Affordable housing would be used as an inducement to attract new employees as well as to retain those presently employed."[13]

In this proposal, the consortium would create a non-profit development corporation to develop the housing on a break-even basis. The consortium would then offer individual units to employees and, if necessary, put the remainder on the open market. The consortium would retain its investment in the rental (both commercial and residential) portions of the property.

In addition to developing the housing, the consortium would provide mortgage assistance to employees. Rental income would offset the cost of borrowing money, which would be used either to directly provide mortgages or to shave interest points off market-rate mortgages.

## CONCLUSIONS

In their role as developers, the teams had limited success in responding to the housing needs of women in non-traditional household forms. In general, they

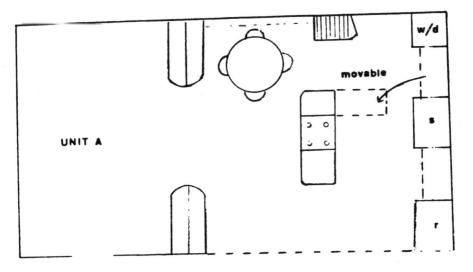

## KITCHEN DESIGN

SCALE ¼"=1"

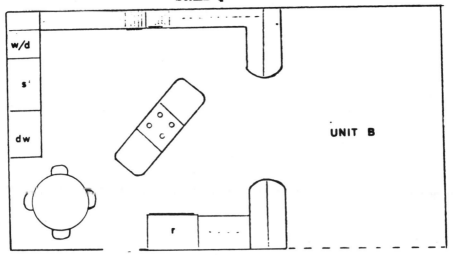

Washer dryers are stackable units.

All exposed corners are rounded for child saftey.

Movable counters are on wheels and can be arranged around stove
   unit as desired.

Empty half of kitchen can be used as more formal dining, play
   area or den.

Exhibit 16.15—Flexibility was the key feature of the kitchen designs.

presented plans for spacious individual units. Incorporating the concept of "flexible space," the teams planned rooms without set functions to allow occupants to use space as they wished. However, with the exception of kitchens, rooms were not innovatively designed. In fact, the teams viewed the kitchen as the only room in existing housing where they could make design improvements. The focus was in the kitchen, Janet Galanor observed. Her project, and the others, drew heavily on Susana Torre's ideas on kitchen design.

The teams also had difficulty financing their projects; to some extent this difficulty explains the near-absence of design innovation. The two projects for rehabilitating apartment buildings highlight the difficulty of achieving innovation when funding is limited. Both teams had creative ideas which they failed to implement because of the limited resources of their target groups and the lack of subsidies. The proposals for transforming a convent to congregate housing and a factory to condominiums were more innovative; they also depended on uncertain funding schemes.

Where the projects do depart from conventional housing lore is their view of the importance of location and availability of services; the fact that all projects include a neighborhood profile reflects the concern for location. The projects recognized that female-headed and dual-career families and single women require access to jobs, stores, services, and public transportation. The projects all were in urban locations which could meet this accessibility requirement. In addition to locating housing where services existed, the teams attempted to bring services closer by incorporating them into the housing itself. Thus, the Riverside Drive multi-family building renovation project included home child care, and the Stamford condominium project included daycare, a staff person to run errands, and commercial spaces for services used by residents.

Clearly, the Stamford project offers the most and best services to its residents, who have the highest incomes of the non-traditional household groups. Without subsidies, and without changes in the nation's housing priorities and programs, only those who have the ability to pay will be able to enjoy the most desirable housing.

## NOTES

1. New York City Real Estate Board.
2. Office of Management and Budget. Message to the Mayor, Fiscal Year 1984, New York: April 26, 1984, p. 137. Some of these units also may have received J-51 tax treatment.
3. Students could chose their buildings from a list of *in rem* properties supplied by the New York City Department of Housing Preservation and Development.
4. Denise Boyce and Irene Fanos, "Housing Design with Institutional Constraints for a Mixed Population," p. 7. (New York, 1982).*
5. *Ibid*, p. 2.
6. *Ibid*, p. 1.
7. Linda Bucciarelli, Margaret Elwert, and Janet Galanor, (no title), p. 1.*
8. Ibid, p. 2.

9. Lisa Boyd and Douglas Roby, ''66 Havemeyer Street: A Proposal for Congregate Housing for the Elderly,'' p. 2. (New York, 1982).*

10. Ibid, p. 10.

11. Ibid, p. 6.

12. Linda Goodman and Camille Sprio, ''Housing the Dual Career Family: An Adaptive Reuse Proposal,'' p. 6. (New York, 1982).*

13. Ibid, p. 9.

*These are papers students prepared for the Hunter College Women and Housing Seminar, 1983-1984.

# PART III

# Implementing Plans for Housing the Unsheltered Woman

When probing design solutions, affordability issues are paramount. With the target groups' income ranges of $4,000 to $27,000, finances play a strong role in defining design. Matching innovative concepts with economic realities is difficult indeed, and weaving the experiences of practitioners who have been through the development process with the sometimes utopian scenarios that design-visionaries promote is a challenge. This section will provide examples of this kind of effort.

On the pessimistic side, developers Lynda Simmons, Carol Lamberg, and Linda Field decry the narrow focus of government housing programs and call for their redefinition in terms more appropriate to today's needs (Chapter 17). Architect Judith Edelman concurs with this analysis (Chapter 18). She reproduces her experiences of attempting innovation in New York City's Two Bridges urban renewal site and speaks about the dangers of formulating plans which do not mesh with those of funding agencies.

A more optimistic presentation comes from South Bronx Development Office Project Director Rebecca Lee. She maintains that their landmark project, Charlotte Street Gardens, is a viable option for moderate-cost shelter (Chapter 19).

Finally, Michael Stegman, of the University of North Carolina, produces a policy-analysis exercise comparing the cost and efficiency of financing programs (Chapter 20). He incorporates into this piece the argument that the beneficiaries of the Housing and Urban-Rural Recovery Act of 1983 are not clearly defined, and he warns that help for the low-income household is dependent upon the skills of local program officials who design programs to meet the needs of the poor.

Despite a strong desire on the part of many contributors to this section to create "life settings for people . . . for easy supportive use by individuals, families, and groups,'' the realities of the financial world temper this goal. Clearly, most developers have yet to welcome even the slightest changes in housing design. They are tied to traditional solutions, an allegiance that can be attributed to economic as well as social conservatism.

As a result, several authors tend to conclude that while adapting housing designs to new needs is a worthy enterprise, it has to be pursued along with a parallel thrust—the resolution of more fundamental issues relating to income and the concurrent issue of equity in the workplace and home. In fact, some make the case that planners, public policy makers, and other professionals have yet to effectuate practices which recognize new trends because women themselves have yet to become an effective constituency. One step to building this support is found in the two appendices following these last essays. They are, in effect, position statements around which a gender-related lobbying program might be fashioned.

# 17

# Theory and Practice of Housing Development: Changing the Physical Environment of Our Lives

Lynda Simmons, Carol Lamberg, and Linda Field*

Almost everything in the world is real estate—land and buildings. Real estate is owned and cared for (or neglected) by individuals, families, organizations, businesses, and governments. Fortunately, there is still a good deal in the hands of Mother Nature. What is not real estate is very small, compared to what is real estate. What is not is mainly furnishings of real estate—such as tables and chairs—or of people—such as clothes.

Real estate is another name for the physical environment. This environment is the setting of our lives, the stage on which is played all our dreams of joy and despair, suffering and hope. It is a heavy responsibility to create that stage, to shape our buildings and the spaces between them, to care for, or to leave alone, the "natural" spaces of the earth. The character of the stage, by influencing our possibilities, helps form our characters and our lives. As Winston Churchill said, "We shape our buildings, and they shape us."

About 15 years ago, several streams of thought came together to begin to create a general consciousness of "the environment." More and more people began to realize that the quality of air, water, green spaces, and other primary natural manifestations was essential to a good quality of life. They built upon the work of conservationists of the early twentieth century whose "environmental consciousness," combined with their wealth and power, preserved the lands that now make up our national park, forest, and wildlife refuge systems. The recent resurgence and broadening of our environmental awareness expanded our interest

*This article is drawn from a panel discussion. Lynda Simmons is the author of all but the last two segments. Linda Field wrote "How Can a Woman Developer Have an Impact on Women's Housing Issues?" Carol Lamberg wrote "Some Examples of Developers' Experience in Promoting Enlightened Social Goals."

to oceans, rivers, flood plains, and the atmosphere; it arose again in response to, and in context with, clear threats to their purity and proper management.

Poets and artists have felt and expressed the environmental influence, both "natural" and manmade, since the beginnings of human awareness. For the last 150 years, sociologists, social workers, and political reformers, with their deep perception of the crippling effects of bad environments upon human development, have spent volcanic energy seeking to change our environments.

About 15 years ago, psychologists began to investigate "the environment" as well. Their environment is the entire physical setting of life, but most of their work has to do with the manmade environment, perhaps because the pioneer environmental psychologists were urban people. Thus, attention to undeveloped nature is balanced by an equally necessary attention to the urban setting of hundreds of millions of lives. All of them, from different points of view, have expressed in their lives and works a comprehension of the power of the physical environment upon human potential.

Speaking personally, I became an architect because of my own sensitivity to the active role of the physical environment in my life—emotionally, financially, intellectually, and spiritually.

## THE PHYSICAL ENVIRONMENT AND VALUES

Our built environment is programmed by society's current institutions for the purpose of transmitting both their values and their structures to succeeding generations. The transmission of values is a primary—although as yet largely unconscious and unrecognized—product of the creation of buildings and spaces designed to facilitate the activities needed and valued by society.

Our present residential environments were built, by and large, to satisfy the needs of the nuclear family which was once almost the universal basic social unit. It never dealt with all of the population. There have always been a great many more single people—young, middle aged, and old, living alone in groups—than most people realize. Little in our homes, neighborhoods, and cities reflects the needs of these other groups. Nuclear family needs are reflected in the number and character of "single-family" homes, whether free-standing, rowhouses, or apartments. The internal arrangement of these dwellings, with their shared kitchens and baths, assumes that household members are on intimate terms with one another.

Building design also indicates which people and activities our society values. The devaluation of women is reflected in windowless apartment kitchens. (Can you imagine kitchens being designed to be dark and poorly ventilated if men did the cooking?) As late as 1974 there were urinals in the ladies' rooms of the Harvard Business School. In the mid-1950s, when that particular building was built, authorities could not imagine that women would ever study there. Is this plumbing still there in 1984?

Selected national laws also suggest who is important according to society's values. In the 1970s the federal government required ramps and elevators instead of stairs in public, and some private, facilities for the benefit of handicapped people, who comprise 5 percent of the population. Women, who are more than 50 percent of the population, have been dragging children and groceries up flights of stairs for generations. No one passed laws to lighten their loads with ramps and elevators. The handicapped achieved these exceedingly expensive amenities mainly through the campaigns of disabled veterans—men. Deserving, yes; more deserving than mothers and grandmothers? That is the question.

Our built environment consists of spaces which also reflect values. Without gathering spaces, people do not gather. Without connecting circulation spaces, people do not connect. Without play and sitting spaces outdoors, people stay inside or sit on fireplugs, or play in the street, with cars. In some very powerful ways, our present New York City environment limits us because of its lack of spaces appropriate to certain needs. Clearly, buildings and spaces can cause neither interactions nor social and individual development; but they can encourage them by providing the stage upon which they may occur. And buildings and spaces can and do prevent and make it difficult for people to meet and to develop.

Our value systems are influenced by the character of our physical settings. Often if we cannot do something or do not live with it, we assume—or pretend—that it is not important. Further, the next intellectual step is to cease to investigate the relevance of the phenomenon. In New York City, for example, there are many residents bound to the city by poverty. They do not get to the country much, if ever. They have experienced little of, and therefore place little value on, the benefits of quiet, trees, and open spaces—the gifts of nature which have been so important to most people throughout history. Yet, for those with resources, nature remains of great importance. The 1950s phenomenon now known as "white flight" from our inner cities was due not only to whites' wish to escape contact with southern blacks moving north, but also to their desire to experience trees, grass, and open spaces, and to have their children grow up in contact with nature and its cycles. The latter desire continues to operate in modern society. You can see it in the summer crowd in the Hamptons and in the second home boom across the country. New York City bills itself as a "Summer Festival," and it is. It is also a summer prison.

Just as the physical environment shapes social values, the physical environment itself is shaped by social values. In periods of social stability, the physical environment is shaped by universally accepted values, and it reinforces them. In periods of transition, when values are changing, that is, when economic and political systems and their ideological supports do not conform to the needs of significant numbers of people, the physical environment is viewed by many as inadequate and unsupportive. That is where we are today.

We are all engaged in the difficult and conflicting process of creating new values. Specifically, we are now focusing on the role of women in America and the expansion of their possibilities in all realms of human activity. To put it another way, we want to end the era of male supremacy and move toward realizing the ancient dream of fulfillment for all. This desire has been forced to the forefront by economic and social transformations such as the movement of large numbers of women into the work force, the lower fertility rate, and the opening of new options for household arrangements.

These events are bringing about a new world. Right now we are between the old and the new. That is, we are very much still in the phase where we must change social values and their embodiments in society's ways of doing business before we can make significant physical changes on a large scale. Nevertheless, we must struggle for small changes where we can. They affect lives, and the struggle itself is an important way of changing values. It creates increased consciousness of the *active* influence of the built environment on women.

## THE DEVELOPER, VALUES, AND CHANGE

In our society, the catalyst of physical change is often the real-estate developer. The profession of the real-estate developer is a high calling (despite individual failures): the role is a crucial one. Developers often begin the process of physical change by initiating a project, acquiring land, and creating a program which determines the uses for which architects will design. They find the financiers, lawyers, architects, and contractors necessary to bring the project into being. Then they move foward and supervise the process of creation, solving the problems as they come. At the end, if they are successful, society has a new use in real estate, the individuals using it have better lives because of it, and the developers personally or organizationally have made some money, most of which goes to produce more environmental changes in the future. Whether for profit or not-for-profit, the developers' role is the same: to bring about change in the physical environment. To do so, they shape land and materials according to a plan through the power of money within a set of rules created by society.

In my field, the public-sector development system, the dominant view regards "housing" as shelter for poor, male-headed, one-wage-earner households. People in positions of power—they are predominately men—have an attitude that says in effect, if you are not our ideal, we will not give you what you need. We will give you what *our* ideal needs. Then you can strive to be the ideal household that we envision. And if you can do that, you will benefit from what we have designed to give. The real people involved in the process, of course, do not consciously think these things; yet these ideas are implicit and embedded in their actions and results.

These decision-makers and "the system" simply have not caught up with the implications of the changes in women's roles of the last 30 to 50 years. In 1984, for the first time, more than half of the American women worked outside the home. This change manifests the vast (and largely unremarked upon, perhaps because inadvertently masked by the women's movement) drop in American living standards over the period. Today it takes two fulltime workers to support a household; after World War II, one (male) worker earning a good salary could support several others, usually his family. Additionally, household composition reflects increasing proportions of single parents and elderly single women. In my field, there has been almost no recognition of the needs of these groups.

The issue here is that the physical environment of housing and other facilities does not support the lifestyles required or desired by women today. This condition will not be solved by making small and obvious changes. I, along with many women architects, have spent a great deal of time studying and redesigning kitchens. Years ago, I concluded that fixing the kitchens will not help, except as it helps to get men into the kitchens. What is necessary is to transform the role structure which says that a woman's place is in the kitchen, and that women should focus on kitchens.

The problem lies in the social-value system. It must be changed to make women's lives easier and better. Such a change in values must create supportive financial and administrative systems; then significant physical change can occur.

We could leave everything in our physical environment *as is*, and *transform* women's lives by allocating a relatively tiny amount of resources to two things. The first, would be to employ *people* to start and coordinate a fulltime support staff for women and men organizing into neighborhood or building-wide mutual self-help groups. They would get the kids to school, to the dentist, organize delivery and pick-up of laundry, dry cleaning, groceries, and even plan dances and parties. Having to do all these things physically, and often work fulltime as well, leaves women no time and energy to do anything else. That is how they keep us down. Time and energy are the essence of richer lives. Karl Marx said, "Time is the womb of human development." (I am an admirer of Adam Smith as well.)

The second is to provide daycare centers. They can be placed in existing buildings for less money than we think, provided we overcome some excessively costly regulations. The controlling professional groups' struggle for higher standards has been historically important; new concerns must take precedence now. Having children in centers where the toilets are not perfect is better than having children at home taking the consequences of the hostility of their mothers who regard them as the sources of imprisonment and poverty.

Unfortunately, the development system we are working in now was shaped by the very values we want to change. It is set up to prevent "housing" funds from being used for social-support services because, I think, it could make us independent of male heads of household. Instead, this system could, and one day will, regard housing as the *life settings* of people. It could recognize that thoughtful, well-designed life settings encourage—for women and for men—greater self-esteem, more capability, personal power, happiness, and greater social and economic productivity.

Changes in the built environment that will have a major impact on improving women's lives will not come from architects, communities, developers, and government officials tinkering with the physical and economic details of dwelling units. Although this "tinkering" often does create better dwellings, and raises consciousness, it is useful mainly as it promotes the broader concept of "housing" and its role.

## TOWARD A BROADER CONCEPTION OF HOUSING

What do we mean by "housing"? Is it buildings only or does it include the life that is lived in them? I would rather use the term *community*, as encompassing the *private existence and social interaction of people in the physical settings of their lives*. My thesis is that we can eliminate confusion and develop a clear focus for *thinking* and *acting* if we say that we are not going to use the term "housing" anymore, because traditionally that means only buildings. The term *community*, however overused now, is one which can convey the meaning: the social, physical, and financial interaction of people, buildings, and money. It represents an evolution in thinking about shelter. The traditional concept of housing as mainly a decent roof over one's head has now served an important historic purpose. It cannot give us the future we want for *women and men;* for that, we need a new concept, a new idea which meets present needs that have evolved from the success of the old.

In our thinking, we must make the distinction between the physical and the social aspects of community. We then can use that clarity to create positive interactions between the two. With this approach, we will initiate two major departures from existing practice. First, we must not just build buildings. Instead, we must design life settings for easy, supportive use by individuals, families, and groups in their private lives and social interactions. This is a *program*, the beginning of good design. Another part of good design is *beauty*, which is biologically important to the full lives of all human beings, not just upper- and middle-income human beings.

Secondly, we must build gathering and meeting places into housing. We must design these spaces to include the social support of services appropriate to the life-cycle-stage and income groups who will live there. This second task is much harder to accomplish than the first because it requires reallocation of resources. This is always difficult because of vested interests. The fact that funds could usefully be diverted from our criminally unproductive "welfare" systems makes it no different in this case. Yet the concept provides a way of thinking about, and responding to, the needs of all groups to be served.

In fact, private developers are far ahead of subsidized housing sponsors here. Today, market-rate housing is sold by providing user services: social and health clubs, and/or concierges, and other locally desired features. A concierge is simply the private sector's solution to finding someone to leave dry cleaning with, an element of the support network advocated earlier.

How different is this approach from the present one? Why have social and physical systems historically been separated? We spend vast amounts of resources on both. We know that if the systems were coordinated, the impact of those resources would be geometrically increased in their ability to create good for all of us. Why do we do it? If support systems are set up in housing for women—daycare, service support—women will clearly and unambiguously be able to be functionally independent of men if they wish to be. Setting up support systems strikes at the heart of men's ability to dominate.

Reasonable and helpful men become adamant defending, for instance, the New York State bond resolution that says that proceeds of bond sales can be used only for housing and "appurtenant facilities." Supermarkets are "appurtenant facilities"; they are everywhere in the city and state Mitchell-Lama projects. But, daycare centers are not. It took three years to get a daycare center approved for Phipps Plaza West (one of my projects in New York City) because state administrators had to be convinced it was an "appurtenant facility" (Exhibit 17.1). The reason for their resistance was correct in their context: they believed that supermarkets could be counted on to pay rent. In contrast, they thought daycare centers were chancier. Housing might have to help support them.

But what of the values embodied in these laws and decisions? Why not support daycare? If women have to work to support the family, they must be freed from the burdens of childcare. The consequences of not doing so are clear and great. Society pays through the nose for not having daycare centers: the costs of welfare, food stamps, and other transfer costs to support women to stay home "at leisure" with their children. Society bears other less tangible costs, those of arrested individual development, loss of pride, self-esteem, and consequent costs of jails and drug rehabilitation centers.

There are other reasons for the opposition of men to daycare centers. One, I believe, is that a daycare center is perceived as a woman's need and therefore is devalued just as women are devalued. Another, with which the feminist community may not have yet dealt with sufficiently, is that a significant body of opinion holds that infants' best development requires the consistent, nearly continuous presence of its primary caretaker, probably its mother. Women must face this. We must recognize that men's reaction to our "liberation" includes dismay because they hold beliefs about mothers and children which have yet to be refuted. We could face all this better though, if we were not invisible and devalued in our general human functions which now begin to take us into sanctuaries of male power.

The truth and consequences here are so clear that only deeply held values which obscure "eyesight"—that we see what we already believe is a well-established fact—could prevent anyone from seeing them. Women's votes will soon cause everyone's eyes to open.

## IMPLEMENTING CHANGE

In translating these theories into practice, we must recognize that in the public-housing-development arena government agencies provide major obstacles. For example, the U.S. Office of Management and Budget (OMB) rigorously enforces the separation of housing and social services despite the efforts of some people at HUD and HEW to bring the two together for years and years. In 1980, after ten years of negotiations, the two agencies finally were allowed to sign an agreement on limited cooperation for social services in some public housing projects. We have been told that even then it happened only because the secretary of HUD—Patricia Harris—became the secretary of HEW and personally mandated the coordination. Agencies like OMB may be seen as the linchpin of male supremacy in our government institutions. If we are practical instead of wishful thinkers, that is where we must work for change.

Focusing *only* on the physical aspects of housing as a cure for the physical problems of women in housing will not and cannot work, because it will make only small changes. Valuable as these are, they are still small. But when the transformation of values has proceeded further, we will create *new physical communities* in our neighborhoods which will provide real support for women and men. These new communities will not be so different as some may think, but they will include the critical functions of social and family life—indoor and outdoor gathering places, recreational and ceremonial spaces, offices, and workers for social support systems. This is the essence of good planning.

At the core of our efforts to change values is the assumption that women's traditional roles are as important as men's, even as we move toward enlarging our possibilities beyond tradition. Our goal is to foster a social system that eliminates the segregation of function and supports all *human* possibilities. We will not achieve it until we force recognition of the importance of the social system which supports only the traditional conceptions of women and not the new and expanded reality of women's lives.

At present, my colleagues in development, Linda Field and Carol Lamberg, and I work within a development system created to perpetuate the values and arrangements of the 1930s. The three of us try to make the system work anyway. We bend the system and use it as much as we can. Linda and Carol will describe some of what it takes to do that, how it feels, how much we can get away with, and what are the limits of bending. Because the fact is, as long as the housing-development financial system continues to embody values of the past, it will al-

Exhibit 17.1—Author Lynda Simmons supervised the planning, development, and building of the 1,610 apartments in this Phipps Houses project.

ways be only bending. Carol is a brilliant financial-bender: her accomplishments and the Settlement Housing Fund's have made many lives better all around New York. Linda has taken the step of moving into the world of big-money risks and, hopefully, rewards. (Most of us, as women, were brought up to be terrified of that: we sense what it takes for her to do it.) She is the central force in her otherwise all-male development group.

## HOW CAN A WOMAN DEVELOPER HAVE AN IMPACT ON WOMEN'S HOUSING ISSUES?

A developer is in a position to make choices among alternative investments. These choices are limited not only by economic constraints but also by political-administrative conditions, particularly in programs that seek to address the most needy sectors of the population. Integrating women's concerns into the development process, then, requires that a developer decide on a target population and its needs and understand the practical mechanics of the process, above and beyond the financial questions. Thus, while a developer can be sensitive to women's housing needs and temper his/her decisions accordingly, there are immutable barriers to innovation that will impede progress until they are changed.

Many of these obstacles are the results of a lack of political conviction (or downright prejudice) on the part of policy makers. Many of them exist because decision makers in both the private and public sectors refuse to recognize that it is not physical structures, but the social network, which has the greatest impact on people's lives.

Women, in particular, are victims of this ignorance. This is less a problem for affluent women than for the poor. The former can afford daycare, transportation, homecare workers, and high-price leisure. For the latter, the infrastructure question is posed differently. They are largely captive in their environment, a condition dictated by the restrictions of income and the affordability of housing.

An examination of the process by which this target population, the low- and moderate-income woman and her family, achieves housing and the characteristics of this shelter is useful. It provides an excellent example of the interplay between private and public decision making. It also assists in the assessment of just what impact a developer can have on women's housing issues.

In the private sector, a poor woman's choices are normally limited to the most remote, unsafe, inconvenient, and poorly served neighborhoods—often the areas with the oldest, most dilapidated housing. In the subsidized sector, however, she may have more choices about neighborhoods and housing characteristics. In fact, probably the most important contribution a developer can make is in the site selection for subsidized housing. The housing quality of the surrounding neighborhood, the network of social services, transportation, and schools should dictate site selection.

Unfortunately, in the area of subsidized housing, the developer does not have total control over where projects can be placed. Choices must be in conformity with federal regulations. Every locality eligible for Section 8 or 202 funds, for example, must have a housing-assistance plan (HAP) which generally dictates the sorts of sites that can be selected. In New York City, HAP gives priority to city-owned land. This land is mostly located in the deteriorated areas which are the poorest in terms of accessibility and availability of transportation and social services. Additionally, the potential sites available for developers are usually horrible because federal cost limits are so low that designing an economically feasible project requires cheap land.

Despite these heavy constraints, a feminist developer can try to find areas even in the most deteriorated neighborhoods where the residents have developed social networks to provide daycare and other supportive services. In New York, a feminist developer can do more than careful site selection for individual projects. At the present time, the city follows a scatter-site strategy. A more effective policy would be to cluster services and housing in various locations throughout the city. This concept could be easily implemented in New York City. Each community board has several areas that could act as foci of further development. In fact, the City Department of Housing, Preservation, and Development has already experimented with it in various areas including the West Tremont section of the Bronx.

The importance of the site-selection decision is further underscored by current practices in subsidized housing programs which prevent the provision of desired services within a given project. For instance, it is not mandatory to provide space in a project for social services other than community rooms. Furthermore, rigid rules limit how much space can be devoted to community rooms in family housing. (HUD programs allow only about 20 square feet per family—regardless of the size of the family—per building.) Other codes restrict the amount of money that can be spent on outdoor public spaces. Finally, ancillary facilities are closely regulated. Commercial use is approved only when a lease can be attained in advance from a high-grade, long-term client who unquestionably will be able to pay the rent. Clearly, this last condition is set to insure economic viability, a requirement of banks as well as federal housing administrators. Basically, there is no willingness among government administrators to provide the rental subsidies to support non-revenue-producing spaces of any kind.

The reluctance of the federal, state, and local governments to provide adequate funding for social-service programs is the real barrier to expanding developer responses to contemporary gender-related needs. It is not possible for developers, no matter how socially motivated, to compromise the bottom line, and to include amenities when a program cannot be financially stretched to contain them. While developers can press programs to the limit, they cannot pass the line between a profitable and an unprofitable project. This line varies among types of programs.

Some housing programs are more constrained with regard to social facilities than others. The reason for the differences probably lies in public attitudes. Nowhere is this irony more evident than in senior-citizen and family-housing programs. The popular perception of the elderly has traditionally viewed them not as poor, but as people on "fixed incomes," a position they are in through no fault of their own. This view holds that retirement and inflation have made the elderly victims. Consequently, they deserve full-support systems. As a result, subsidy programs encourage developers to provide lavish spaces for social activities in senior-citizen housing. In contrast, the population eligible for subsidized family housing is in large part female heads of households, a high proportion of whom are welfare mothers. Family-housing programs exhibit a strong prejudice against making available and clustering social and physical resources. This prejudice seems to come from the prevailing view that these people are fortunate enough to get housing; they do not deserve social services as well. Certainly they do not deserve amenities. The bare minimum of shelter is what they should get.

In some places such as New York, subsidized multifamily housing has fared relatively well despite these problems. Here, the Housing Preservation and Development and City Planning Departments require a number of features including public laundry rooms, pram rooms, community rooms, and outdoor recreational areas. To go beyond this, however, the developer would compromise the profitability of the housing project. This would result in delay or cancellation.

In judging the ability of a woman developer to address women's housing issues, one must remember that she is playing in a game whose rules are the same for everyone. She has to play to win. She cannot play to almost win or to barely win. For this reason, her effectiveness is limited to a few judgmental calls, mainly in the area of site selection. Therefore, those desiring innovations in housing will have to depend on the public sector to set and establish programs for such changes.

## SOME EXAMPLES OF DEVELOPERS' EXPERIENCE IN PROMOTING ENLIGHTENED SOCIAL GOALS WITHIN THE SYSTEM

Housing development in New York is like politics: nobody agrees on anything. Developers have to get approvals from various agencies and individuals who often hate each other and always impose conflicting requirements. In addition, they must comply with a myriad of statutes and regulations, especially if they are using government financing or city-owned property. A female developer faces additional problems in the world of contractors, building inspectors, financiers, political figures, and other professionals whose image includes cigar smoking, blunt language, and a somewhat sexist view about women. What is a poor feminist to do? How does she develop housing that responds to women's needs? When one adds sexism to the ordinary obstacles that face New York City residential development in the 1980s, the problems facing a woman developer and her constituency are challenging to say the least. But in spite of the obstacles, women fare quite well in this field.

Take for example the case of the Settlement Housing Fund. Staffed entirely by women, the SHF has managed to develop 3,500 apartments since 1969, ranging from small cooperatives to large rental projects, from moderate rehabilitation to new construction. It has integrated these projects racially and economically. It has rescued failed government projects. It has established a data base on housing for the handicapped. It has changed legislation and regulations. It has worked closely with both profit-motivated investors and non-profit developers. All its efforts have been successful socially and financially.

Despite this record, the Settlement Housing Fund has had problems in every stage of the process. It has suffered through the horrors of owning marginal buildings. It has even had to go into housing court to evict tenants, a very hard task for a socially oriented organization.

In looking back over the various projects that SHF has worked on, there is a common thread. Together with community partners, it establishes social and physical priorities for each project early in the game; then it fights to achieve them, even if it has to bend regulations to make the system work. Among the questions it has faced are: one organization wanted to build a geriatric clinic as part of its housing for the elderly; a sponsor of family housing in Harlem wanted alternate Section 8 limits in order to integrate the project economically; another wanted tenants to buy their building and convert it to a co-op in spite of being surrounded by devastation and in spite of a wide range in their incomes. Joining with these partners, SHF won in all these and many other instances. This success resulted from its willingness to compromise on nonpriority issues, and its knowledge of how to work the system without selling out.

While some of the Settlement Housing Fund projects do not have prize-winning exterior designs, they all have really good interior designs. Most importantly, they all have achieved their priority goal. My priority is to build liveable low-cost housing, and I never feel apologetic for taking advantage of whatever below-market financing exists, even if it forces aesthetic compromises. It is more important to get quality housing built, especially if it is for moderate- or low-income families, than to hold out for the most preferred design. Architectural elements such as building height or exterior design materials may not please the artistic sensitivity of every architect, critic, and planner, but a building that provides dwellings that otherwise may not have been built is a victory. Sometimes I have had to put aside personal preferences and prejudices. For example, in the geriatric housing project, the kitchen design was terrible. I was willing to go to war with the contractor and the architect. Before doing this, I showed the plans to a group of elderly people. They loved it. I gave up fighting on that one.

As a developer who also has social goals, I can offer a framework of questions to act as a guide in the formulation of housing goals and strategy for implementation. These questions will apply whether you want a kitchenless house, shared housing, manufactured housing, or a standard unit.

First, is the project economically feasible? Are the costs of land purchase, development, operation, and debt service within the rent-paying ability of the target population? (The only way to find out if the tenant can afford the rent is to add up all the costs.) If not, are government subsidies available for the intended income groups? Second, does the project comply with the current laws and regulations? If not, could changes be effected within a practical timetable? Third, what are the politics? What is the best way to approach decision makers? What compromises will be necessary? Promoting a project that is the least bit unusual requires an enormous effort, extensive overtime, extra homework, and constant monitoring.

As to implementation, the first step is to assemble the highest quality professional team with a track record of solid accomplishments. The architect, contractor, attorney, financial consultant, and managing agent should have gone through the process before, especially if the developer is relatively inexperienced.

The next step is to develop a timetable. Try to stick to it. One problem to avoid is getting too involved in minutiae. Do not, for example, rework the numbers until they are perfect. They may change.

Finally, remember that while the process is complicated, creative piggybacking on various government programs and engineering public and private financial devices will allow the attainment of some of your goals.

# 18

# Barriers to Architectural Innovation: The Case of Two Bridges

Judith Edelman

Any useful analysis of the built form of housing must be based on an understanding of all the forces that have an impact on making planning and design decisions. This paper represents an architect's perception of the effect of these forces. It holds that the constraints imposed by regulations of funding agencies, political pressures, decreasing resources, and bureaucratic fumbling result in decisions that have little to do with sound planning, let alone innovative design goals. In fact, there have been virtually no opportunities to actually build innovative housing for low- and moderate-income people, although creative design concepts have long been explored on the drawing board.

This case study will describe the planning and architectural history of the Two Bridges Urban Renewal Area located in downtown Manhattan. My firm, The Edelman Partnership, has been involved with this area as architects and planners since 1970. The area had been designated for urban renewal some 12 years earlier. Several development schemes had been abandoned, the site had not been cleared of existing buildings, and no new housing had been constructed. Shortly before we became involved, the city awarded the sponsorship for the area to the Two Bridges Neighborhood Council. The Settlement Housing Fund joined as co-sponsor in 1973.

The urban renewal area consists of several blocks bounded on the south by the F.D.R. Drive, with the Manhattan Bridge directly to the west. There are spectacular views of the East River, New York harbor, and downtown Manhattan. It was divided into Sites 1 through 8 for planning and phasing purposes (Exhibit 18.1).

In 1970, a time of relative expansion—although that was very soon to change—we started our work with enthusiasm and optimism. Working closely

Exhibit 18.1—Two Bridges: site diagram.

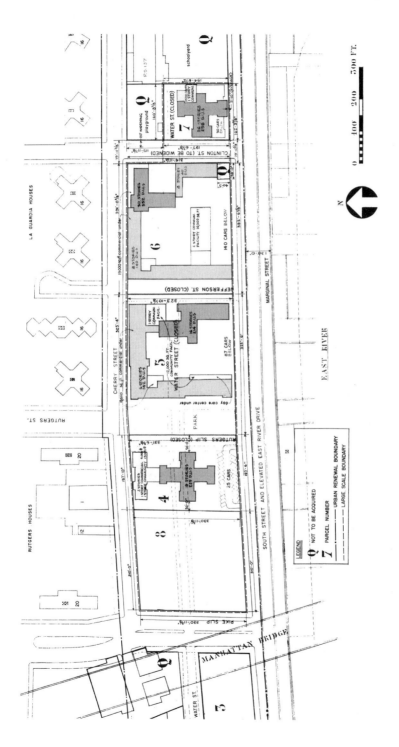

Exhibit 18.2—Two Bridges: site plan, 1971.

with the Neighborhood Council, we developed criteria for apartment types, income-level mix, racial mix, density, and community and commercial space. An unusual number of large apartments and a density lower than the zoning permitted became key elements of the design program. Our firm's architectural and urban design goals included: achieving a coherent, integrated relationship between buildings and open space; respecting and reinforcing the streetscape by building to the street line (on Cherry St.); providing commercial and community space that would enhance the liveliness of the street; careful orientation for sun and views; a balanced variety of building heights; and, of course, well-planned apartments and well-designed building exteriors.

We started on a large scale development plan for the area, working intensively with the Design Department of the New York City Housing and Development Agency.[1] We improved and refined, producing revised drawings and study models weekly for about a year. By 1971, we had a site plan and preliminary building designs that we were all very satisfied with (Exhibit 18.2). The plan was approved by the City Planning Commission in May 1972.

Most of this design effort was focused on sites 5 and 6 which were designated for Mitchell-Lama-funded buildings with a range of income limits and some deep subsidies. Sites 4 and 7 were designated for public housing; the New York City Housing Authority has its own very particular constraints dictating the form of the buildings, which I will touch on later. Sites 1, 2, 3, and 8 were not designated for housing use and will not be included in this discussion.

The plan for Two Bridges created a wall of lowrise buildings on the south side of Cherry Street, with a continuous facade of much-needed local retail space at grade, and a highrise residential tower and lowrise community building on sites 5 and 6. Portions of the lowrise structures were connected to the highrise elevators to minimize the numbers of elevators and entrances. The natural grade, which falls one story between Cherry Street and South Street, was decked over on sites 5 and 6 to provide south-facing open space above covered parking. Each community building had its own clearly defined outdoor space accessible only through the building. The commercial areas were serviced from the underground parking. The configuration of the towers minimized their impact on one another, limited the perimeter facing north, and provided through ventilation in the larger apartments by means of a skip-stop, alternate corridor scheme combined with duplex apartments (Exhibit 18.3).

Now we had an exciting, beautiful scheme. But while we had been deeply involved in perfecting it and getting the final approval of the H.D.A.'s Design Department, the city's fiscal crisis was brewing. The H.D.A. Cost Department put the whole project aside as being too expensive. The fatal flaw in the process had been the total lack of communication between the two H.D.A. departments.

Meanwhile, during the hiatus on sites 5 and 6, the New York City Housing Authority was prepared to proceed. But sites 4 and 7 had occupied buildings on them with commercial and industrial tenants difficult to relocate. A "scatter

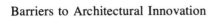

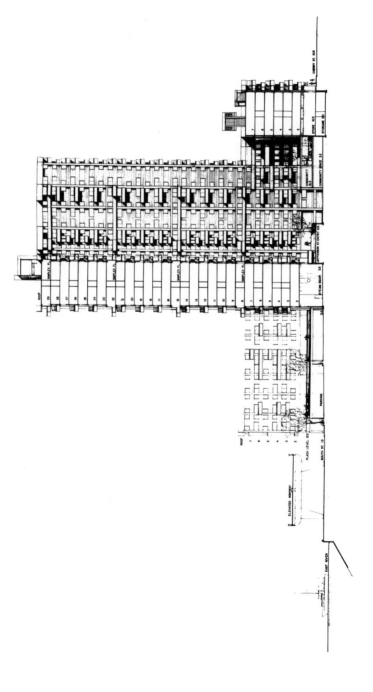

Exhibit 18.3—Two Bridges: section-elevation of site 5 buildings, 1971.

Exhibit 18.4—Allen Street building.

site'' was acquired nearby on Allen Street, very close to the Orchard Street-
Grand Street shopping area. On the basis of a planning study, made for the city
by a private consulting firm, which indicated only a few residential tenants on
site, the decision was made to build on that site first rather than in the urban renewal area. The study proved to be incorrect; the existing tenements were almost
fully occupied. In spite of the two-year delay caused by the error, the project for
this site was the the first to go ahead. A controversial issue during design was
street-level commercial space. The Two Bridges Neighborhood Council was
strongly in favor of it; we believed it to be desirable from an urban design point
of view; but the Housing Authority and City Planning Department opposed it.
The building was completed in 1974, with no commercial space. It is of reasonable size, modestly scaled, with a normal relationship to the neighborhood as
compared to a multibuilding project (Exhibit 18.4).

While the Allen Street building was under construction, we began work on a similar one for site 7. In this case, a delay of over a year was caused by HUD's imposition of new regulations regarding noise level which effectively declared all inner-city sites uninhabitable. Two Bridges was particularly vulnerable because there truly is a lot of noise from the F.D.R. Drive and the Manhattan Bridge. After lengthy negotiations, HUD agreed to accept certain noise attenuation measures within various decibel ranges.

The Allen Street and site 7 buildings provide a vivid demonstration of the influence of agency regulations on built form. The New York City Housing Authority has some admirably humane standards for apartment design. One of them inevitably leads to the characteristic Housing Authority plan shape; the rule is that all apartments larger than one bedroom must have at least two exposures; the result is the cruciform plan with many corners that is to be seen all over New York. Another rule is that interior kitchens are not permitted except in the smallest apartments; the result, at least in our designs, is combined kitchen/dining areas open to the living rooms. We prefer this solution to the alternative closed-off eat-in kitchen. (Regrettably these particular standards are not currently being enforced in turnkey projects).

The obstacles to further housing construction caused by the city's fiscal crisis and the apparent demise of city and state Mitchell-Lama programs were compounded by the national moratorium on housing subsidies imposed by President Nixon. There seemed to be no way to get anything started for sites 5 and 6.

But a way was found. There was a much-publicized federal attempt to stimulate innovative construction techniques called "Operation Breakthrough." Small demonstration projects had been built using several different prefabricated systems at various locations around the country. In April 1973, HUD established priority allocations from Section 236 funds for five sites in New York, including 550 dwelling units for sites 5 and 6 in Two Bridges. The Shelley System was to be used and construction of 250 units was to commence in two months, by June 1973. National Kinney Corporation, which had some financial arrangement with the Shelley System, was to become cosponsor-developer.

The Shelley System consisted of factory-made concrete boxes fabricated in a plant outside of the city, trucked in, and stacked in a checkerboard pattern one on top of another. Historically, there had been virtually no prefabricated-systems building in New York City largely because of the opposition of the building-trades unions. However, the special case of "Operation Breakthrough" and the dearth of construction activity at the time overcame the unions' resistance.

This was very good news, but it was accompanied by some very serious problems. The most obvious was the time schedule. But two other things were even more disturbing. A consequence of using the box system was the abandoning of our own building-design concepts which could not be even approximated given the constraints of the system. Due to the city's failure to do relocation and site

Exhibit 18.5—CAMCI building under construction.

clearance necessary for the project as originally conceived, the site plan was abandoned. The only available space was the southern portion of site 6; so, a line was drawn east to west creating sites 6A and 6B. There was no choice but to build a single, isolated slab-shaped building with poor orientation. Fifty percent of the apartments would have no sunlight and no views. Apartment layouts and room sizes were strictly limited by the box dimensions. Expediency and piecemeal decision making had taken over and would govern the development of the urban renewal area from this time on.

A ceremonial groundbreaking was held in June to satisfy the commencement

Exhibit 18.6—Site 5.

of construction requirement. We redesigned the project and managed to complete working drawings. In October 1973, with Building Department approvals, construction was really ready to begin when National Kinney decided to substitute another prefab system for the Shelley System. The reason was never made clear. The Shelley System was out of the picture.

In order to keep the "Operation Breakthrough" funding, it was necessary to find another HUD-approved factory-made system. The solution was the CAMCI System, fully owned by Starrett Brothers and Eken, who became the builder. CAMCI is a sensible system composed of pre-cast, flat concrete panels, but it has even more limited capabilities than the Shelley System. The only feasible configuration for the building was an even longer, thinner rectangle, again in a far from ideal position of the site. We designed the project all over again, and this time it was built. In spite of the constraints, we did achieve quite liveable units and a handsome exterior. This project was one of the first prefabricated-system buildings in New York City as well as the last funded by the Mitchell-Lama program (Exhibit 18.5). Although National Kinney had had a funding commitment for 300 additional units, Two Bridges could not accommodate them because of the city's failure to act on site clearance.

After yet another interval of no activity, after construction of the last Mitchell-Lama, we went to work on the first HUD Section 8 new housing in the city. (The Section 8 program, now defunct, provided direct-rent subsidies as well

Exhibit 18.7—Interior site 5 with other habitable room.

as construction funding. The funding limits seemed cruelly inadequate, but they were to get much worse.) The city had made some progress on clearing site 5, so Two Bridges was eligible and ready to receive the first Section 8 allocation for 490 dwelling units (Exhibit 18.6). During the transition from the Shelley System to CAMCI, the same developers and builders were retained for site 5. National Kinney continued as developer, Starrett continued as the builder.

Starrett imposed constraints on the building form that ultimately had to be accepted if the apartments were to have any amenities beyond minimum requirements. The negative results are two enormous parallel slabs, too high. The space between is too narrow. Corridors are too long, and there are too many apartments per floor. The buildings are isolated forms with hardly any relationship to the street. The only commercial space is one small store. The parking is on grade on both site 5 and site 6, eating up much of the open space, whereas the original plan had provided decked-over parking.

We did manage to provide apartment layouts with unusually generous space, attractive finish materials (i.e. hardwood flooring), sun in all of the rooms at some time of the day, and river views from most of the units (Exhibit 18.7). We took advantage of a gimmick called "other habitable room," invented by speculative builders to circumvent the zoning-room limit. There was no need for the zoning advantage, but we used the gimmick to increase the mortgage limits

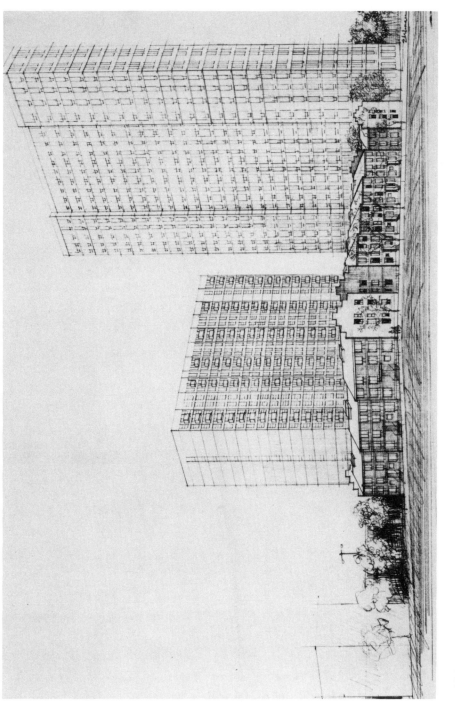

Exhibit 18.8—Two Bridges: site 6B buildings with site 6A (CAMCI building) and site 5 in background.

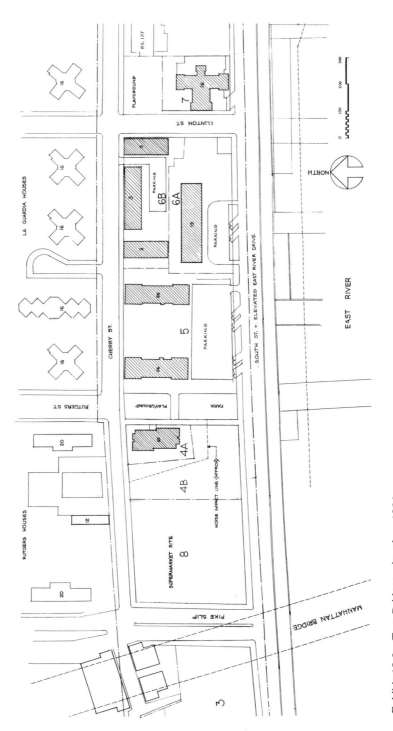

Exhibit 18.9—Two Bridges: site plan, 1954.

Exhibit 18.10—View from the Brooklyn Bridge.

and to gain living area for the apartments without changing the dwelling-unit mix that had been approved. However, there was a negative tradeoff for the use of this gimmick. The OHR is in the position where the dining area would be. In order to comply with HUD's definition, we had to separate it from the interior kitchen with a wall and door and from the living room with a folding partition. In comparison with the Housing Authority's kitchen/dining area, this kitchen is closed off and dark. The relative positions of cooking and living areas are exactly the same, but the effect is very different; again, this is an illustration of the impact of agency rules.

After the completion of the site 5 building in 1979, there was another hiatus. Site 6B never did get its allocated "Operation Breakthrough" units. Despite the R10 zoning, the most dense category, the Two Bridges Neighborhood Council wanted moderate density on 6B because so many units had been concentrated on 5, 6A, and 7 that the population was already very high. We studied 8- and 11-story schemes for a while, but in 1980 HUD imposed a 6-story limit. We did some 6-story studies, but HUD kept raising new objections and showed a great reluctance to approve anything.

Then the most bizarre example of expediency-forced decision making occurred. Some funding under the HUD Section 235 ownership program was offered. This program provided low sales prices, subsidized debt service, and other carrying charges. It required a time schedule that the HUD Multifamily Division admitted it could not meet. But the HUD Single-Family Division worked faster;

if the buildings were limited to three stories, the funding application could be processed through that department even though the proposal was for apartments. So a group of three buildings of three stories each were designed containing 66 dwelling units (Exhibit 18.8). Construction started in 1983. Moderate density was indeed desired but, where the needs are so great, putting 66 units where 400 could legally be built seems absurd. They are attractive little buildings, but completely out of scale in their context and overwhelmed by their 26- and 19-story neighbors.

Site 4 never did get its public housing as called for on the original urban renewal plan but did receive, in 1984, an allocation of funds for a HUD Section 202 elderly housing project of 10 stories containing 109 units (Exhibit 18.9). This will complete the housing construction for the Two Bridges Urban Renewal Area (Exhibit 18.10).

After 14 years, about 1,200 units of desperately needed subsidized housing has been produced. It is good shelter, with well-planned apartments—better than much "luxury" housing which suffers from its own constraints. But the overall plan has been so compromised that our goals for an enhanced urban environment were lost by the wayside. The original proposal could only have been realized if consistent long-range policies existed on the local and federal levels of government, with genuine commitment to good housing. We could then be designing and building housing as well as we know how and could be implementing our goals and planning concepts instead of seeing them constantly eroded.

## NOTE

1. This agency is now the Department of Housing Preservation and Development.

# 19

# The Affordable Option: Charlotte Street Manufactured Housing

Rebecca A. Lee

In a community widely known as a symbol of America's urban ills, a subdivision of single-family homes is under construction. While the idea of building a suburban subdivision in the South Bronx may seem strange, this subdivision, it is hoped, will serve many purposes. First, it will provide decent, affordable housing for middle-income households who require shelter and who would like to become homeowners in the area. Second, it will spur economic recovery in the nearby commercial area by reinforcing the residential market base. Finally, it will improve public regard of this troubled community by demonstrating private investor confidence in the area. While rebuilding communities through middle-income homeownership is not the only answer, it can be a key to successful neighborhood redevelopment given the limited collection of government financing tools seemingly available for urban revitalization over the next few years.

The subdivision, known as Charlotte Gardens, is the brainchild of Edward J. Logue, president of the South Bronx Development Organization (SBDO). SBDO was established in 1979 by the City of New York to formulate and carry out projects and programs to aid in the South Bronx's revitalization. SBDO has devoted its efforts to housing, economic development, employment training, and human services, spearheading the new construction of 250 townhouses (using Section 235 mortgage subsidies) in four neighborhoods, creating a 21.5-acre light-manufacturing industrial park, and operating a successful work/training program for public-assistance recipients.

Charlotte Gardens is located in a 190-acre area of the South Bronx known as Crotona South. In 1980, SBDO and the planning firm of Raymond, Parish, Pine, and Weiner (RPPW) initiated a planning study of the area in consultation with the local Community Board and a local community development corporation, the

Mid-Bronx Desperadoes. The plan called for a variety of housing types—from new construction of 500 single-family rowhouses, to the substantial rehabilitation of 630 apartments—as well as nearby commercial and industrial redevelopment. The range of housing types was designed to accommodate not only low-income families, but also households with two workers whose annual incomes total $20,000 or more.

The heart of the Crotona South plan was the homeowners community to be created. SBDO had a specific market in mind: (1) families who were living in the South Bronx but whose incomes had reached the upper limits of Section 8 qualifications; (2) families already paying stiff rents in Section 236 buildings constructed by the New York Urban Development Corporation; (3) families with roots in the South Bronx who had fled in the 1970s during the worst of the arson, but who wished to return; and (4) families who just wanted to become homeowners.

In a rare display of unanimity, SBDO, community leaders, and city officials agreed that homeownership would serve the dual purposes of strengthening the community and meeting housing demand. This agreement was based on two observations. First, homeowner neighborhoods in the Bronx had remained relatively stable despite the devastation that had occurred around them. Second, SBDO's Section 235 townhouse construction program had met with tremendous local acceptance: all were sold, a number of them to families with incomes too high to qualify for the Section 235 subsidy.

The 1980 presidential election and subsequent demise of the Section 235 program caused SBDO and city officials to rethink the implementation of the Crotona South plan. SBDO concluded that the only way to create affordable homeownership opportunities was to create less expensive houses. What Ed Logue had in mind was manufactured houses—1,152 complete single-family, three-bedroom raised ranch homes with full basements trucked to the site in two pieces and permanently placed on a tailor-made foundation. But none had ever been developed in New York City, a notoriously complex market in which to build, and the Crotona South community leaders were skeptical about the quality of manufactured houses versus stick-built houses.

In the fall of 1981 Logue approached the Local Initiatives Support Corporation (LISC) for a grant to commission an architect's examination of the feasibility of constructing manufactured homes at Crotona South. This was the beginning of a unique, close partnership between LISC and SBDO which, with other partners, public and private, has led to the creation of the Charlotte Gardens subdivision.

LISC is a national, non-profit lending and grant-making corporation funded by private corporations and foundations. An outgrowth of the Ford Foundation's extensive efforts in the field of community development, LISC operates in 25 program sites around the country, from the state of California to Boston. Through a network of local advisory committees in these LISC ''areas of con-

Exhibit 19.1—A rendering of the affordable option for Charlotte Street.

centration,'' LISC helps independent, community-based development organizations undertake housing construction and rehabilitation projects, for-profit businesses, and industrial and commercial development. LISC aims to assist these groups in improving the physical and economic condition of the area in which they operate. One of LISC's first ''areas of concentration'' was the South Bronx.

Logue's architect—Herbert A. Tessler—examined the cost and quality of manufactured houses produced in New York State, Pennsylvania, and Ohio. His conclusion was that the manufactured homes were of superior quality to stick-built housing; the manufacturers used materials of high quality, and the extra strength built into the homes so they could withstand a 250- to 300-mile journey resulted in a sturdier product. In addition, there were significant cost savings: materials could be bought by the manufacturer in great bulk and lower cost; the construction time (and thus interim financing costs) was much shorter; and there was much less material and time loss (weather and theft) in a factory than on a construction site.

Finally, because the home would be built to order in the factory, there was flexibility in the design. Buyers could choose extra features. Thus, in one case, when women from the South Bronx advisory committee saw preliminary plans and complained that residents would not be able to watch their children as they cooked in the kitchen, the solution was an easy removal of a wall.

LISC provided additional grant funds to SBDO to explore the building code and other difficulties associated with building manufactured houses in New York City. Meanwhile, SBDO worked with community leaders to assure them that these were not to be the cheap, unattractive mobile homes of the 1960s but, in fact, an "in-town Levittown."

The risk was great, particularly since the Charlotte Street site had been visited by two presidents and numerous presidential candidates; and it had been proclaimed the "shame of the nation" by President Jimmy Carter in October 1977. Yet four years later, it remained untouched, buried under acres of previously demolished tenements and garbage dumped illegally by private parties.

To replace the 500 Section 235 townhouses, SBDO proposed "Charlotte Gardens," a subdivision of 90 single-family ranch houses on 6,800 square-foot lots (Exhibit 19.1). To accomplish this, Crotona South would have to be "downzoned" to R1-2 (single-family development found only in New York City's posher suburban-type neighborhoods, such as Riverdale). The large lots would allow SBDO to build the homes without brick facing—a major cost savings. The lots also responded to market demand for "real" yards, not the stamp-sized lots offered with the Section 235 townhouses already in construction elsewhere in the South Bronx.

This plan did not emerge without overcoming several obstacles. First, the choice of manufactured units had to be defended and an appropriate producer selected. All of this had to be tied into specifying a product that would conform to both the city and state housing codes. The latter consideration became increasingly important when SBDO discovered that any unit it commissioned would fall under the New York State Manufactured Housing Code, a law designed to deal with the problems arising when manufactured housing produced in one city is shipped to another and does not meet the second city's codes. SBDO juggled design, construction, and legal considerations as it worked to develop the subdivision plan under the various constraints.

There was some concern about how this development would fit into its surroundings. There was a small, tenuous homeowners' community to the west of Charlotte Street. In the immediate area, however, the sad fact was that although the streets were once lined with six-story buildings, each having 40 apartments, there were only two buildings on 18 acres. In terms of its impact on the surrounding area, therefore, the only thing that would happen was that if this development worked, the property values for those few buildings would rise.

In addition to testing the acceptability of the South Bronx site, SBDO and LISC were interested in testing the acceptability of the cost of the homes. SBDO estimated early on that the units would cost between $40,000 and $45,000 and be affordable to families with incomes in the area of $22,000. This would include two-income households with each worker earning about $11,000—a standard salary for even unskilled people in the city. The monthly operating costs were estimated at $225 a month. This figure was based on estimates from Consolidated Edison for utilities, repairs, normal carrying costs of the home, and on SBDO's Section 235 experience.

Hoping to make these homes affordable without subsidy, SBDO had fixed a price such families would be able to afford and then worked backwards looking for ways to cut construction costs. For instance, fireproofing would have added to the costs. In order to avoid fireproofing, the homes were placed on lots of at least 6,800 square feet. To bring costs down further, the houses were redesigned so that more work could be done in the factory.

A further reduction was achieved by reducing the cost of sewer connections. By looking at old city maps showing the original buildings and their sites, SBDO's architects were able to pinpoint the existing sewer lines. Hooking up to these lines represented a savings of between $5,000 and $6,000 dollars per unit.

The pivotal point in the project came with LISC's agreement in 1982 to underwrite the cost of placing two model homes at the site. LISC's loan was secured by the homes themselves—which were on lots leased by the city to SBDO. This was a classic high-risk LISC loan.

But the model homes proved a great draw. In the three months after their opening in April 1983, thousands of families visited the homes and 520 applied to purchase one. The local cosponsor, MBD Community Housing Corporation, screened all the applicants and culled a list of 90 households, all first-time buyers with annual incomes ranging from $25,000 to $54,000.

In the end, SBDO concluded that this development could not proceed without public subsidy. The city and SBDO sought and received an Urban Development Action Grant of $1,350,000 in 1983 to underwrite the cost of demolishing the remaining old buildings within the project area, patching the streets, replacing the sidewalks, planting street trees, and providing non-amortizing $10,000 equity participation second mortgages to 88 of the homebuyers. (HUD refused to extend the UDAG to the two model homes, so the second mortgages were available to 88 buyers.)

In addition, the city sold the building lots to SBDO for one dollar each and extended 421(b) tax abatements to the homes, entailing a ten-year phasing in of property taxes. The State of New York Mortgage Agency (SONYMA) reserved money for 88 first mortgages (at 9.9 percent) from its single-family mortgage revenue bond program. At a selling price of $51,975 (the development cost is $71,900), the homes are inaccessible to families earning less than $25,000 a year.

## CONCLUSION

Clearly, Charlotte Gardens is not for the poor; it is housing for middle-income families. Although this kind of housing does not serve those who currently live in public housing, it does serve a different market. Until recently, the market for affordable single-family, housing had been totally ignored in the city, despite the fact that homeownership had long been associated with stable neighborhoods. In addition, neighborhood advocates had embraced economic integration as a prerequisite for successful community revitalization.

In addition, SBDO is not seeking to move people out of their apartment buildings into private homes on a large scale, nor to import people to the South Bronx to buy this housing. The goal is to keep those South Bronx families who want to stay in the area and who could afford better housing, but who in the past have been forced to move out of the area because such housing did not exist.

Finally, SBDO and LISC believe that providing better housing for some might have a filtering effect in the community. For example, if a family moves from an apartment on the Grand Concourse to Charlotte Street, it might mean that another family would move from a partially-abandoned building into a better apartment on the Grand Concourse. Thus, this development might, in a small way, represent the beginning of bettering the housing situation of a large number of South Bronx residents.

While Charlotte Gardens is not directly targeted to non-traditional families like the female-headed household, in fact, 10 percent of the first 90 buyers are single heads of households. The racial/ethnic background of the majority of the buyers is black or Puerto Rican, while a high proportion of the buyers are employed by the city or a quasi-public authority.

As with all development undertakings in complex urban areas, the Charlotte Gardens development, still in construction, has emerged quite different from its original conception. Its success as a housing development is still unknown, but we can point to its success already as a product of public and private partnerships and as a symbol of the South Bronx's renewal, and proof of the re-emergence of private investor confidence in the area.

## REFERENCES

See "Crotona South: Final Planning Report & First Year Action Program," published by the South Bronx Development Organization, 1250 Broadway, New York, NY 10016 (212/868-6350).

For further information, contact the Local Initiatives Support Corporation, 666 Third Avenue, New York, NY 10017 (212/949-8560).

# 20

# New Financing Programs for Housing

Michael A. Stegman

In recent years, America's housing problems have been increasingly defined in terms of affordability.[1] For a high percentage of women whose income places them among the poorest of the nation's households and among those paying a disproportionate amount for shelter, some form of housing subsidy may be necessary to treat their housing problems adequately. One need only cite the alarmingly high poverty rates in the United States to underscore this point. Forty percent of all individuals living in families with a female household head—nearly 12 million individuals—were poor in 1982, an increase of 16 percent since 1979.[2] This compares to a national poverty rate in 1982 of 15 percent. Thus, in addressing housing issues, including those related to gender, understanding how subsidies work is essential. Since providing subsidies involves questions of economics, budgeting, and program administration, that understanding must include knowledge about the intricacies of housing finance, the mechanics of the budget-making process, and the independent influences (not necessarily intended by Congress) exerted on housing outcomes by program regulations. The following pages contain an exercise designed to illustrate how various financial variables interact to determine the cost of housing to the consumer.

The analysis begins with a new, multifamily rental unit and determines the level of subsidy that would be necessary to make the unit affordable to a low-income family. Next, two different types of subsidies are described: an interest or rental-assistance subsidy to the private mortgage lender which continues over the life of a project mortgage, and a one-time capital grant to the housing developer which reduces the size of the necessary mortgage but not the interest rate on it. The illustration then pays special attention to the ways these two subsidy approaches are treated in the national budget-making process, showing that the choice of subsidy seems to depend more on larger economic and political considerations than on cost and efficiency factors. Next, the analysis demonstrates how major modifications in program regulations affect who will benefit from housing subsidies. Finally, the new housing production programs contained in the Housing and Urban-Rural Recovery Act of 1983 (HURRA) are assessed, and the challenges these pose to communities dedicated to the supply of low-income housing are discussed.

## DEFINING LOW INCOME

Before we can compare different subsidy approaches, we first must identify the rent-paying ability of the intended client population. For purposes of this paper, the target group is families that have low incomes, a concept that is not always easy to grasp when applied to housing-assistance programs. A brief discussion of how income-eligibility has been historically defined will illustrate why one cannot take for granted that low-income housing programs always serve families with low incomes. Since 1974 the federal government has defined "low income" as relative to the median income of all families in the area where a subject family resides. The government considers a family of four "low-income" if its total household income is below 80 percent of the area's median household income. That same family is considered "very low-income" if its income is below 50 percent of the area median.

Until recently all income limits were adjusted for household size so that lower limits applied to single individuals than to larger families. That is no longer always true. In what resulted in a change in low-income housing policy by regulation rather than by law, in 1981, the U.S. Department of Housing and Urban Development issued regulations to implement a statutory requirement that 20 percent of the units in each rental housing project financed through the sale of tax-exempt bonds be set aside for low-income families in a way that essentially redefined the concept of low income. It did so merely by establishing 80 percent of median income as an absolute, rather than a relative, income criterion. That means, at least with respect to bond-financed rental housing, a single person with an income equal to 80 percent of the area's median income is considered to be as poor as a family of four with the same income. Since, for program purposes, these households' respective rent-paying abilities are identical but the smaller household's space demands are far more modest than the latter's, housing sponsors are likely to meet their 20 percent low-income requirement by housing elderly singles and couples in efficiency or one-bedroom units rather than building units for poor families.

Exactly why that is so can be illustrated with a simple example. Assuming an area median income of $18,000, then a household with an income of 80 percent of median, or $14,400 qualifies for a low-income unit. HUD requires rent-subsidized tenants to contribute 30 percent of their income to rent, and since we can assume the tenant could not afford to pay more, that household could afford a maximum rent of $360 a month. Since household income and, hence, maximum rents do not vary with household size, a developer may choose between building for the single person or small household market and building larger, multi-bedroom units for the same $360 rent. Who would not target the elderly under these antifamily program rules?

Whether or not one agrees with the policy, it is important to understand that HUD applies less restrictive low-income limits to otherwise unsubsidized bond-financed rental projects than to, say, Section 8 housing because tax-exempt interest rates provide too shallow a subsidy to make family units affordable to low-income families, defined in the more traditional manner. In essence, then, the magnitude of the available federal subsidy influenced HUD's definition of "low-income."

In a somewhat similar manner, it is not unusual for states to define "low income" in terms of available subsidies. Recognizing that rising construction costs and interest rates, combined with declining federal subsidies, could price housing beyond the reach of their traditional low-income markets, state housing finance agencies (HFAs) routinely back into a definition of "low income." It is not uncommon to find HFAs defining "low income" as the minimum income required to occupy a new unit of housing they can produce after taking full account of all interest and other non-federal subsidies available to them. Thus, for example, if the required monthly rent for a new apartment financed by an HFA is $460, and the assisted household is expected to spend 30 percent of its adjusted income on rent, then "low income" would be defined as any income under $18,400 ($460 × 12 ÷ .30) regardless of what the area median income might be.

In short, low income has been variously defined in law and regulation. Given the poverty statistics cited earlier, it is reasonable to conclude that a gender-sensitive housing policy should define low-income relative to household size. For purposes of this paper, we will classify a four-person household as having low income if its adjusted income is below $10,000 a year. That amount is slightly higher than the average 1982 income of public housing tenants in New York City ($9,416) and just above the official national poverty income threshold for a family of four, also in 1982 ($9,862).[3] Using 30 percent of adjusted income as the required contribution to housing cost, at the maximum low-income limit, a family of four can afford to spend $250 a month for rent or housing payments.

## DEVELOPMENT AND OPERATING COSTS

The depth of the subsidy required to make a new housing unit affordable to a low-income family is a function of its development cost, financing terms, and maintenance and operating costs, including normal profits. For both new construction and substantial rehabilitation we will assume a total development cost of $35,000 a unit. That is lower than the average cost of a new low-rent public-housing unit nationally and probably close to the national average cost of new unsubsidized multifamily rental units. A 90 percent ($31,500) fixed-rate mortgage at 13 percent interest for 30 years produces a monthly debt service of about $348. Adding $200 a month to account for taxes, insurance, maintenance, operating costs, and before-tax cash flow produces a rent requirement of nearly $550. Using a 30 percent rent/income ratio, a household would need an income of nearly $22,000 a year to afford this unit. Clearly, to bring the rent for new housing down to a level affordable to households earning less than $10,000 a year requires a very deep subsidy or a combination of cost-reducing measures.

Although this article is limited to an analysis of the role of financing in housing cost, it should be noted that increasing attention is now being paid by housing policy makers to a variety of nonfinancing ways of reducing end costs. In a recent paper, William Gainer, of the U.S. General Accounting Office, illustrated how development cost and rents could be reduced by 10 percent through a combination of more intensive land use, reductions in dwelling unit size, and selected building-code concessions—all measures that could be negotiated at the local level.[4] Gainer also estimated that full local real-estate tax abatement could lower rents by another 7 percent. The practice of rent skewing (the subsidization of lower-income tenants by higher-income ones) also is a cost-reducing measure; it is being required of developers by some agencies that finance multifamily housing in markets that are strong enough to bear such distorted pricing patterns.[5]

## SUBSIDY MECHANISMS

### Interest Subsidies

Returning to the foregoing example, we can see that subsidizing interest paid on a building loan by the developer could have a powerful affect in reducing monthly costs. For example, a subsidy that would lower the interest rate from 13 percent to, say, 4 percent would reduce the mortgage payments from about $350 a month to $150 a month. This subsidy would lower the rent enough to be affordable to a household with a $14,000 income. The cost to the government of this 9 percent interest subsidy would be about $71,000 over the thirty-year mortgage term, or about $200 a month. Although that is already substantial, a far bigger subsidy would be needed to get the mortgage down to what a household with a $10,000 income could afford. Driving the interest rate to the developer still lower, to 1 percent, would reduce required debt service to just $84 and produce final rents that are affordable to households with incomes of slightly more than $11,200. To accomplish that further reduction, however, the interest subsidy would cost the government $268 a month and nearly $97,000 over the mortgage term.

### Principal Reduction Grants

There is a less expensive way of subsidizing mortgage interest rates that could have a similar effect on tenants' rent. The government could make a one-time capital (or principal reduction) grant to the developer that would reduce the amount of initial mortgage principal needed to pay for the required new construction or rehabilitation. The mortgage loan would be made at market interest rates; the size of the principal reduction grant would be a function of the difference between that rate and the desired subsidized rate. Thus, for example, if market interest rates are 13 percent and the subsidized rate is 4 percent, using the same $31,500, 30-year market-rate loan as our base case, the capital grant will be $17,900, which means that the market-rate loan will be $13,600. That is, monthly payments on a 13 percent, 30-year mortgage loan for $13,600 are the same as those on a $31,500 loan at a 4 percent interest rate. That means a one-time capital grant of $17,900 received at the start of construction has the same cost-reducing effects to the developer as a series of $200 interest-subsidy payments to the mortgage lender which began at completion of construction and that total $71,000 over the 30-year mortgage period. To get closer to the rent affordable by a household with $10,000 income per year, the effective interest rate could be lowered to 1 percent by increasing the principal reduction grant to the developer to $24,200. That would substitute for a 30-year interest subsidy of $268 a month, which totals $96,480.

## TREATMENT OF SUBSIDIES IN THE BUDGET

To understand why deep subsidy programs traditionally have not been funded through the less expensive capital grant mechanism, one must understand how housing-assistance program costs are accounted for in the federal budget. Three concepts are important in this discussion. The first is *new budget authority*. This is the amount of money the Congress agrees to pay in future years for expanding low-income housing-assistance programs in a given fiscal year. What makes the concept unique is that it represents the full, multiyear cost of the new housing subsidy contracts that the government has approved for execution in the new budget year. *Contract authority* represents the appropriation needed to pay the current year cost of all the new subsidy contracts for which new budget authority has been approved by the Congress. Finally, federal *housing outlays* are the subsidies being paid each year for all assisted housing that is still under subsidy contract regardless of the year that budget authority was initially granted. Since housing payments represent the cost of assistance contracts entered into in previous years, in any given year those costs are largely beyond congressional control. This also means that because it takes at least 24 months for new housing approvals to result in actual outlays, a decline in new budget authority this year will not show up as a reduction in federal housing outlays for at least two years into the future.

President Reagan's budget for fiscal 1985 proposed new budget authority of $9.1 billion to support 136,000 new multiyear housing-assistance contracts.[6] The contract authority (or initial year's subsidy obligation) associated with those units is $806 million. Finally, in fiscal 1985 HUD's housing outlays on behalf of the nearly 4 million families now living in assisted housing across the country will total $9.3 billion.[7]

In our simplified example, the budget authority required to support a 30-year interest subsidy to reduce the monthly cost on a $31,500, 13 percent loan to an effective interest rate of 4 percent is $71,000 (approximately $200 a month for 360 months). The budget authority required to deepen the subsidy to an effective 1 percent interest rate is nearly $97,000 (approximately $268 a month for 360 months). In the former case, the contract authority (first year's subsidy) needed to support an additional unit of assisted housing would be just $2,400 ($200 a month × 12), whereas for the 1 percent interest rate, it would be $3,216 ($268 a month × 12). Since the alternative subsidy mechanism under discussion requires the government to make only one payment, in the year construction begins, the contract and budget authority requirements of a principal reduction payment program are the same. Again, referring to our earlier example, a capital grant of $17,900 that reduces the initial market-rate mortgage loan requirements from $31,500 to $13,600 would lower monthly carrying charges on the developer's loan the same way subsidizing the interest rate down to 4 percent on the original principal would. The $17,900 represents both the new *contract and budget authority* associated with the capital grant subsidy system. In the case of the 1 percent loan, the required contract and budget authority would be higher—$24,189.

## THE POLITICS OF HOUSING SUBSIDIES

In short, although the long-term cost of a capital grant-type subsidy program is less costly than an interest subsidy or other form of continuing assistance, the fact that the first-year cost of the former is greater means fewer new assisted housing units can be supported per dollar of available appropriations. Thus, as long as there is strong congressional support for keeping the level of new low-income housing production high, a strategy that lessens the immediate budgetary effects of those programs will be favored over one that keeps down long-term costs.

Because assisted housing is unfairly singled out for special treatment in the federal budget—few other human services programs require full appropriation of multiyear subsidy costs at the front end—low-income housing programs that depend on continuing subsidies are frequently attacked as too costly. Witness a May 1983 column by George F. Will that criticized President Reagan for not cutting assisted-housing budgets even more than he had proposed to do:

Since 1937, $363 billion has been committed—note that word—to federal subsidi-
zation of housing. Ninety percent of that has been obligated in the last eight years.
And all but $90 billion remains to be spent. That is, the government has obligated
itself to spend $273 billion the next 40 years and that is without a new bill enriching
the menu.[8]

Although it might appear that as housing subsidy costs mount, political opposition to large-scale housing programs increases, I think the corollary is closer to
the truth: Whenever political support for low-income housing programs declines,
the arguments about their excessive long-term costs intensify. Attacks on costly
construction programs usually are accompanied by calls for housing allowances
and other strategies that do not involve new construction.

After he placed a moratorium on all low-income housing production programs
in March 1973, President Richard M. Nixon addressed the failures of low-income housing programs, including their excessive costs and tendencies to
mortgage the future, and proposed a new policy direction:

In place of this old approach, many people have suggested a new approach—direct
cash assistance. Under this approach, instead of providing a poor family with a
place to live, the federal government would provide qualified recipients with an appropriate housing payment and would then let them choose their own homes on the
private market. . . . The plan would give the poor the freedom and responsibility to
make their own choices about housing and it would eventually get the federal government out of the housing business.[9]

Eight years later, President Reagan's Commission on Housing picked up on the
same theme in its 1981 final report:

The fiscal 1982 budget notes that outstanding obligations under Section 8 contracts
now total $121 billion. Adding in the continuing costs of the bond issues that built
public housing and other forms of housing assistance, the unfunded liabilities of the
federal government for housing subsidies reach nearly a quarter of a trillion dollars.
The weight of these accumulated obligations has begun to restrict the amounts the
government can fund for assistance to other families.[10]

Advocating a national program of housing allowances, the commission indicated that the lower unit cost of cash assistance would "enable twice as many
poor people to be helped by the same housing budget."[11] Yet even a casual
glance at any of the Reagan housing budgets suggests that the substitution of
housing allowances for new production programs is viewed by the administration, not as Nixon saw it—a way to get the federal government out of the house
*building* business—but as a way of eventually getting the federal government out
of the housing business altogether.

The President's budget for fiscal 1985 ($30.2 billion) proposes new budget
authority for assisted housing that is 37 percent less than a year earlier and nearly
80 percent less than in the final year of the Carter administration. The budget in-

cludes support for just 12,500 new and substantially rehabilitated units, down from more than 100,000 such units in fiscal 1981.[12] At the same time, only 87,500 additional households would receive housing allowances (or vouchers as the administration refers to its direct cash-assistance program proposal) compared to 83,000 families four years earlier. In short, when the high cost of producing low-income housing is used to justify a shift to a lower-cost subsidy alternative, it does not always follow that more low-income households will receive assistance as the President's Commission and others before it have frequently implied. More often, it means a cut in both the number of newly built units that will be authorized and the number of additional families who will be served by assisted-housing programs.

I do not think it is a coincidence that interest in the use of capital grants to stimulate new supply tends to increase at the same time large-scale new production programs fall out of political favor. That is because the modest volume from the new production initiatives put forth during these periods of social retrenchment are generally small enough to keep demands for new contract and budget authority down to politically acceptable levels. That is the situation that exists today, after four years of the Reagan presidency.

### Combining Subsidies

We have previously indicated that, holding production costs constant, the size of the required front-end grant to make otherwise unsubsidized housing affordable to lower-income families is partly a function of the spread between market and subsidized interest rates and partly a function of the income group the housing is supposed to serve. In our earlier example we showed that to reduce effective interest rates by 9 points on a $31,500 loan required a principal reduction grant of $17,900, which is equal to 51 percent of the development cost (which equaled $35,000 a unit). A principal reduction grant equal to 69 percent of the development cost is necessary to reduce effective interest rates down to 1 percent. It follows, therefore, that a capital grant big enough to subsidize housing for very low-income families could come close to or even exceed total development cost. That is because some families, especially public-housing tenants, are unable to afford any debt service at all as part of their rent payments. That is why the federal government subsidized the full capital costs of public housing developments and partially subsidized operating costs as well. The average public-housing tenant in New York City pays $145 in rent, although it costs an average of $260 per month to operate the unit he occupies.[13]

Even when delivered in its more cost-effective form as an up-front grant, the main limitation of an interest subsidy is its inflexibility. Whether the size of the subsidy is defined by the magnitude of the desired reduction in effective mortgage interest rates or more arbitrarily capped at some dollar limit or percent of development cost, if the subsidy is not permitted to change with a family's rent-paying abilities over time, then tenants must bear the full effects of inflation on operating and energy costs. If tenant incomes do not keep pace with inflation, either their rent/income ratios will increase or (if they are either unable or unwilling to pay higher rents) project sponsors will be forced to reduce operating costs by lowering maintenance standards. If inflation and deferred maintenance practices persist, lower quality can lead to higher vacancies, lower rent collections, and, eventually project failures. That is, in part, what happened to many multifamily projects sponsored under the Section 236 interest-subsidy program during the mid-1970s. To reduce the severe effects of runaway inflation on operating costs in Section 236 projects, Congress first approved the use of rent supplement funds and later enacted the "flexible subsidy" program, a special set-aside of Section 8 rental assistance funds, to increase the rent-paying capacities of families living in these financially distressed projects.

The key point here is that the supplemental assistance programs eventually approved to help bail out financially distressed interest-subsidy projects were sensitive to how much tenants could afford to pay for housing. Although these programs were not planned to be used in tandem and, indeed, were contrary to the then-prevailing federal policy (which frowned on double-dipping or piggybacking housing subsidies), the beginnings of a more cost-effective, flexible system that combined interest subsidies with rental-assistance payments was born out of crisis efforts, albeit not always successful ones, to stabilize the operations of failing Section 236 projects.

### The Housing and Urban-Rural Recovery Act of 1983 (HURRA)

After months of bitterly contested negotiations with the administration, in November 1983 Congress killed the Section 8 new and substantial rehabilitation programs because of their very high multiyear cost and approved two new vehicles for producing assisted housing both of which use the capital-grant subsidy approach. Contained in Title III of the Housing and Urban-Rural Recovery Act of 1983, the new rental production program provides for one-time grants to developers who will construct or substantially rehabilitate housing in areas that HUD designates as experiencing a severe shortage of decent rental housing. Twenty percent of the units built with assistance under the program must be made available to low-income families, and a maximum rent for those units is set at 15 percent of the area household median income. That translates to $250 a month when the household median income is $20,000 a year. Because the federal subsidy is limited to a maximum of 50 percent of development cost, in many higher-cost localities unsubsidized tenants will have to subsidize the rents of the low-income families to make the projects feasible. The need for such cross-subsidization can be illustrated by referring once again to our hypothetical project.

Recall that a capital grant equal to 51 percent of the total development cost was needed to reduce the effective interest rate in our project from 13 percent to 4 percent. According to our assumptions about taxes, maintenance costs, and operating costs, this one-time subsidy would lower monthly rents to $350, a level affordable to a family with an income of $14,000 a year. Without any additional outside subsidies, the only way that 20 percent of the units in an assisted project can be made available at a rent of $250 a month, which a $10,000-a-year family presumably could afford to pay, is for the unassisted families to pay higher rents to make up the deficit. Thus, if the assisted project requires an average rent of $350 a month and one-fifth of the units have a maximum rent of only $250 a month, then the remaining four-fifths of the units must average $375 in rent. That means every non-low-income family in the assisted project will be subsidizing the rent of each low-income family by $25 a month.

Because of the need for tenants to subsidize each other, the new program is another example of how federal subsidy limitations can affect the capacities of a housing program to assist low-income families. Without deeper subsidies developers cannot be expected to dedicate a larger fraction of their units to low-income families because that would require raising the rents for the non-poor even higher. The same arises if developers try to make their designated units available to families with, say, $5,000 to $7,000 income. The difference between the maximum rents these families could afford to pay and the average rent levels needed for the project to be economically viable would have to be borne by the market-rate tenants, whose tolerance for cross-subsidization is surely limited.

Unlike its rental development counterpart, the new moderate rehabilitation program contained in Title III of HURRA combines a front-end grant program with a special set-aside of Section 8 housing certificates to enable moderate rehabilitation to be accomplished without displacing existing tenants. Rehabilitation grant funds are allocated on a formula basis to cities with populations of 50,000 or more and to states, which administer the program in nonmetropolitan areas. Grants are generally limited to $5,000 and 50 percent of the unit cost of rehabilitation. For each $5,000 of capital grant funds allocated to a community, one Section 8 existing housing certificate or housing voucher will be given to the local housing authority for use in the program. The certificates represent HUD's commitment to pay the difference between post-rehab rents, which should not exceed Section 8 fair-market rents, and 30 percent of tenant income. But, unlike the special rental assistance Congress provided to selected financially distressed Section 236 projects and to all Section 8 new construction projects, which was tied to the housing, the new program assigns the assistance to the tenant. Families are free to use their rent certificates to help pay the higher rents in their newly rehabilitated units or are free to take them to any other housing in the community that meets applicable Section 8 rent and quality standards.

By separating the rehabilitation incentive (the capital grant) from the rental assistance (the Section 8 certificate) but allowing them to be used in tandem at the tenant's discretion, Congress is trying to contain costs by instilling in the program a market discipline. This discipline derives from the fact that since rental assistance payments are not guaranteed to the housing developer, post-rehab rents must be competitive in the local unsubsidized rental market, or else the newly renovated units will remain vacant. Front-end grants must be sufficient to reduce net development costs to levels supportable by unsubsidized rents, or project rents will be too low to support necessary mortgage, maintenance, and operating costs. Overimproved units that require higher-than-market rents to be profitable will not be supported under the new program as they have been under earlier subsidized housing programs.

## CONCLUSIONS

In building new rental housing with the aid of a rental development grant, the developer must make only one out of five units available to low-income families. To reduce rents on these designated units to their lowest possible levels, projects will have to have the benefits of tax-exempt financing and the full cooperation of local governments to reduce unnecessary code and related land-use regulations that increase project costs without providing corresponding community benefits. Without substantial local participation in development efforts, it will be very difficult to provide new housing under the program for very low-income families with young children.

By not restricting the rental assistance available in HURRA's new moderate rehab program to rehabilitated housing, Congress had implicitly declared that the program's primary goal is to increase the supply of standard housing and, secondarily, to improve the quality of low-income families' housing. The program assumes that some rent increase will inevitably accompany housing rehabilitation and that the increase will be only high enough to bring previously depressed rents for substandard housing up to levels that are being charged for standard units in the local market area. Congress is counting on careful project underwriting by local governments to make sure housing is not overimproved relative to its location. By prohibiting rent controls and other means of regulating post-rehab rents, the program has the potential to subsidize improvement efforts that would have been initiated in gentrifying neighborhoods without public assistance, and to permit lower-income households to be outbid by higher-income families for their own housing and thereby to contribute to displacement. In such neighborhoods it is usually the elderly and young families with children who are replaced by young professionals and singles. Whether the portability of rental-assistance payments maximizes mobility and housing choice and dampens inflationary price pressures on the rehabilitated stock or becomes a cheap form of relocation payments to involuntarily displaced families will depend largely on the skills and dedication of local program officials and the kinds of complementary programs they bring to the housing development effort in these difficult times.

## NOTES

1. See, for example, *Report of the President's Commission on Housing*, Washington, 1982, p. xxii.

2. "Poverty in the United States: Where Do We Stand Now?" *Focus*, Institute for Research on Poverty, University of Wisconsin-Madison, vol. 7 (December 4, 1984), p. 4.

3. *Ibid.*, p. 3; and New York Urban Coalition, "The New York City Housing Authority," *Neighborhood*, vol. 6 (November 2, 1983), p. 9.

4. Cited in *Housing Affairs Letter*. No. 84-16, April 20, 1984, pp. 9-10.

5. *Ibid.*, pp. 9-10.

6. "The 1985 Housing Budget and Low Income Housing Needs," Special Memorandum, November 21, 1983, Low Income Housing Information Service, Washington, D.C., Table 2.

7. *Ibid.*

8. George F. Will, *The Washington Post*, May 26, 1983, p. A-29.

9. "Message from the President of the United States Transmitting Recommendations for Improvements in Federal Housing Policy," September 19, 1973, p. 8.

10. *Report of the President's Commission on Housing*, p. xxiii.

11. *Ibid.*, p. xxiii.

12. "The 1985 Housing Budget and Low Income Housing Needs," Table 3.

13. "The New York City Housing Authority," *Neighborhood*, p. 9.

# Epilogue

At the end of each year the seminar members produced a statement which captured the conclusions of the group. The first paper has been included in various chapters and introductory sections of this volume. The second statement was placed in two position papers developed for specific political arenas. They are produced here in the Appendix. One is a national summary about gender-related housing and was included in the briefing papers for the National Platform Committee of the Democratic Party in June 1984 (see Appendix A). The other paper summarizes the New York City situation and was offered as testimony at the New York Department of State hearings on the Feminization of Poverty in June 1984 (see Appendix B).

Using these documents the seminar participants will continue to press for housing policy targeted to meet the needs of women. For example, many former seminar participants are working with New York's Women in Housing and Finance organization to plan an architectural competition designed to promote plans and projects responsive to women's lifestyles. Others will carry this message elsewhere. It is hoped that in the future, work of this nature will make a difference in how American women are sheltered.

> *Frances Levenson*
> Vice President for Urban Housing
> Goldome Bank
> Co-Chair, Hunter College Women and
> Housing Seminar

# Appendix A

# The Unsheltered Woman: Summary of Gender-Related Housing Problems in America

- There are more than 22 million female householders in the United States.

    They include: 9 million single parents and their 12 million children; and 13 million single women, 7 million of whom are elderly.

    They constitute almost one-third of all American households, a number that has grown dramatically since 1950.

- There are 23 million households in the United States who live in substandard housing or pay a disproportionate amount of their income for shelter. Female householders make up more than 40 percent of this group. Almost 10 million female householders have a housing problem (see note).
- Female householders are severely underrepresented among homeowners in the United States.

    Only 48 percent of them own their own dwellings while over 65 percent of all American households are owners.

    Although renter tenure has been declining for most American house-holds, female householders have become a larger proportion of renters. They now constitute 40 percent of all renters.

- In addition to housing quality and tenure data, many other environmental factors must be considered in the definition of housing problems, including consideration of location, services and neighborhood quality. Unfortunately, there is little data available on these topics.

> In the future, the U.S. Department of Housing and Urban Development and the Bureau of the Census should be mandated to collect data that reveals the presence of basic services—public transportation, daycare, protection from crime, and others—by gender or household type.

- Female householders experience housing problems because of their low economic status and patterns of discrimination.

  > Female householders have a median income ($8,931) which is only 47 percent of the national median income ($19,074).

  > Three-quarters of all female householders earn $15,000 or less; only 40 percent of all American households and 20 percent of married couples earn under $15,000.

  > Lacking credit history, women are discouraged from entering the mortgage market.

  > Certain groups of women, such as the single parent, face active discrimination in the rental market.

- Any housing policy targeted to maintain and increase the supply of low-cost housing or to assist low- and moderate-income groups in gaining decent, affordable shelter is of particular significance to women.

These goals can be accomplished in a variety of ways:

> by income policies such as housing allowances or borrowing subsidies;

> by financial arrangements which reduce the cost of loans for rehabilitation or new construction;

> by construction, rehabilitation, and maintenance of public housing;

> by planning and developing new housing arrangements such as accessory apartments or inter-generational housing;

> by expanding rent-increase exemptions and/or real-estate tax exemptions for female householders;

by stronger legislation to eliminate discrimination in the credit and rental markets; and

by mandating more cooperation between the Departments of Housing and Urban Development and Health and Human Services to coordinate shelter and service programs.

*Note:* Substandard housing is defined as follows:

1. Physically deficient due to a) the absence of adequate heating, plumbing, or electrical systems as outlined by HUD guidelines; or b) the absence of separate kitchen or bathroom facilities.
2. Overcrowded because there is more than 1.1 person per room in a dwelling.
3. Cost-burdened because homeowners pay more than 40 percent of their income for the mortgage and maintenance of their dwellings, or renters pay more than 30 percent of their income for rent.

# Appendix B

# The Unsheltered Woman: Summary of Gender-Related Housing Problems in New York City

- There are more than 1 million female householders in New York City.

  They include: 308,000 single parents and their children; and 604,000 single women, 312,000 of whom are elderly.

  They constitute 40 percent of all New York City households, a number that has grown dramatically since 1950.

- There are 1.2 million households in New York City who live in substandard housing or pay a disproportionate amount of their income for shelter. Female householders make up more than 52 percent of this group. Almost 606,000 female householders have a housing problem (see note).
- Female householders are severely underrepresented among homeowners in New York.

  Only 13 percent of them own their own dwellings while over 23 percent of all New York City households are owners.

  Although renting is the predominant tenure status in New York City households, female householders constitute 44 percent of all renters.

- In addition to housing quality and tenure data, many other environmental factors must be considered in the definition of housing problems, including consideration of location, services, and neighborhood quality. Unfortunately, there is little data available on these topics.

In the future, the U.S. Department of Housing and Urban Development and the Bureau of the Census should be mandated to collect data that reveals the presence of basic services—public transportation, daycare, protection from crime, and others—by gender or household type.

- Female householders experience housing problems because of their low economic status and patterns of discrimination.

   Female householders have a median income ($8,098) which is only 54 percent of New York City's median income ($14, 885).

   Three-quarters of the female renters earn $15,000 or less; only 41 percent of all New York City married couples earn under $15,000; 57 percent of the female owners earn under $15,000; only 13 percent of the married couple owners earn under $15,000.

   Lacking credit history, women are discouraged from entering the mortgage market.

   Certain groups of women, such as the single parent, face active discrimination in the rental market.

- Any housing policy targeted to maintain and increase the supply of low-cost housing or to assist low- and moderate-income groups in gaining decent, affordable shelter is of particular significance to women.

These goals can be accomplished in a variety of ways:

   by income policies such as housing allowances or borrowing subsidies;

   by financial arrangements which reduce the cost of loans for rehabilitation or new construction;

   by construction, rehabilitation, and maintenance of public housing;

   by planning and developing new housing arrangements such as accessory apartments or inter-generational housing;

   by expanding rent-increase exemptions and/or real-estate tax exemptions for female householders;

   by stronger legislation to eliminate discrimination in the credit and rental markets; and

by mandating more cooperation among the state departments to coordinate shelter and service programs.


*Note:* Substandard housing is defined as follows:

1. Physically deficient due to the absence of exclusive use of plumbing (this
   standard undercounts the problem).
2. Overcrowded because there is more than 1.1 persons per room in a dwelling.
3. Cost-burdened because homeowners pay more than 35 percent of their income for the mortgage and maintenance, or 30 percent for maintenance of
   their dwellings, or because renters pay more than 30 percent of their income
   for rent.

# Selected Bibliography

Birch, Eugenie L., ed. "Planning and the Changing Family," *Journal of the American Planning Association*, 49:2 (Spring 1983): 131-184.

> The effects of demographic changes are related to selected planning concerns, including transportation, social-service delivery, and zoning.

————"Woman-made America, the Case of Early Public Housing Policy," in Donald E. Krueckeberg, ed. *The American Planner, Biographies and Recollections*. New York: Methuen, 1983.

> The role of women in the development of housing policy is discussed.

Diamond, Irene, ed. *Families, Politics and Public Policy*. New York: Longman, 1983.

> This is the most recent publication on the implications of the changing definitions of the family. Discussants are of liberal and Marxist persuasions. Suggested essays are "Contemporary American Families," "Women and the Reagan Administration," and those about housing, child care, and the need for a family impact statement in decision-making arenas.

Hayden, Dolores. *The Grand Domestic Revolution: A History of Feminist Designs for American Homes, Neighborhoods and Cities*. Cambridge: MIT Press, 1981.

> This provides an excellent background on feminist-based concepts for altering the built environment.

Keller, Suzanne. *Building for Women*. Lexington, Massachusetts: Lexington Books, 1981.

> Of particular interest are articles by Keller and associates on the failure to incorporate women's needs into major construction projects.

National Council of Negro Women, Inc. *Women and Housing: A Report on Sex Discrimination in Five American Cities*. Washington, D.C.: U.S. Department of Housing and Urban Development, 1975.
> This is an old but still useful assessment of the plight of women in the housing market in American cities.

Schmertz, Mildred, ed. "Roundtable: Housing and Community Design for Changing Needs," *Architectural Record* (October 1979), pp. 97-104.
> This article contains opinions of nationally recognized leaders discussing the implications of the demographic revolution for specific urban concerns.

Smith, Ralph E., ed. *The Subtle Revolution: Women at Work*. Washington, D.C.: The Urban Institute, 1979.

Sternlieb, George, James W. Hughes, and Connie O. Hughes. *Demographic Trends and Economic Reality: Planning and Markets in the 80s*. New Brunswick, New Jersey: Center for Urban Policy Research, 1982.
> Both Smith and Sternlieb et al. provide excellent background about the demographic revolution and include basic data on women.

Wekerle, Gerda R., Rebecca Peterson, and David Morley. *New Space for Women*. Boulder, Colorado: Westview, 1980.
> One of the first readers on the subject, it is important for its comprehensive treatment of the topics.

Wright, Gwendolyn. *Building the Dream: A Social History of Housing in America*. New York: Pantheon, 1983.
> This is a survey of American housing by a feminist architectural historian.

# Index

Quality, housing. *See* Housing quality
Queens. *See* New York City

Race: elderly and, 56-57, 62; income by, 62; living arrangements by, 17-18; tenure patterns and, 41
Raymond, Parish, Pine, and Weiner, 277
Reagan (Ronald) administration: budget cuts of, 288-89; Commission on Housing, 289; fiscal 1985 budget of, 288; housing budgets of, 289-90; neighborhood women's program and, 183; role of volunteerism in the, 221
Real estate. *See* Environment, physical
Rehabilitation, housing 229-46; daycare centers and, 232, 235; dual-career families and, 238-43; elderly and, 235-38; innovation and, 230-32; New York City, 229, 230-32. *See also* Architecture; Design, housing.
Rein, Martin, 155, 158, 173n9, 175n29
Rent: control in New York City, 57-58, 66; elderly and, 59-60, 64-67, 67n2; income as related to, 63-67; New York City public housing, 290. *See also* Financing programs, housing: subsidies; Shared housing
Renters: cost burden of, 45n4; elderly as, 53-67; housing quality and, 36-37; tenure patterns and, 39-43
Richards, Ellen, 135, 147
Roby, Douglass, 235-38
Rockefeller Brothers Fund, 180
Rooming houses, 196-97
Roybal, Edward R., 161

Saarinen, Eero, 138
*Savvy* survey of executive women, 69-77
SBDO (South Bronx Development Organization). *See* Charlotte Street Gardens project
Schadelbach, R.T., 84, 87
Schindler, Pauline, 148
Schindler, Rudolf, 148
Scientific housekeeping, 147
Section 8: construction guidelines for, 102; female-headed households and, 175n25; HAP requirements for, 259; HURRA and, 291-93; low-income definition and, 285; MDUs and, 219-21; new and rehabilitation funds of, 271-72, 291; rent/income guidelines of, 63; shared housing programs and, 219-21, 222
Section 202, 67, 259, 276
Section 235, 275. *See also* Charlotte Street Gardens project

Section 236, 269, 291, 292
Segregation, 138
Seifer, Nancy, 180
Senior Citizen Rent Increase Exemption Program (New York City), 65-67
Services: female-headed households' need for, 153-76; housing and need for, 153-76, 182-83, 245, 259. *See also* Design, housing
Settlement Housing Fund, 258, 261, 263. *See also* MDU
Sex, 8-9, 12-17, 54-55
Sexton, R.W., 205
Shaffer, Gail, 189
Shalala, Donna E., 1
Shapiro, Joan, 211
Shared housing programs, 217-23; government's role in, 222-23; MDUs and, 219-21; New York City, 217-23; New York State, 222-23; non-profit sponsors' roles and, 221-22; urban cooperatives for single-parent families and, 218-19. *See also* Elderly; Female-headed households; Material feminists
Shelley System, 269, 271
Simmons, Lynda, 123
Single parents: age of, 157; educational level of, 157; as householders, 155-60; housing options for, 156; identification of, 156-58; income of, 157-58, 174n23, 175n25, 175n29; race of, 158; similarities and differences among, 155-56; standard of living of, 158, 174n23, 175n25, 175n29; urban cooperatives for, 218-19. *See also* Female-headed households
Single-person housing, 191-216; apartment hotels, 204-7, 216n27; boarding houses, 194-96 for women, 197-99; highrises, 205; lodging houses, 199-203; MDUs 219-21; New York City, 191-216; rooming houses, 196-97; SROs, 191-93, 207-14. *See also* Shared housing; Single women
Single women: income of, in Denver, 94-95; Lenox Hill Neighborhood Association and, 225-27; low-income, 191-216. *See also* Executive women; Householders
Sites: importance in highrise living in New York City of, 113-14; selection of, 259, 260
Skyline Urban Renewal Area. *See* Denver, Colorado
Smith College: Institute for the Coordination of Women's Interests, 148-49
Society for Improving the Homes of American Mechanics, 202